INSTANT ADVERTISING

Other Books in the Instant Success Series

Successful Franchising by Bradley J. Sugars

The Real Estate Coach by Bradley J. Sugars

Billionaire in Training by Bradley J. Sugars

Instant Cashflow by Bradley J. Sugars

Instant Sales by Bradley J. Sugars

Instant Leads by Bradley J. Sugars

Instant Profit by Bradley J. Sugars

Instant Promotions by Bradley J. Sugars

Instant Repeat Business by Bradley J. Sugars

Instant Team Building by Bradley J. Sugars

Instant Systems by Bradley J. Sugars

Instant Referrals by Bradley J. Sugars

The Business Coach by Bradley J. Sugars

INSTANT ADVERTISING

BRADLEY J. SUGARS

McGraw-Hill

New York   Chicago   San Francisco   Lisbon   London
Madrid   Mexico City   Milan   New Delhi   San Juan
Seoul   Singapore   Sydney   Toronto

The McGraw·Hill Companies

3 4 5 6 7 8 9 0   DOC/DOC   0 9 8 7 6

ISBN 0-07-146660-6

This publication is designed to provide accurate and authoritative information in regard to the subject matter covered. It is sold with the understanding that neither the author nor the publisher is engaged in rendering legal, accounting, or other professional service. If legal advice or other expert assistance is required, the services of a competent professional person should be sought.
—From a Declaration of Principles jointly adopted by Committee of the American Bar Association and a Committee of Publishers.

McGraw-Hill books are available at special quantity discounts to use as premiums and sales promotions, or for use in corporate training programs. For more information, please write to the Director of Special Sales, McGraw-Hill Professional, Two Penn Plaza, New York, NY 10121-2298. Or contact your local bookstore.

Library of Congress Cataloging-in-Publication Data

Sugars, Bradley J.
   Instant Advertising / Bradley J. Sugars.—1st ed.
      p.   cm.
   ISBN 0-07-146660-6 (alk. paper)
   1. Advertising copy.   2. Advertising.   I. Title.
   HF5825.S879   2006
   659.1—dc22   2005025276

To business owners everywhere.

Congratulations on your courage.
The path to freedom is yours.
Just keep walking, running, crawling, and moving along it.

Success willl happen when you least expect it.

▮ Contents

▌Let's Get Started

If you've ever run an advertisement, you'll know the pain of waiting for calls, of hoping people will come in, of expecting the sales—and the profits—to begin flowing...and then, *nothing*.

Every single businessperson I know has suffered the pain and agony of a failed advertising campaign. The problem wasn't that the campaign failed; it was that the entire future of the business had been wagered on the success of this *one* campaign.

What you'll learn through this book will totally relieve you of the worry, the anxiety, and the pressure of having to create a winner.

By the time you get to the end of this book, you'll know all the so-called secrets the professionals use to create amazing sales from their advertisements.

It's really quite simple when you know how.

It's as easy as 1, 2, 3

This book is divided into five sections. I've done this in an attempt to relay all the information in such a way that you'll not only absorb the message but also see how effective it is when implemented. And that's the key. It's no good having hundreds of great ideas if you do nothing with them.

In fact, too many ideas will paralyze you if you don't get started as soon as you can. Some authors want you to wait until you reach the end of the book before you get started. I'm almost the opposite; as soon as one idea jumps out at you, use it, get started, change your ads, and test a new strategy.

As the great Jim Rohn once said, "Never wish life were easier; wish that you were better." In my books, reading is the first step to achieving great results. Doing something with what you read is the second, and measuring the results, adjusting them if you need to, is the third.

So, let's get started.

Part 1—The Basics

For you to write great ads, there are some absolute truths that we've learned over the years that you just have to take into account. You see, without them we'd be arming you with a great weapon but not giving you any bullets.

In this first section you'll learn about strategies on how to create a concept that is worth advertising: a concept that is not just eye-catching, but wallet-catching.

Every little idea here sets you on the path to creating a strategy that will give your ads the power to perform. It's almost like getting inside the brains of the great advertising gurus and working out how they think, how they create strategies, and how they get ads to sell more than ever before.

In this section you'll learn the nine different strategies we use to create winning ads. Choosing a strategy is the first step to designing a winning ad. But you've still got to understand the basics.

Part 2—Business Principles

In the second section you're going to go on a journey of discovery—a journey that will unlock for you the secrets of business fundamentals that so few have ever really understood. In fact, it's scary how few business owners have ever learned what you're about to.

I'd call them secrets, but they're not really. In truth, they're just commonsense ways of looking at business.

Not until now has anyone really taught these simple concepts in such a comprehensive way. In fact, these fundamental concepts have been around for years, yet very few people apply them to their businesses. Most just seem to think that if they worked a little harder, worked a few more hours each day, life would get better.

Wrong.

Doing the same thing will produce only more of the same.

This section is specifically written to dispel the myth that hard work beats strategic work, and the myth that anyone can succeed in business.

You see, *ignorance* is not bliss. *Ignorance* causes bankruptcy in business. That's why we're so glad to be able to teach the absolute fundamentals in such a way as to make sure you become successful.

Another hint: Please also read my first book *Instant Cashflow* and play my board game "Leverage" to make sure these lessons are well entrenched in your mind.

Part 3—Writing Successful Ads

This is the biggest section of the book. It's where we get down to detail. It's where you'll learn what to do, how to do it, and what specifically makes one ad work while another one fails.

We teach everything, including how to write the headlines, with examples. We'll show you the right way to craft an offer, the best way to make your sales pitch, and how to incorporate your call to action at the end of every advertisement.

This is the meat in the sandwich, so to speak.

Take your time and make notes. Go back and reread the sections that are of prime importance to you. With the right mindset and strategy from Section 1, the right business principles in place from Section 2, and the ideas you learn here in Section 3, you'll be well on the way to creating winning and profitable ads that'll bring you heaps of customers and, more importantly, a bag load of cash.

Once you've mastered this, it'll be time to get the right look.

Part 4—The Layout: Making It Sell

So, you've got the strategy, the offer, the words, and now it's time to put it all together.

The layout can make or break an ad.

You're about to learn that changing just one tiny element of your ad's layout can affect sales by as much as 60 percent. That's right. You'll learn about fonts, borders, what to use, and what not to use.

You'll learn how to use pictures, what pictures to use, where to place them, and so much more. Remember that these simple details can make or break a winning formula.

Part 5—Final Points to Remember

I wanted to make sure you get the best of all worlds, so we've also covered radio and TV advertising as well.

Advertising is an amazing science: one that can make you a fortune, or one that can burn all of your profits.

Be sure to keep your advertising costs down and your sales and profits up. Advertising is great, but it's not everything in business. The most important thing to remember is to make a profit.

A major piece of that puzzle is to write great ads that bring you great customers—ones who will stay with you for life and invest greatly in the things you sell.

Your journey towards extraordinary ads, great customers, and super profits begins here.

Good luck and enjoy the ride.

INSTANT ADVERTISING

$$\boxed{\textbf{Part 1}}$$

∎ The Basics

1. Strategy

Most people wrongly believe that good ads have to be funny, well written or visually dramatic. The truth is, the very best ads work because of the strategy behind them.

Here's a good analogy. If you've prepared a delicious meal and your dinner guests are hungry, they won't care what kind of plates you use. Put another way, if your message and offer appeal to the people you're writing to, it barely matters how you present them.

Of course, there are things you can do to make your ad clearer, more direct, and more interesting, but these are definitely secondary concerns. If your strategy is wrong, the best penmanship combined with the best graphic design in the world won't save you.

Imagine trying to encourage teenagers to invest $400 a week for their retirement. On the surface, it sounds like a reasonable idea, but realistically, you'd be lucky to get a single interested adolescent. The strategy is completely wrong. First, you're going after the wrong people, and second, the amount you're asking for probably exceeds their weekly incomes.

That's an extreme example, but a good one to highlight the problem with most advertisements: saying the wrong thing to the wrong people.

Usually ads are saying nothing much to no one in particular. That's a far more serious issue. If you've been writing the kind of ads that just say, "Hi, there. My business name is X, and my phone number is Y," you shouldn't be surprised if your ads haven't been successful. These types of ads rarely do anything, except fund a newspaper or magazine. People will *not* read them unless you promise to give them something.

Behind all of this is a strategy. So let's look at what the word *strategy* means. It is defined as a plan: what you want people to do and how you're going to get them to do it.

Let's take an example. A local butcher wants to place an ad. Not being the smartest businessman around, he simply writes his name at the top and his phone number at the bottom. He sits back and looks over his ad. This will bring in heaps of customers, he mistakenly thinks. Of course, nobody bothers to look at his ad, as it's completely uninteresting.

He's missing a strategy. So let's work one out for him. First, we need to think about what it is he's trying to achieve. Put simply, he wants to encourage people to come in and buy their meat from him. But we have to be more specific when we talk about people. Thinking about it, he's really interested in the people who do their weekly grocery shopping in the local area.

So, how's he going to encourage these people to come in? They're probably already quite satisfied shopping at the supermarket four minutes down the road. He needs a good reason for them to come in and see him. How about a special offer? For every $10 you spend on meat, you get a $3 credit. That's not bad—people would probably go out of their way to claim that. Throw in a larger choice of meats, cheaper prices, higher quality, and friendly service, and you've got something that looks like a strategy.

Once people have come in and taken up his special offer, they're more likely to come back again the following week. He may not make a killing on the first ad, but he will see *some* customers, as opposed to *none*. Over time, this strategy will pay off with repeat and referral business.

So give it some thought—what is your strategy? *Whom* do you want to do *what*, and *how* are you going to encourage them to take that action now?

2. Stop Being Clever

One of the most common mistakes people make when they first start writing advertising copy is being too clever. They try to impress people with their ability to write humorous or clever advertising copy, rather than simply getting the sales message across.

So why do they fall into this trap? Well, it's simply what they've learned from what they've seen, heard, or read. It's what they've been exposed to in magazines, newspapers, and on television and radio.

You see, all around the world advertising agencies spend thousands of dollars trying to produce award-winning advertisements. These "clever" advertisements are not designed to make sales for their clients but rather to impress judges. The judges themselves have no interest in how successful a campaign has been. They simply look for the best play on words, the biggest, the brightest, or the funniest advertisements.

They miss the point of the whole exercise: making sales.

Advertising is about one thing and one thing only: getting people to buy your product or services—getting customers coming through the door and spending money with you.

The problem with clever advertising is simply that it doesn't make people buy. To prove my point, consider how many ads you read, see, or hear in the course of an average day. If you consider the number of billboards, in-store displays, window signs, taxi-signs, and outdoor signage you go past on an average day, you probably won't be surprised to hear that you, like most people, are exposed to over 1500 advertisements each day!

Now how many of those do you stop and take notice of? How many can you actually recall seeing? Probably not too many. In many cases, people would be lucky to remember 10. That's not many out of 1500. It's hardly surprising we can recall only a handful; after all, if we were to stop and pay attention to every ad we were exposed to, we'd spend our entire day reading advertisements.

So the problem with clever advertisements is that people simply don't have the time to stop and think about what the ads are trying to say. If your ad doesn't get the sales message across quickly, it will fail to achieve its true purpose: additional sales.

To give you an idea of how this works, consider these two headlines for a fish and chips shop that is trying to advertise a two-for-one fillet of fish promotion in a newspaper:

"If you think there's something fishy about this offer, you're right."

Compared to:

"Buy one fillet of fish, get another one FREE!"

Now the first headline uses a clever play on words. A fishy offer in relation to a fish sale is quite humorous. But people have to stop and think about what it means.

Chances are that rather than reading the rest of the ad, they'll simply turn the page and keep going. Compare this to the second headline, which gets the message across quickly. People thinking about what they were going to have for dinner that night would be tempted to read on.

The second ad might not be as glamorous, but it works.

It's all about getting people to read your ad, and then take action. If people have to decipher what you've written, they'll simply pass your ad over and forget about you altogether. Writing ads is not about making people laugh, or having them think you're a genius. It's about communicating with them in the fastest, clearest way possible.

Average people are not skilled in reading comprehension. If it's not spelled out for them, they won't be able to understand it. You need to realize that writing ads is not about you the writer, it's about making people understand. If you want to write for your own selfish reasons, then copywriting is not for you. You'd be better off writing novels or short stories. There's no place for big egos when it comes to writing ads.

If you want to be a copywriter, you need to forget about beautiful writing styles and creative expression and focus instead on getting your message across in a fast and efficient manner. It might not win you any awards, but it will win you a lot of satisfied clients and repeat business.

3. Promote Something *Big*

Tasteless, boring, unimaginative, dull advertisements never made anyone any money. But that doesn't stop people from running them. In fact, people seem to consistently run common, uninspiring ads, seemingly without ever asking themselves the question, "Would I respond to this ad?"

Let me show you what I mean.

Imagine people running an ad to sell wood-turning equipment. Now they could run the standard product/price type of ad, but would this inspire anyone to call? Hardly! However, with a little bit of forethought and planning, they could put together an event that would motivate people to respond.

For example, they could package up a number of products and/or services that would be worth boasting about. Perhaps a jigsaw, a lathe, and some chisels for an unbeatable price, *plus* free woodturning lessons. Now that would be something *big*!

Once you've got something worth promoting, then you can start to really boast with exciting headlines. Things like "HUGE SALE" or "BEST EVER DEALS ON (X)" will get people reading and, more importantly, will get them buying.

But package deals are only one means of promoting something *big*. Demonstration Days, Market Days, and Open Days will also give you something to really *sell* in your ad.

A lot of people are put off doing these types of promotional days because they feel that it would be too expensive or too difficult to put together. But it's really not that much of a challenge when it comes to organizing one of these events.

To start with, suppliers will quite often assist with the cost of a promotion, providing they see some benefit in them by getting involved. It surprises me how many business owners don't realize that suppliers often incorporate a marketing levy into their prices. This levy is usually around one percent or one and a half percent of the purchase price of the goods they sell.

Now they won't come out and tell you this, but if you ask them to subsidize your advertising, they will normally come to the party. Also known as cooperative advertising, this will normally take one of two forms.

The first is a straight payment to assist with your marketing costs. Your suppliers will in this instance offer to pay a percentage of any ads you run to promote the event, provided their product is mentioned or their logo appears.

The second is often the most popular and involves stock at cost price rather than a financial contribution. This is normally easier for them to fit into their budgets, and once you've sold the goods at normal retail you'll have made back the money anyway. The reason this is often better from the retailers point of view is that suppliers are more generous when it comes to this form of assistance. Whereas they may have paid $100 towards an ad, they'll often be willing to give you goods at cost, which when sold, will give you many hundreds of dollars in additional profits.

However, monetary assistance is just the beginning. Most suppliers will often send one or two representatives along to demonstrate their products. They will give you extra stock on consignment for the sale and then actually set up and man their own display. This has two major benefits for you, the business owner: It makes the day more interesting for the public and it alleviates some of the staffing problems you might otherwise have had.

Regardless of whether you put on a show to end all shows, or simply put together an exciting package, you must never run "just an ad" and always, always promote something *big*.

4. Sell One Thing at a Time

It always pays to keep your ads as simple as possible. Trying to get too much information across will cause your ad to fail, as people will tend to either get bogged down when reading it, or they'll become confused.

Often people will have many products or services that they are looking to sell. Trying to fit them all into the one ad or letter is detrimental to the campaign as a whole. Better to just cover one key product or aspect of your services, and then tell them about the rest when they call or come into your store.

What we're trying to achieve with most advertising is to get people to contact us. You shouldn't attempt to get people to buy straight from your ad. We still want to qualify those people who respond to our ads. For example, if we run a headline that says, "Attention people looking to buy a new VCR," we should only get people responding who are in the market for a new VCR.

But we don't want to give them too much information, because they'll then feel that they can make a decision about your product without needing to come in and see you. Let me show you why we should avoid telling them too much up front.

Imagine that you are selling home entertainment units. You place an advertisement and one of your competitors places an ad in the same publication. You list all your product's features and benefits, as well as all of the optional extras that come with your system. Your competitor tells them very little and invites them to call or come in for further information.

People read your ad and feel that they know a lot about what you have to offer. Based on this, there's no need to call you. Instead, they'll call your competitors to compare their system to yours. At this point you might still rate yourself a chance to make the sale.

But when they call your competitors, they are immediately caught up in a slick sales script that results in the customer making a purchase. You have now lost the sale because you gave too much information away and you never got the chance to talk to the prospect.

So it pays to always sell only one thing at a time. If you're selling a product or item that has many accessories, mention only the key ones in your ad. Tell them about the rest when they come in. For instance, if you were selling paint, you would also most likely sell brushes, rollers, drop cloths, thinners, etc. But although you sell all these other items, you would not mention them in your ad. You'd cover these when prospects come into your store.

The less you put into your ad, the less confusing it is for the prospect. The less confusing, the greater the chance of success. Let's face it, nobody wants to deal with anything that's difficult. If something looks too complex, people will shy away from it.

5. Relate to Something Local

Have you ever noticed the peculiar views of sports fans in relation to players on opposing teams? A sports fan who supports one team will usually love the players on that team. As much as they love the players on their team, they'll hate players from an opposing team.

Often they will go along to watch their team play and sit there hurling abuse at the opposing players with great vigor and passion. But if the opposing player they've been abusing is selected to represent their country against another country, they'll quickly turn from the abusive, crazed individual they'd been earlier, into that player's greatest fan. Why?

It's all about being a local.

People will generally support "locals." They'll favor people who live on their street over someone who lives across town. They'll support someone who lives in their town over someone from another town, a person or group from their state over a person or group from another state, and so on.

So what does this have to do with advertising? Simple. You need to appeal to people's sense of loyalty if you want them to buy your product or service.

To demonstrate what I mean, imagine you were advertising in a small country town for a large client based in a big city some distance away. Now, if the product or service you're advertising is already being provided by a local company, you'll have a lot of trouble getting the locals to purchase from you. Even if what you're selling is bigger, better, more reliable, and less expensive, you'll still have difficulty overcoming the loyalty factor.

You see, the people you're advertising to feel a loyalty to their town and those people and businesses operating in that town. If you want to break into that market, you need to appeal to their sense of loyalty.

6. Skim the Cream

One of the most popular techniques employed by copywriters is commonly known as *skimming the cream.*

This is where you go after an existing market, a market where people have already decided to buy and are now just working out whom they'll buy from. And it's a popular market because they've already identified themselves as buyers.

For this type of advertising the emphasis is not on "Why you need to buy X," rather it's on "Why you should buy X from us."

To give you an example of how this works, let's imagine for a moment that you sell washing machines. Using the skim-the-cream technique you'd use a headline such as, "So you need a new washing machine."

A headline like this will attract only those people who are looking to buy a washing machine right now (or at least in the very near future).

You're not trying to convince people who already have a functional washing machine to buy a new one. You're targeting only those people who have already decided to buy. It's now simply a matter of getting them to buy from you rather than from someone else.

Your body copy will focus on why people should purchase their machine from you rather than your competition. While you'll cover the benefits of your brand of washing machine (or whatever it is you're selling), you'll also explain why your company is the best one to deal with.

You need to cover all the advantages of dealing with your store. After-sales service, layaway, and free delivery are all the sorts of things that you'd mention in your ad. There's less copy needed to describe the benefits of having a new washing machine because your prospect has already decided to buy one. You can now devote more space to explaining why yours is better.

If you want to take this technique one step further, you can target those people who are in the market only for your particular brand, or model, of product. For example you might have a headline that reads, "So you're looking for the best deal on a new Simpson LI5000 washing machine."

An ad like this will bring you very qualified inquiries. But caution needs to be taken with this approach because the more targeted your headline becomes, the fewer people it will attract.

The whole idea with this sort of advertisement is to find those people who have already made up their minds to buy—those people who are already educated on the benefits of having a new "X." But it would be wrong to assume that all customers in the market for your product or service will be educated to the extent of knowing the exact make and model they want to buy.

It's better in this situation to keep your headline reasonably broad. You don't want to scare off any potential candidates by being too specific.

Often the sale will simply come down to price. If you have the best price on the market, you could do worse than simply running a targeted headline followed by the price and then your contact details. You'd still put a few benefits into the body of the ad, but not as much as you would if you were running an educational type of ad.

Remember with this sort of ad, you have to target your prospects with your headline. You need to let people know what it is you're offering. A misleading headline for this type of ad will fail badly. People need to know what it is you're selling just from the headline. A headline like, "Sharon Smith Airs Her Dirty Laundry" will not work because it doesn't target anyone. It also makes people feel duped when they read on and discover that you're selling a washing machine.

It can also be useful, if using a direct mail approach, to assume the sale. By this I mean that you would write your ad as if your prospects have already decided to purchase your product/service, even if they might not have. A headline like, "I know you've been thinking about moving to a new house" is a good example of how this style of writing works. The prospect might not have been thinking about it, but by assuming the sale you can often get people to read on. If your argument or offer is good enough, there's a chance you can convince people to take the action you're looking for.

One of the main benefits to this form of advertisement is the fact that people who respond to your ad have already identified themselves as being good prospects. You get a lot fewer people coming in saying, "I'm just looking," or, "I'm not really ready to buy just yet."

The people who come in need your product or service, which means your sales team will be dealing with people who are more likely than not to buy. This type of ad virtually sells off the page. People will often walk in the door ready to buy, with very few questions that need to be answered.

But there is a downside. There may not be all that many people in the market for the product you're offering at any one time. Some people, who might have purchased if they had of come in and spoken to your sales team, might not respond because they hadn't considered buying your product. For these sorts of people an educational type of ad works better.

7. Education

The opposite of the skim-the-cream technique involves educating people about your product or service, why they need it, and why they should get it from you.

This type of ad plays on some very basic fears that most people experience—the fear of being ripped off and the fear of looking stupid.

You see, no one likes to feel ripped off. People want to think that they've got a good deal. They don't want to walk out of your store with a product, only to think a few days later that they've made a mistake. By educating the consumer, you overcome this fear. People will feel that they have all the information they need to make an informed decision.

People are also fearful of looking stupid. Often people will put off buying a product or service because they think they'll look foolish if the salesperson asks them a question they can't answer. An educational ad arms them with the knowledge they need to feel confident.

You need to understand that people won't buy if they feel they'll be making the wrong decision. By educating them through your advertisement, you'll overcome the fear that holds them back from taking the next step. You also get to do it in a nonthreatening way.

Often people are put off by salespeople who ramble on about the product and then look for the close. By teaching customers about your product or service, you can then simply have a discussion with them and they will feel that you know what you're talking about. You don't need to convince them; you simply need to go over things in a little more depth and let the prospects sell themselves on your product/service.

Another important benefit of this type of ad is that you get to explain everything your product can do. I've met a lot of salespeople who know their product inside out and simply assume that their prospects do too. But often their clients only know the basic functions of a product.

Mobile phones are a good example. A team member in one of my companies recently purchased a new mobile phone to replace an old broken one. He was looking for the phone number of another team member he spoke to on a fairly regular basis. I mentioned that I was surprised that he didn't have the number already programmed into the phone and he looked at me in amazement. He had no idea numbers could actually be programmed into a phone. And as to the many other functions his phone offered? Well, that's another story!

A similar situation occurred with a cabinetmaker I was working with. He complained that he didn't sell many bathroom cabinets. I asked him what he had done to promote this service, only to find that he hadn't done any marketing. Further investigation revealed that his clients hadn't even realized that he offered this service.

Because he only advertised in the "Kitchen" section of the Yellow Pages and didn't market his bathroom renovations at all, many of his clients had no idea he did both. And to make matters worse, many of his clients actually went to another cabinetmaker to get their bathrooms done after my client had done their kitchens! Not because they weren't happy with my client's work, but simply because they didn't know any better.

So what don't your clients know about your product or service? By using an educational type of ad, you can teach people everything there is to know about your business. You can even train them in how you'd prefer to do business with them. For example, you might like to make appointments with people rather than have them simply dropping into your store. By explaining this in your ad, you can teach them to do business your way.

Don't ever assume that people know as much about your business as you do. Telling them everything you can do for them in your ads can dramatically increase your sales.

Educational ads can also teach your clients which questions to ask. The main advantage here is that you can teach them to ask the questions that you want them to ask—all those questions you already have the answers to. You can also get them asking your competition questions that they'd rather not be asked.

To give you an example, imagine you're selling computers. Now for the sake of the example let's assume you have one major competitor. This competing company sells computers that don't come with a factory warranty (yours do), they don't come with original software (once again, yours do), and they are made from inferior components. Added to that, the company doesn't offer delivery or on-site maintenance (that's right, you do). The one thing they do offer is lower prices. So how do you overcome the price difference with an educational advertisement? Try this headline: "Here are the top 5 questions you should ask before buying a new computer."

Then list the five questions about things you offer and they don't. See how this will get people to ignore your competitor?

It comes down to the fact that people like to feel knowledgeable. Just as people fear looking foolish, people like to look like they know what they're talking about. While some people can come across as know-it-alls, there's a little bit of know-it-all in all of us (or at least the desire to know more than someone else).

But what about our washing machine ads that we mentioned earlier? We saw how these worked in the skim-the-cream technique, but how would we advertise them using the educational technique? Simply by using a headline like, "Is your washing machine doing its job?—Here are 4 ways to tell."

We would then go on and list the four things that our washing machine can do that the competition's machine can't. Pretty simple really. But for some businesses, this can be taken a step further.

I did some work once with a photographic store. The store owners did quite well with their existing skim-the-cream advertisements where they focussed on product and price, but some of their lines and additional services were not as well supported. So we started running a weekly advertising column in the local paper, disguised as a hints and tips section on photography.

We covered things like new products or processing techniques and used the ads to educate the public on additional services the store offered.

After just a few weeks there was a flood of people coming in asking for the services and products that had been featured that week. Sales increased dramatically and people started to collect the column on a weekly basis. Not only did sales increase, but also the number of queries they received about products and topics that hadn't been covered. Why? Because the store had begun to enjoy another major benefit of this type of advertising, being viewed as the expert in the field.

When you talk about your product in a knowledgeable way, people start to view you as an authority on the subject. By writing educational ads, people soon start to look at you as an expert and will start coming to you for advice.

Now there is one huge benefit to being viewed as a guru on a particular product or service. That is, people will not only ask your advice, but they'll also tend to do exactly what you tell them to do. If you tell them they need to upgrade their computer system, they'll do it. If you tell them they need to start using a more expensive type of photographic film, they'll buy it.

The only downside to this form of advertising is the time wasters who come into your store for free advice. Often people will come in, not to buy a product, but simply to pick your brains. The solution is to charge for your time. Often you'll make as much out of consulting as you will out of selling your products.

8. Tell a Good Story

I've seen many occasions where people have tried to sell on facts and figures alone, when telling a story would have made the sale for them.

The interesting thing about people is that they like a good story. There are very few people who are interested in straight facts and statistics.

It should be obvious to everyone that stories often sell better than straight sales ads. Think about a newspaper for example. How many people buy a newspaper for the ads? Very few. If you're in the market for a particular product or service, you might buy the paper to find out who is selling it and what price range you're looking at.

The majority of people buy newspapers for the articles. When you really think about it, the very name *newspaper* means news stories printed on paper.

But many people don't realize this and try to *sell* in their ad copy like there is no tomorrow.

Now, I'm not saying you shouldn't sell. It's just that there are different ways to do this. Most people don't like being sold something, but they love to buy things. Can you see the difference? People will buy from you if they trust you and if you can show them how they'll benefit from using what you have to offer. They will not buy if they distrust you or if they have some reservations about the true benefits.

Let's look at an example of what I mean. Examples are usually an easier way to visualize what a person is trying to say. Imagine that you're selling business shirts, not cheap ones but fairly expensive shirts in comparison with others in the market.

Now if you simply placed an ad that looked at the product and price, you'd be unlikely to make many sales. You could explain the "7 reasons why your shirts are superior" but there's another way to advertise your shirts that would work better still. Tell them the story behind how they're made. Let the story explain why they are worth every cent, even though they're more expensive than others. You might write something like this:

Why it takes almost a year to make each one of these shirts:

My father had inherited our shirt-making business from his father, who had inherited it from his father before him. We never produced many shirts in the old days, mainly because each shirt had to be hand sewn. But with technology, shirt making became easier. Machines took over from people and productivity went crazy. Why one of these new machines nowadays can produce more shirts in half a day than an average factory could have produced in a year 50 years ago.

Yes sir, things have certainly changed. But not at my Dad's factory.

See, Dad's father didn't go in for all those "newfangled devices," as he called them. He didn't see how a machine could stitch as accurately as a person could. After all, he would say each piece of material is different; each requires a different sort of stitching.

Well, I finally had to admit he was right. I couldn't convince myself any longer that machine-produced shirts were as good as the ones we made in our factory. Sure, we still only produce 750 shirts a year, but each of them carries a two-year guarantee on fabric and stitching.

See how this advertisement tells the story behind how the shirts are made, and why they cost a little more? Imagine if the rest of the ad went on to tell how much cotton was used in each shirt, how the fabric was the very best quality, how it took years for the material to be treated, and how buying cheaper shirts costs more in the long run.

Now, it would have been easy enough to simply run an ad that said the quality of the shirts is better, therefore they're a bit more expensive. But it would not get the whole story across. While this ad does not have the slick polish of many ads, it has a warmth and honesty about it. It's also very easy to read. Best of all, at no stage does it try to *sell*. It gets the sales message across without going for the obvious pitch.

The ad also starts off talking about a common problem that many people would have experienced in their lives. By starting off this way, it builds rapport and trust through common ground—talking about experiences that the reader can relate to.

So what is your interesting story?

It's not a matter of just rambling on about what you do. You need to have a point to your story. You need to share something with the readers in such a way that they can't stop until they reach the end.

A really good story ad does just that. It keeps you reading and creates a mental picture that takes you away from where you are now and puts you right there as things are happening. It should tell you what you need to know, cutting out all the fat and simply sticking to the story itself.

The vision you create should show the readers how things could be if they take the action you're recommending. They need to see that their lives will be better or using your product or service will solve a problem.

Every business has a story to tell; you just need to tell it.

9. Show How You'll Solve a Problem

People don't buy a product or service because they need it.

Now, this statement may seem odd to some people, but it's true. People don't buy things because they need them; they buy things to solve a problem.

Using our washing machine as an example, imagine if the common practice in the world today were disposable clothing that's worn once and then thrown away. Now if this were the case, would people buy a washing machine because they want to own a washing machine? No. People buy a washing machine to clean dirty clothes. Dirty clothes are a problem and the washing machine offers a solution. If clothes never needed washing, no one would ever buy a washing machine.

As someone once said to me, "People don't buy a drill because they need a drill. They buy a drill because they need a hole." So, what is your drill and what is their hole? This is the question you need to ask yourself.

Selling through advertising is easy if you work out what people's motivations are for buying. As soon as you can target that motivation, you can focus on that and make the sale.

So what problem do people have that your product/service offers a solution to?

Now, sometimes the answer can be quite obvious. For a pizza store the problem is hunger and the solution is the store's pizza. But in other cases you need to dig more deeply. But whatever it is you sell, there is a problem that needs to be fixed, and this is what you need to focus on.

Selling is all about making people recognize something in their lives that they're dissatisfied with. If they don't have a high enough level of dissatisfaction, they won't buy what you're trying to sell. By highlighting this dissatisfaction and adding to it, you're taking them closer to the sale.

Once you've built up their level of dissatisfaction, (which by the way can build rapport through common ground experiences) you need to offer a vision of how much better their life would be if they purchased your product or service.

For example, imagine a masseur who specializes in the treatment of back pain. If he spoke about the constant discomfort, the frustration of not being able to get to sleep, and the stress it places on those around you, and then talked about what life would be like free of that pain, there's a good chance that he could convince back pain sufferers to take advantage of his service.

If you need a chain saw that can cut all day without raising a sweat ...
You need a Batcher 500...

Let's face it. Most chain saws are all show and no go. Sure they look good in the showroom, but it's what they do at work that we're interested in. That's where the **Batcher 500** really stands out. It's made tough and just loves to work. Doesn't matter how hard you push a Shindaiwa, they never give up.

You can cut good size logs all day with the **Batcher 500**. It's powerful 47.9cc engine throws out an amazing 2.6 kilowatts of power. And unlike some other brands on the market, **Batcher** put as much work into their personal chain saws as they do with their commercials. You'll be hard pressed to push the **Batcher 500** anywhere near its limit. Best of all, it cuts through the tough stuff without the worry of constant overheating.

You can tell by the extras how good the machine is. You get a rugged 18" bar, and a top quality chisel chain.

None of this cheap stuff you find on a lot of saws you see nowadays. And it's got 6 point anti-vibration system, so your arms don't ache at the end of a long day.

The **500** really is a top machine. To prove it the people at **Batcher** offer a 7 day money back guarantee and extended 2 year warranty. How many companies would do that?

Special Offer...

For the next 14 days if you take this ad into any participating dealer, you'll receive a **FREE** carry case valued at over **$75!!!** But you'd better be quick, this offers only available for the next 14 days or while stocks last. So call in today, and see what real quality's all about.

Contact your dealer or call 1 800 555 5555

He simply needs to show them the steps they need to take and the sales will eventuate.

Problem solved. The headline of this ad will immediately attract the attention of people who are frustrated with the reliability of their chainsaws. The headline alone promises to solve the reader's problem.

10. Fulfill a Dream

In all the time I've been on this earth, I've never yet met someone who didn't have a dream. Now the dreams may vary and quite often they do. But all the people I've ever spoken to have had some burning desire that they've craved to fulfill.

For many people their dreams will never be realized. I suppose that's why they're called dreams in the first place. But deep down, everyone hopes that her dreams will come true.

Imagine for a moment that you could grant someone her wish; that you could actually give someone the thing she has dreamed of having. Imagine what someone would be prepared to pay for that!

You see, some dreams will ultimately be unattainable. For example, you might have a dream of holding the world 100-meter sprint record. Now you may or may not be a good runner. But regardless of how good you are, what you're really aiming for is to be better than anyone else in the world who has the same dream. Unfortunately, with a dream like this, only one person can realize it.

But not all dreams are unattainable. Some just need to be presented at the right time and in the right way. Let me show you what I mean.

You own a company that sells outdoor patios and you place an advertisement in the local newspaper that simply says, "Outdoor Patios, at Great Prices." Now, there happens to be a young lady reading through the paper and she sees your ad. She barely pauses for a moment at your ad before turning the page and reading on.

She comes across your competition's ad a few pages later. But his ad is different. His ad says something to the effect that, "Imagine how your friends will flock to your home to enjoy your new outdoor entertaining area." This time she doesn't turn the page. This time she stops and picks up the phone and dials the number at the bottom of the ad. A few short weeks later she's sitting back admiring her new patio, while your competitor is happily banking her money.

So why did his ad work, and yours fail? After all, she did see your ad first.

The reason is quite simple. This young lady was never very popular at school and even now that she's been in the workforce for quite a few years, she doesn't have many friends. But all her life she's dreamed of being popular. She's spent countless hours dreaming of what it would be like to have parties at her house where everyone who's anyone would attend.

Now, you were advertising the same product as the company that eventually made the sale. But you approached it in the wrong way. You simply focused on the facts, whereas he focused on the dream. Now maybe she won't be more popular now that she has an outdoor patio, but in her mind she's satisfied that she's taken another step towards realizing her dream.

So how does that apply to your product or service? What dreams do your potential clients have that you could fulfill? It all comes down to basic wants, needs, and desires.

For most people, feeling popular and being accepted by their social groups is all-important to them. Very few people are happy to be alone. People also want to feel good about themselves. They want to feel that they've achieved something.

Almost all dreams are based around basic desires that most people have, even if they don't admit it to themselves. Any advertising that can appeal to these desires will have a great chance of making sales. But you need to be careful when trying to fulfill a dream. If you go over the top, people will quickly see through you and feel that you're trying to rip them off.

11. Offer Great Value

It never ceases to amaze me how many people I see advertising basic services or products no different than that of any number of other similar businesses. And they expect people to purchase from them simply because they're advertising. There are so many companies who don't offer any value out of the ordinary, who simply run ads and wait for calls. This is exactly what they end up doing, sitting around waiting for calls that never eventuate.

I'm certain if you asked these people why prospective clients should choose their business, they'd be able to come up with any number of lame reasons, none of which really make them stand out. Yet these very same people would be expecting exceptional value whenever they go shopping.

Part of the reason why people fall into this trap is because they mistakenly believe that offering great value costs a lot of money. They feel that if they offer anything out of the ordinary, they'll be cutting into their margins. Now in some cases they would indeed make slightly less from each sale, but at least they'd be making sales!

The ironic part of their whole way of thinking is that they probably already offer great value and simply don't realize it. In some cases, they're simply not promoting it.

A good example is a business that sells a product and then offers advice on how best to use it. Hardware stores are often guilty of this. You can go into a hardware store and talk to one of the salespeople about a project you're undertaking and he will give you heaps of advice and then sell you the products you need. Now, there may not be anything exceptional about the products he sells, but what price would you place on his advice?

If he simply promoted the fact that he gives expert advice, at no extra charge, he would be offering sensational value that would be certain to generate extra sales. To make it really effective, he could place a dollar value on his advice and then offer this as a free service for people who brought their ads into the store when they came to make a purchase.

You simply need to make your customers aware of the things you do that your competition doesn't. In other words, you need to define your Unique Selling Proposition, or USP.

Your USP is the one thing that is truly different about you, or at least the one thing that you can promote as being different.

A successful USP should be:

- Truly unique.

- Exciting to your target market.

- Something that will get people talking.

- Something that can't be easily copied, or if it can, it will be an obvious rip-off on the part of the offending business.

A lot of business owners wonder why they need a uniqueness at all—shouldn't there be room for dozens of "me-too" businesses? The fact is, there isn't and the me-too businesses will ultimately go to the wall.

What about your business? When you started, did you begin with a uniqueness—a real point of difference—or did you just start as a me-too competitor?

Here's an interesting illustration of why uniqueness is so important. When a new grocery store opens, it has to share sales with all the other grocery stores in the area. If there are already three stores, and two of them are struggling, what makes you think you have a better chance? All you've done is split the potential sales further. Now, instead of the total grocery market being split between three, they have to be split between four.

If you promote your business as a "me-too" business, you can forget it. The days of competing on price and service are at an end. These days with so many options customers can almost always get it cheaper and from someone who'll do it better.

The major point is clear: You must offer *great value*. If you have no uniqueness, you have no reason for existence, and as new competitors come into the market, you'll continue to sink.

You can offer great value through package deals. You simply have to offer more value for the same money. Of course, this is where your margins may become an issue. But consider this:

What if you have old stock sitting on a shelf and it's not moving? Rather than leave it there taking up space, why not offer it as an extra incentive for people to buy? This way you can make an offer that people perceive as being great value and at the same time freeing up your shelves for faster-moving items.

Another option is to offer a special deal from another business. Imagine if a hairdresser offered a free facial at a nearby beauty salon for customers who had a cut and color. They wouldn't have to pay for the facial; they'd simply need to approach the beautician with the idea of sending the hairdresser a whole lot of new clients.

When you think about it, this makes a lot of sense for the beautician. To understand what I mean, consider this: Each time the beautician places an advertisement, it costs her money to generate new clients. Now if she places a $100 ad that brings her 10 new clients, each client has cost her $10 to attract. Now if the actual *hard cost* of her facials is $5.00, she saves $5.00 for each free facial she gives away! When you consider how much that new client will spend with her over the next few years, she comes out well ahead.

So simply put, making a great offer doesn't need to cost you money, just a bit of time and thought. At the end of the day, it will be time well spent.

12. Underpromise and Overdeliver

Advertising is all about making sales. You should never place an ad for the sake of placing an ad. You should place an ad only with the view to making sales.

So with this in mind, you need to realize that getting people to call is only half the battle. You need to be able to sell to them once they've responded to your ad.

One of the easiest ways to do this is to underpromise in your ad and then overdeliver when they contact you in response to your ad.

You need to keep something up your sleeve for when prospects call or come into your store. To do this, tell them just enough in your ad to get them to contact you. This should be the case with almost all of your advertising anyway. If you tell them too much in the ad itself, they can make their decision without needing to speak with you. Now you might ask, "Isn't that the idea?" To put it simply, the answer is *no*.

You want to be able to talk to prospects so you can sell them on your product or service. Many people will read an ad and interpret it in different ways. So there's a chance that people reading your ad may think they can make the decision for themselves, yet they haven't really received the message you are trying to deliver.

By talking to them in person you get the chance to find their motivation for looking at your service in the first place.

If you can get the prospects to call, then you can find out what motivates them and you can play on that in your sales pitch. If you've then kept a few things up your sleeve, you can use these extras as a way to get them over the line.

Car lots do this particularly well. Often people will be looking at a car, be on the verge of making a decision, and the salesperson will offer to throw in a few extras. Advertising draws the prospect in, but overdelivery closes the sale.

It's a matter of working out what you can offer, over and above what you're offering now, that will be seen in the prospects' eyes as overdelivering. It's really quite easy. A person who mows lawns for people could offer to change their light bulbs when he finishes the lawn at no extra charge. A bakery could throw in a donut with every two loaves of bread it sells. Anything at all that you can offer will help get people to purchase. Remember, it's not enough to get people simply to call you; you need to make the sale to those who do.

Sales are not just about those people who respond. This can also lead to extra sales through referrals.

Imagine if you responded to an advertisement in the Yellow Pages for mechanical repairs. You take your car around and leave it to be serviced. You might expect to have to catch a taxi back home and then come back later when your car is finished, but this mechanic is not your normal run-of-the-mill mechanic.

When you arrive, you're taken to a clean and comfortable waiting room with leather lounge chairs. You're offered a cup of coffee (brewed, not instant) in a beautiful china cup. The mechanic then asks you a series of questions about the sort of driving you do, any major repairs you've had done previously, and a host of other questions regarding your car.

When the initial interview is completed, you're told that it will be approximately three hours before your car will be ready. The mechanic tells you that he'll send a car around to take you back home. You're a little hesitant. The last time you got into a mechanic's car, you ended up covered in grease and stinking of gasoline.

Imagine your surprise when a clean, current-model sedan pulls up out front.

You're taken to your house and told that the car will come back and get you in three hours. Do you think you might tell a few friends about your experience?

Your ad may draw people in, but it's the overdelivery when they purchase from you that will lead to additional sales. Advertising is so often about more than simply those people who respond in the first place.

13. The Bottom Line: If It Works, Rerun It

I remember working with a cabinetmaker who was running advertisements in his local newspaper. He asked me to write some new ads for him. Before starting, I asked to see the ones he was currently running.

I looked over these ads and was surprised to see that they were quite good. So good in fact that I felt compelled to ask him what sort of response he was getting.

He informed me that he was averaging around 7 to 10 calls per week. Not a bad strike rate, I thought, considering how many people were actually looking for a cabinetmaker at any one time. He went on to explain that the ad I was looking at had brought him a better response than any ad he'd used in the past. Not only was he getting a reasonable number of calls per week, but he was making quite a few sales and the ads were very profitable.

I asked him if the ad was getting fewer calls now than it had in the past. He said it wasn't. The response he was getting each week was as good as he'd ever received with it. I was a little confused. The ad was getting a good number of callers, many of whom were then buying from him, and he was making very good money from the ad.

So why did he want to change it?

He had simply grown tired of seeing the same ad over and over again, and felt that his potential prospects would be sick of it too!

Now, you might look at this and realize how ridiculous his thinking was, but I've seen this happen time and time again.

The simple fact is that once you find an ad that works, you should keep running it. You'll get sick of it well before your clients do.

When you think about it, to stop running an ad that's making you money simply because you're tired of it doesn't make any sense. It would be like a professional photographer deciding she was sick of taking wedding photographs, even if weddings were where she made the bulk of her money.

What many people fail to realize is that at any one time there are only a limited number of people who will be looking for a particular product or service. People can read a newspaper day after day and never see your ad until they happen to be in the market for what you're offering.

If you were advertising washing machines, you wouldn't expect everyone reading the paper to be in the market for a washing machine at the same time. In fact, you'd be lucky if two percent of the people looking through the paper were thinking of buying a new one. So, if your headline were something along the lines of "Here's why you should buy your new washing machine from XYZ retailers," you wouldn't expect to get too many calls. Not because it's not a good headline, but simply because not many people will be looking for your product.

However, if someone were in the market for a new washing machine, your ad would jump off the page at him, and he would more than likely call. It's what's commonly referred to as people's Reticular Activating System, or RAS for short.

Without going into too much detail, your RAS is simply a way of getting your mind to focus on something that is important to you at that time. You don't need to consciously focus on what it is you're after; often it will just happen. But your RAS is very powerful and can be consciously or unconsciously set to track for all sorts of things.

I'll give you an example of how this works. Recently I decided to buy a new car, a silver Porsche Boxster. Now, until I decided to buy one, I hardly ever saw them on the roads. But once I'd bought it, I saw them everywhere. The reason: Before I started thinking about silver Porsche Boxsters, I never noticed them. They were always there; I just hadn't seen them.

It's the same with your ads. Even though you're running the same ad week after week, people will not notice it until they're in the market for your product or service. As soon as they're looking for what you offer, they'll call. So even though you're tired of your ad, if it's making you money, you need to keep using it.

14. Test, Test, and Test

If there are only three things you get out of this book, this *must* be one of them. Once you understand this simple principle, you'll be able to make money from your advertising all the time, with every ad you ever run.

Over the years I've spoken to many business owners who've tried advertising in various mediums, only to stop using them because they didn't work.

Often their competition was using the very same mediums and got great results. But ask these business owners if they advertise in their local paper or on the local radio station and they'll tell you it doesn't work.

So if the newspaper doesn't get results or the radio station ads fail to get a response, why are there are so many companies still using them? Surely they've worked out whether or not they're getting results?

The fact is that it's normally not that the medium or the strategy doesn't work; it's simply that their ads weren't good enough in the first place.

The secret to getting a response to your advertisement is to test a number of ads until you find the right one.

You see, a lot of people write an ad and believe that it will work well for them. They place it in the paper and sit back waiting for the calls. All along they've believed that it will work; after all, a lot of their current clients read the paper. But when it fails to improve their number of leads, they stop running the ad and blame the paper for the poor response.

But how did they think the ad was going to work? You can never know until you put it to the test. If it doesn't work, you simply change the ad and run it again. You keep testing over and over until you find the ad that works.

I've seen many businesses blow huge sums of money on expensive campaigns that never worked. They've simply wasted their cash. They'll run full-page ads in major publications costing thousands of dollars, only to find that the ad was a shocker in the first place. If only they'd tested it (or its key parts) to start with, they could have saved themselves all that hardship.

So let's look at the things you need to test.

First, you need to test your headline. Your headline is the most important part of your advertisement. We'll get onto how to write a great headline later. For the moment you need to be aware only of its importance and the fact that it's crucial that you test it.

You also need to test the offer you're making. Some offers that you think will get people in will quite often not work, but some that you didn't think would work will quite often bring a huge response. You can't be sure until you test them.

Test different publications. If you find that one newspaper gets a lot of calls and yet another containing the same ad doesn't, fair chance that it's the publication and not the ad. The position is something else you need to test. Try your ads in the business pages, the classifieds, or the early general news sections. I've seen many times where clients have simply taken an ad that wasn't working, placed it in a different section of the paper, and suddenly they started getting a great response.

Test your ads with and without photographs. Test them with and without a border, and so on. There are so many things that can alter the results you achieve, but you can't possibly hope to know what these are without testing them first.

You can have all the theories and beliefs in the world, but until you put them to the test, you can't be sure if they'll work.

15. Test with Flyers

So you understand the importance of testing your advertising to find out what works. We've also looked at some of the things you need to test. Now, let's take a look at some of the ways you can test your campaigns before you spend hundreds of dollars on them.

Flyers are one of the best ways to test campaigns. They're cheap, they're easy to produce, and you can test many different headlines and offers at the same time.

If you're considering placing a large advertisement in the newspaper or Yellow Pages, it could be a good idea to test the ad first using flyers.

Now you need to understand that flyers probably won't bring the same response as you'd expect from, say, the Yellow Pages.

Go to the mailbox of any household on a Saturday morning and it will generally be overflowing with flyers and catalogues. While the average person may read some of them, most will end up in the garbage. Of those that are read, very few will ever be acted upon. There are many examples of companies who send out 40,000 flyers and only get 4 responses.

A successful flyer campaign will, of course, perform much better than this, but even an effective campaign will not generate a 100 percent response rate. A realistic target would be between 2 percent and 7 percent for the average campaign.

You need to remember that it was not your intention to run a flyer campaign in the first place. You only want to test the campaign as a whole before you run your true campaign elsewhere.

The true beauty of using flyers is that you can have a number of different headlines and different offers all being tested in the marketplace at once.

Sit down and write the ad you're looking to run, along with a number of different headlines with different appeals as well as a few different offers. Now combine the various headlines and offers and produce 8 to 10 variations and combinations of your ad. Once you have these together, you simply need to mail them to different areas. The area that brings the best response will show you which headline and offer works best.

But you need to consider a few more things before you go and run your full campaign. First, you need to send all your test flyers out at the same time. Different days can bring different responses that can affect the results of your test. You should also keep in mind the areas where you're placing your flyers. A more affluent area may bring a better response than an area with cheaper housing. In this case, it won't have as much to do with the headline or offer as it will with the area in which your flyers were placed. You need to try to keep the tests as even as possible.

But headlines and offers are just a few of the things you need to keep in mind if you're going to test using flyers. Let's look at a few of the others.

Colors

It could be argued that because people see in color, your flyer should be printed in color. While this would seem a worthwhile argument, it pays to remember that most newspapers are printed in black and white, and they don't have any trouble getting people to read them.

Printing your flyers in color will cost quite a bit more than standard black text on white stock. The aim of your flyer is to bring customers into your business. The less you spend on attracting them the better. If your headline promises a benefit, your copy conveys your message, and your offer is worthwhile, it's fair to assume that you don't need color.

If you were going to use any color at all, you'd be well advised to print in full process color. Research has shown that the difference between two colors and black-and-white advertising material is minimal and doesn't justify the extra expenditure.

Printing on colored paper is an inexpensive way to brighten up your flyer. Be careful which color paper you choose, as it can make your flyer difficult to read. Keep this in mind if you decide to print your text in color. As a general rule, you're far better off printing your text in black, as this will increase readability. Of course, this whole exercise is designed to test your print or Yellow Pages ad. If you don't intend to print those ads in color, then leave your flyer black and white.

Layouts

Many people fall into the trap of trying to jazz up their flyers by adding different shapes and elements. Unless you have a good deal of artistic ability, you're best off sticking with a simpler layout. Putting your headline at the top, your coupon in the bottom right corner, and your pictures in the middle may not sound exciting, but it will generally bring better results.

Try to do your layout in blocks. By this I mean placing the headline, copy, pictures, and coupon in a blocked, or balanced layout on the page. Keep your layout tight and don't leave too much empty space on the page. You're paying for these flyers, so use every bit of them.

If you want to try something out of the ordinary, you should pay a graphic designer to do it for you. Professional designers can be quite expensive. If you want to save money, contact a college or university that runs a graphic design course. This way you may be able to find a second- or third-year student who will do it for a reasonable price.

Of course, it's a good idea to make your flyer look as much like the proposed ad campaign as possible. After all, the headline and offer aren't the only things you need to test.

Size

The size of your flyers will depend on how much information you need to include. I would normally recommend your flyers fit on paper that is 5.8 × 8.3 inches, an A5-sized piece of paper.

You probably wouldn't place an ad in the newspaper that was larger than 5.8 × 8.3 inches, so you shouldn't have any problem fitting all you need to say into this space.

You can fit two flyers on one standard letter or A4 sheet of paper. This will save you quite a bit on printing costs, as you'll only need half as much paper as you would if you were printing on A4.

Stock

Stock is the term used for the type of paper or card that you print your flyers on. There are numerous types from which to choose. Should you use glossy paper or plain paper? Plain card or a textured card? These are just some of the questions to be answered when choosing your stock.

Just as there are a variety of materials, there are also a variety of prices, ranging from the very expensive to the downright cheap. Because your campaign is simply designed as a testing process, go for the least expensive option.

Once you've tested your flyers and found out what works, you'll be ready to run your full campaign, safe in the knowledge that your headline and offer will get results.

16. Test with Codes

As we mentioned in the previous section, one of the most effective ways to test your advertising is by using flyers. But you can also test your ads in newspapers, magazines, or with direct mail letters. In fact, you should always be testing your ads. But if you're running a few different ads in a few different places or publications, how do you know which ad is getting which result?

One of the ways to work out where your best inquiries are coming from is to code your ads or direct mail letters. You do this by placing a code at the bottom of each ad or letter.

Let me explain what I mean.

Let's imagine you're an accountant. If you were running a number of advertisements in a variety of publications to find out which ad gets the best response, you'd simply place a different code at the bottom of each ad. Now let's imagine that the offer in your ad was a free booklet on new taxation laws.

To find out which ad was getting the best response, you'd simply get people to cut the ad out and send it in to take advantage of your offer. You'd then have a way to check which ads were getting sent in and which weren't. By recording which codes ran in which publications, you'd be able to work out which ads were working best.

This idea works particularly well when used with coupons. You simply have a coupon at the bottom of your ad or letter that people fill out and send in. Or if you want them to come into your store, get them to hand you the coupon to take advantage of your offer. A small code in the bottom corner of your coupon will soon let you know what's working and what isn't.

Coupons, of course, have another advantage. They enable you to get people's phone numbers and addresses so you can add them to your database for future mailings.

Testing by area is another way to track the results of your ads. If you send different letters to different zip codes, you simply ask people what their zip code is when they phone in.

But this idea can also be applied by using a pseudonym. I worked with a motel owner once who had no idea which ads were working for him and which ones weren't. He was advertising all across the country and although he was testing a number of headlines, he had no way of tracking the result. So I suggested to him that he started running ads that said things like, "Ask for Sally," or "Call Bernie."

There was no Sally or Bernie working at the motel. So right away you knew that the people calling were (a) responding to an ad and weren't regular customers calling off a business card, or (b) which ad they were calling from, depending on which name they asked for.

This system worked brilliantly. We soon discovered that two of his advertisements were getting a huge response and the others were getting little, if any. We immediately stopped running the ads that weren't working and changed them to the ones that were. In the space of just a few quick months his inquiries had gone through the roof and his advertising was back on track.

At the end of the day it matters little which method you choose. The main thing is that you have some system in place that lets you know what's making you money and what's costing you money.

17. Test with a Phone Number

Another way for you to test where your inquiries are coming from is by testing the phone number you place in the ad. Now, I don't mean that the number itself will make a difference to your response, although a toll-free number will generally get a better response than a mobile number for obvious reasons. What I mean is having a phone number that is a dedicated line that you use for the sake of testing.

In your business you'll probably have a phone number that people call all the time. It's the number on your business cards or in the phone book. In fact, it's the number that your prospects could have found anywhere. Now it would be impossible to know where they saw your number unless you actually asked them.

But what if you had a phone number that was never used, a number that your husband or wife used to call you, or that maybe you used for outgoing calls?

Let's imagine that you place that phone number in your Yellow Pages ad for one whole year. You don't place it anywhere else. The only way someone who calls could have found that number is through your Yellow Pages ad. What do you think this will teach you about the effectiveness of that ad? You'll know immediately where the calls are coming from, simply because that's the line that's ringing.

Therefore, if you find that over the twelve-month period the number hardly rings, what do you know about that Yellow Pages ad? It doesn't work. It's not a good ad. So you'll know next year that you need to change the ad if you want a better response. Or maybe you've found from testing your other forms of advertising that it's more cost effective to put more money into direct mail advertising and less into the Yellow Pages. Either way, you'll be saving yourself a lot of wasted money.

Now some people reading this will be saying to themselves, "Yeah, but someone might call from the Yellow Pages ad, then write the number down and pass it to someone else. Then that person will call even though she has never seen the ad herself." Does it matter if she has never seen the actual ad? *No*, the call has come about as a result of the ad in the first place. Sure, it's through a referral but she is being referred by someone who responded to your ad in the first place. So the ad has actually worked twice as well in those situations.

What if you don't have a separate line that you can use for testing? Well, the first thing you can do is contact your phone company and inquire about special phone lines. Some telephone companies can actually supply you, at no charge, a dedicated Yellow Pages phone number. This is done to test the effectiveness of

Yellow Pages as a whole. But there are many people looking to get these numbers, so there's no guarantee that you'll be selected.

If you can't get one of these phone numbers, call your phone company and explain what you're trying to do. The company might have a way of setting up something else for you. For example, multiple number duet. This is where you can have two numbers linked to the same phone line but each number has a distinctly different ring. This is just one example. Call your phone company and ask what will be most effective for you.

18. Test Headline Only Ads

Of all the techniques I've used for testing ads, this is by far my favorite. Admittedly I use it almost exclusively for testing newspaper ads, but I've also used it to test titles for books and headlines for Yellow Pages ads.

The idea is simple.

You write a full-sized advertisement, maybe up to half a normal newspaper size. You then write ten to a dozen different headlines. You'll probably also come up with a number of offers that you think will attract a response.

Before you place your full-sized ad in the paper, you need to know that the headline will attract attention and draw the reader in. So, rather than go through the expensive process of running a half-page ad ten different times, you simply run an ad that contains only the headline.

I don't mean that the headline is the only thing in the ad; if that were the case you'd never know if it was attracting attention or not. You also need to include a contact number or address so people can call in.

But your ad will not consist of much more than that. It will simply be your headline, a brief paragraph, and then a contact number. In some cases I'll also include an offer to test at the same time I'm testing the headlines.

It's important when you start testing that you begin with a small ad. Why? Because it costs less, which means you'll lose less if it doesn't work the first time.

Better to blow a small amount of money on a business-card sized ad than to lose a heap of money on a full-page ad.

By running a series of smaller ads and measuring the response, your full-sized ad will have a much greater chance of success.

Now you can't expect the phone to ring off the hook when you place a small ad. If you could get a big response with a small ad, there'd be no point running a large ad in the first place. What you're looking for is a handful of calls to give you an indication of which headline should be used in your final ad. Often you'll just get one or two calls from a headline only ad, but you'll notice that some ads get no calls at all. The choice is simple: Run the headline that got the one or two calls.

19. Measure, Measure, and Measure

I mentioned earlier that there were three key points that you really need to derive from reading this book. Testing, you'll remember, was the first. The second goes hand in hand with the concept of testing, and that is measuring the results.

Testing an advertisement, without measuring the results it's getting, is a little bit like playing a sport and not keeping score. Imagine playing a game of tennis where no one kept score. It would be completely pointless!

It's the same with your advertising. It's no good to simply test an ad and then guess at the results. You need to measure its effectiveness.

If you're like most business owners, you'll be running a number of campaigns at the same time, so you need to know which one is working the best. You must find out where your customers are coming from. If you don't, you're really stabbing around in the dark.

You'll have no real idea which marketing campaigns are working, how well your salespeople are doing, or even how much each sale is costing you.

Once you know these things, you have the power to make decisions, and good ones at that. You'll know which marketing campaigns to stop running, which to improve, and which to spend more money on.

You'll also know where your key leverage point is—that is, the thing that you most need to improve. Perhaps your conversion rate is high but your leads are few. Maybe it's the other way around. Maybe you're doing well in both lead generation and conversion but you're not selling enough high-priced items.

Once you know which area needs work, you can start to make some new, well-informed marketing decisions.

The concept of testing and measuring is really nothing new. You've probably been doing it all your business life. Remember the newspaper advertising you tried that didn't work and the radio spots that did OK? That's all testing is. It's about finding out what produces results and what doesn't, then making decisions based on that information. Thinking that an ad did OK just isn't good enough. You need to know for sure.

You *must* start asking people where they found out about you. If you don't, you'll be in the dark forever. You may keep running an ad that never brings a sale and accidentally stop running a good one. Customers usually come from so many sources it's impossible to judge how an ad is working on sales alone. Perhaps you got more referrals that week, or there was a festival in your town. Every time people buy, ask them this question: "By the way, can I just ask where you heard about my business?" You'll find that all of your customers will be happy to tell you.

But you must be vigilant and disciplined. You can't test and measure half the time. You must do it on a regular basis. It's not difficult. Just remember to mark down a record after every customer interaction. Make sure all employees do the same—stress the importance of it and absolutely *demand* that they do so. Tell them it's essential that they are honest.

I remember working with a carpet cleaning company that generated most of its work through a mailbox drop. The owners had tested and measured a number of headlines and offers, eventually finding the one that worked best. Once they worked out the most successful formula, they continued to use it. But what they failed to do was to continue measuring it.

When they came to me, their business had dropped off quite badly. They explained that it couldn't be their flyer because it had proven itself in the past. When I eventually persuaded them to measure it again, they found that the response over the last 12 months had dropped from 11 percent to just 2 percent! We quickly tested some new flyers and got them back up and running. It highlights the fact that you need to be constantly measuring the effectiveness of your advertisements.

Once you've gathered your results, you need to know how to use them to your best advantage.

The first thing you need to do is work out which ads are not performing. If an ad is getting a very low response (which means the profit margin from sales is not even paying for the ad), stop running it.

Of course you need consider the lifetime value of the customer as well. If, after taking all factors into account, you're not getting results, bite the bullet and stop running the ad. Every time you continue to use that ad, you're literally giving away money.

Now you have two options: Channel your marketing funds elsewhere (like back into your pocket) or improve the ad.

If you choose option two, there are a couple of things you can do to make the task simpler. First, go back over your past ads and think about how well each one worked. Pull out the best couple and see if you can pick what gave them their edge. Next, talk to your customers to get a feel for what would make them take action. What is it that they really want from you? Lastly, look at what your competitors are doing. Do they have an ad that they run every week? Chances are that this ad must be doing OK. What ideas can you steal—sorry, borrow—from it?

Then write a new ad.

Go through this process with each marketing piece that doesn't seem to be working (letters, Yellow Pages, referral systems, flyers, and so on). Discontinue, examine, modify. Discontinue, examine, modify. Once you have a collection of these revised pieces, just sit on them. There's something more important we need to deal with first: the strategies that are working.

Run through each of the working strategies in depth, examining why they are producing results and the others aren't. See if you can pick the one important, attractive point about each. This in itself will teach you a significant amount about your business.

Next, think of a way to run each strategy on a larger scale. If it's flyers, the answer is simple—drop twice as many. That should bring twice the sales. If it's an ad, run it in more papers, or increase its size. If it's the Yellow Pages, book a bigger space next time.

But whatever you do, if it's working, don't meddle. Just do the same thing on a larger scale.

After that, test and measure for another two weeks. Notice if the number of inquiries remains the same, goes up, or goes down. Keep in mind how much it's costing you and whether or not it's profitable.

The idea is to keep focusing on the successful strategies and to simply stop using those that aren't working. For example, you might find after measuring that your print ads aren't working but your radio ads are. The answer is to stop running the print ads. Of course, you need to test and measure first. Eliminating a strategy should happen only if you can't get a result from it after a period of time.

By not running those unsuccessful strategies, and focusing more on those that are working, you'll start to make real profits from your advertising. In fact, you'll probably find you barely miss those dud strategies and the *larger-scale* working strategies will be paying off very nicely indeed.

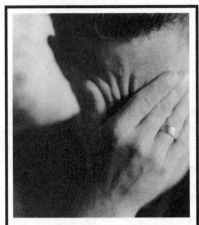

John Smith believed if authorities did more to stop drugs in schools they might save a child's life...

He thought by stopping domestic violence they could save a child's life...

If John Smith would have been able to stop his car he would have saved a child's life.

How Old Are YOUR Brakes?

Chiltern Brake & Clutch Company
212 Smith St., Chiltern

Ph: (035) 856 5759

Ad A.

FREE
Brake Inspection
VALUED AT $38!!!

With the holiday season coming up, and the roads being busy, you want to know that your car is safe. Which is why we are offering you a **FREE Brake Inspection valued at $38**. We'll go over your car's brakes with a fine tooth comb. If we find any faults, we'll discuss them with you before we go ahead with any repairs. So know that your family is safe these holidays, and take a few minutes to pop in and have us do your inspection.

To book in call **Chiltern Brake & Clutch Company** on Ph: **(035) 856 5759**, or call in and see us at 212 Smith St., Chiltern.

Ad B.

The importance of continual testing and measuring is highlighted by these two advertisements. The first time advertisement (a) appeared, it pulled an amazing response. But subsequent testing and measuring of the ad in a number of publications saw it generate no response at all. Advertisement (b), while being less clever, consistently generated a small number of leads, making it substantially more profitable after only a few weeks.

20. Investment

We are about to shatter a belief that's held by business owners around the world. It's what I call the business lie. When we start out in business we are taught two things about bookkeeping: There's an expense column and a profit column. We are told that advertising is an expense and it goes in the expense column. Advertising is not an expense; it's an investment, and it's an investment for a number of reasons.

First, when you place an ad, you want a return on your investment. Or at least that is the general idea when you place the ad—to get a return!

I ran an advertising campaign that cost me $284 and within three weeks I had made $13,800. Another campaign once cost me $4500 and within nine weeks I had made $89,000. Now that's hardly what you'd call an expense!

In fact, when you look at the potential returns on traditional investments like stocks, shares, real estate, or money in the bank earning interest, very few would ever offer the same returns that can be gained through advertising (or good advertising, anyway).

Another reason why advertising can't be classed as an expense is simply that we are taught as business owners that you write off things in the expense column. You would be crazy as a business owner to pay for an advertisement and then write it off, which is exactly what you are doing with an expense column. You are paying for an ad and then saying, "Well, I have written that money off. I don't expect a return on my investment." But that doesn't happen. You do expect a return. And if you are expecting a return, then advertising must be an investment, mustn't it?

When you understand how to test and measure, and you understand that your advertising is an investment, not an expense, then you really can have an unlimited advertising budget. If you know that with every dollar you are going to spend on advertising you are going to get five dollars back, then how many dollars can you afford to spend on your advertising? It's endless; it's all about getting a return on your money.

I worked with a business owner once whose accountant was actually instructing him to run ads towards the end of the year. "Look, you are going to have to pay a lot of tax, so you should run some advertising campaigns," the accountant would say. So he would spend money advertising to reduce the tax he would otherwise have to pay.

Imagine that, the idea of actually placing an ad just to lose money to avoid paying tax. The idea of losing money is repulsive enough, but imagine doing it just to save yourself tax.

What we need to understand is that advertising is an investment and must be viewed as an investment. And we need to be able to measure the return on that investment in dollar terms. Once you understand this, your advertising will be more effective and your profits will begin to soar.

21. Direct Response versus Institutional

If investment versus expense is your business lie, then direct response versus institutional advertising has to be the media lie. Now I know I said before that advertising is an investment, not an expense. And the reason it isn't viewed that way is due to institutional advertising. This gave rise to the lie.

Let me explain what I mean by institutional advertising (there are two different types of advertising: direct response and institutional). Institutional advertising is where you don't really make an offer. There's no call to action in your advertisement. You are just putting your name out there, just getting your name known—you know, brand awareness and that sort of thing. Direct response, on the other hand, is when you place an advertisement and expect a direct response. You want people to call as a result of reading, listening to, or seeing the advertisement.

The reason I call it the media lie is simply because media reps make their money as a result of selling advertising space, or with radio and television, air time. The more they sell the more money they make in commissions. I remember once a newspaper rep coming to see me and saying, "Look, you need to run these ads in the paper. You need to get your brand name out there." Now what happens is you run your ads for about seventeen weeks and then brand recognition occurs. People start to remember the name of your company. They start to remember your brand name.

The benefit to the newspaper rep was that I was going to have to advertise for at least seventeen weeks before I got a result. Institutional advertising in that way does not work. Advertising is then not an investment; it's a promotion. It's simply a donation to the media.

I should point out that while institutional (or *image advertising*, as it's sometimes called) doesn't work for small- to medium-sized businesses, larger corporations can use it with great success. Take for example Coca Cola, which now invests a lot of money on institutional advertising or branding, getting the Coca Cola name out there and keeping it in people's faces.

Part of the reason for this is because Coca Cola vies with only one or two competitors for the market share. You need to understand that companies like Coca Cola have multi-million dollar marketing budgets that are needed to get the brand to its present stage.

The average small- to medium-sized businesses don't have the sort of money that it takes to get this result. While they can spend thousands of dollars running advertisements on television or radio over a period of weeks to get the company or brand name known, they would be far better off investing that money in a direct response advertising campaign that gets an immediate return on their investment.

For smaller businesses, it's just not economically viable to tie money up in advertising that's not going to bring a direct response. They are far better off putting that money into direct mail, flyers and brochures, or print advertisements that bring an immediate result.

For those businesses, it simply comes down to this: Would they rather spend thousands of dollars getting their brand name out there and then waiting for the result in sales, or would they rather spend a few hundred dollars on a direct mail campaign that brings about immediate sales—immediate cash in the bank?

My choice is definitely to get the money in the bank. If I am going to advertise, I expect an immediate response, and so should you.

22. Make It Easy

One of the reasons why many advertising campaigns fail, is that they are simply too complex.

You see, in today's busy world people want things that are easy. People will take action as long as they don't have to really think about it and they don't have to go to any great trouble. It stands to reason that the easier we make it for them to deal with us, the better the response we are likely to get.

So let's take a look at how this might work. Imagine you are running an advertising campaign aimed at selling insurance. If all the reader has to do is simply to call up to make an appointment or come in and see you, then you would expect people are going to respond. It's quite straightforward: You are not asking them to do anything out of the ordinary.

But if you are asking them to fill out documents or to gather previous insurance policies, and then to call to arrange a time for an appointment, sorry but it's too hard. However if the advertisement simply said, "Call now for a free valuation" and then you covered all those things on the phone, chances are they'd inquire.

Remember, you need to tell them only enough to have them inquire in the first place. Once they have inquired, then you can go through all the issues associated with purchasing your product or service.

Another example of how some advertisers make it difficult for people to respond to their ads is putting time limits on responses. I don't mean the "You need to act within the next two days" sort of offer because that's quite effective. But if they have to call between certain hours, lets say between 10 a.m. and 12 noon, then you are placing limitations on them. They may not be available at that time. You are not making it easy for your clients to do business with you.

It's your entire system; it's everything about your business that needs to be easy. You need to make it easy for your customers to just walk in through the door, purchase what they want, and then walk back out. People don't want to spend a great deal of time filling out documents, waiting for you to make receipts, and those sorts of things. You need to have a system where people can just get in and out quickly.

Therefore, it's important that you have a number of staff available so people who walk in can be served, and served quickly. You also need to have a sales process in place whereby it's quick and easy for them to walk out again.

Think about your business for a moment, from the point of view of your customers. One of the first questions that you need to ask yourself is, are you easy to get to? Can people just call in on their way home? Once they get there is there easy parking? Imagine it's a really cold and wet day. You still want customers coming in, but how accessible are you to those customers? Are they going to be soaked to the bone when they get in?

Now these are the kinds of things that make a difference. If you can say to people that there is ample undercover parking, you are going to be attracting a lot of people on a rainy day who want to come and see you anyway. They are not going to go out of their way to get soaked to the bone just to walk in through your door.

Home delivery is another way to make things easier for people to deal with you. If they can simply call up with an order and possibly give you credit card details over the phone, then you are going to have a huge advantage over your opposition.

Mail order, of course, is another great way of making things simple. This can be done in a number of ways, but by far the most popular at the moment is through the Internet. But you need to remember that some people are still wary of the Internet. Many still won't give their credit card details over the Internet for fear of being ripped off. But it's still one that is well worth considering.

Catalogue mail order is one of the simplest and most effective forms of this type of strategy.

Now that you have considered ease of use, it's important that you convey this in your advertisements.

Explain to people how simple it is. Let them know that they can be in and out in just a few short moments, that they don't have to be standing in lines.

As soon as you can start to convince people of this and demonstrate how quick and easy it is to deal with your business, the sooner you are going to increase the response you get from your advertising.

23. Who

This could be considered to be the most important section of this book.

Why? Simply because without a good understanding of your target audience, you couldn't possibly expect to write an effective advertisement. Before you even put pen to paper, you should spend a couple of hours considering those people that you are trying to target with your ad. This must be the first step to putting together any marketing campaign, or for that matter, any business.

Here are some of the things we need to consider when we are looking at *who*. First, you need to understand the way they think, the way they talk, their beliefs, their opinions, and how these opinions are formed.

If you don't already know these things, you'll need to spend some time with members of your target market, talking to them, and getting to know them. Find out what is important to them, what their beliefs are concerning your product or your service (both negative and positive). Take particular note of their way of talking, the common phrases they use, as well as any unique terminology they may use. Understanding the way they talk will be a major advantage when you're actually writing to them.

You also need to find out what their hobbies or interests are. You need to know what they do with their leisure time, how they walk, how they talk, how they think, how they dress, the sort of places they hang out at and, very importantly, the kind of publications they read or the stations they watch or listen to.

These are all the sorts of things that will make your campaign successful. If you don't have a good understanding of them, then your campaign is doomed to failure. Sure, occasionally you might fluke it, but over a period of time if you don't know the members of your target market intimately, you won't be able to communicate with them. Chances are, you won't even be able to reach them.

To give you an example, consider the advertising that you see on the back of taxis or on the sides of buses. Now to understand whether or not this is going to be effective for your business, then *you* must become the *who*.

What I mean by becoming the *who* is to place yourself in a position where you are likely to see the ad. Visualize yourself looking at the ad, taking into account all the relevant factors.

Once you have a good understanding of them, then you know exactly how to appeal to them. It goes beyond that; it also comes down to your store ad and the way you present your services. What's the first thing that people see when they walk in through your door? What's going through their minds? What sort of people are they?

A good example of the need for understanding the *who* and the people that you are going to be working with would be if you were advertising automobiles. It's the sort of appeal that you are going to make that is going to encourage people to take action.

Imagine for a moment that you are advertising sports cars. What kinds of people are going to be buying them? Will they be older, more conservative? Chances are, probably not. Would they be younger people, just out of school? Oh sure, they probably like your sports cars, but chances are that they probably can't afford them.

So the people that you are aiming at are probably people with a high disposable income, people who already have another motor vehicle, and people with egos—the sorts of people who are not interested in fuel economy or safety features.

24. Where

Now that you've identified the *who*, you need to work out *where* you'll find them in their highest concentration. Your prospects may read a certain magazine or trade journal, making advertising in that magazine a wise choice. They might be located in a certain geographical area, which would make direct mail or mailbox drops a more attractive alternative.

If direct mail or flyers aren't an option for you (this may be the case if you're advertising over a wide area or if you have a product with limited appeal), you need to find a publication that reaches them. There may be a number of seemingly suitable publications. So how do you know which to advertise in? You find out through testing and measuring. The easiest way is by trying small test ads in all of them and then testing and measuring the results. Then when you've found the one that gives the highest response, run your full-sized ad in that publication.

Newspapers are among the most common advertising mediums for the small- to medium-sized business. Newspaper advertising can be quite expensive, particularly in metropolitan markets. Basically there are two types of newspapers from which to choose, although there may only be one in some regional centers.

Daily Newspapers

The first of these is daily newspapers. These are papers that are printed six or seven days a week. Circulation can vary greatly from day to day. For example, a paper's circulation (number of papers sold each day), may be 45,000 on a Saturday and only 23,500 on a Monday.

Weekly Newspapers

The second type is weekly newspapers. These are printed only once a week and are quite often delivered free of charge to homes. Because weekly newspapers are delivered to specific areas, they can be a great advertising tool for businesspeople such as tradesmen, accountants, hairdressers, etc.

Daily newspapers tend to have a larger circulation because their articles are more up-to-date. They will also tend to attract wealthier clientele than weekly papers would. If you're selling more expensive items, luxury services, or have a sale that only lasts a few days, then daily newspapers are generally more effective than weekly publications. There is also a school of thought that says because you have to pay for a daily, you're more likely to read it. A weekly paper doesn't cost you anything, so there may be a tendency to discard it right away, or at best, skim over it.

Magazines

Because most magazines are national publications, they will generally be very expensive. The major benefit of advertising in magazines is that they target people with specific interests. Magazines are great if you sell your product nationally, if your product or service has a high price, or if your product or service targets a specific group of people. For example, a company that manufactures bullbars would advertise in a 4WD magazine, and a hose manufacturer would advertise in a gardening magazine. Magazine advertising can also be very effective for companies that sell by mail order.

Trade Journals

Trade journals are one of the least expensive forms of print advertising. Companies advertising in these publications have the advantage of being able to reach a very specific market. While this is a benefit, it can also be a limitation, as they generally won't have a very high readership. To use trade journals effectively, you need to have a great offer. A name, rank, and serial number ad will not be effective in these types of publications.

Newsletters

Schools, sporting groups, and other organizations may have newsletters that you can advertise in. Because of their low circulation and limited content, most newsletters will normally not be worth your time and effort. Advertising in these can be beneficial if you live in a small community or regional center, or if it's popular with a specific industry.

Of course, there will be many times where advertising in one of these publications will not be as effective as flyers or direct mail. For example, if you own a corner store the chances are you'll only attract people who live within a few blocks of your premises. Because there are generally a number of convenience stores in each town or suburb, there's not much point doing any mass advertising through newspapers or magazines. People simply aren't going to drive past their local store to come to you.

In this case, advertising in a newspaper would not make much sense. You have to pay full rate, which is calculated by the number of readers the newspaper will reach. But it doesn't take into account the fact that only a very small percentage of those readers are what you'd class as prospects. In this situation, doing a mailbox drop within a few blocks of your store would make a lot more sense.

25. What

There's no such thing as image advertising. This is the term newspapers and marketing people give to advertising that doesn't do a thing for your business or make you a cent.

This kind of "Hi. Our name is this, we sell this type of product, our phone number is this" advertising is a waste of time.

You need to say something to your potential readers; that is, there must be a strong message you are conveying. This may be in the form of a strong offer, an important point of difference, a list of the benefits of dealing with you, or something newsworthy about your product.

It's essential that *what* you say is appealing to *whom* you are trying to say it to. For example, throwing in a bungee jump with enrollment at a retirement village probably won't work. A free celebration dinner with the elderly person's children and grandchildren might.

Let's deal with each type of message, one by one.

Strong Offer: This is the most commonly used and the one that tends to work the best. Remember that people are totally uninterested in reading ads. They've usually picked up the publication to keep informed and be entertained. But an ad with an offer that stops them in their tracks can really work.

Point of Difference: Can work well when there is a large market for your product as well as many competitors. For example, if you are advertising a steak and seafood restaurant, you'd be hard pressed to stand out. But what if your steakhouse had live entertainment, free drinks from 7 p.m., and the best view in town? That would be worth promoting.

Listing the Benefits: If you don't have a strong offer or point of difference, listing the benefits of dealing with you may do the trick. For example, hairdressers could list the four reasons they give the best haircuts in town, or a beauty spa could emphasise the six ways a prospect's skin will improve after one visit. Most importantly, you must relate the benefits to the customers. Remember, always write your ad about their favorite subject—*them*.

Something Newsworthy: Perhaps you've just opened a new room in your restaurant, or you have a famous author coming in for book signings. Maybe you've just been given an award or one of your staff has done something amazing for a customer. If something has happened that has genuine interest value, tell your potential customers about it. But remember, it must encourage them to come in and buy (Note: Your secretary's third engagement is not worthwhile news).

26. How

Most of this book is about how to put together a newspaper advertisement or a direct mail letter. While the principles are basically the same for all forms of advertising, there are a few things you need to keep in mind when applying these ideas to other forms of marketing.

YELLOW PAGES

A Yellow Pages ad is not all that different from a newspaper advertisement. But there are a few things you need to keep in mind.

First, using a strong headline on your ad can easily double your response.

To understand why, think about this situation. You're shopping for air-conditioning in the Yellow Pages. The first ad you look at has "George's Cool World" in big letters across the top. The second says "Air-condition City." The third has a headline that says "7 reasons to call Harry's Air-conditioning." Which one are you more likely to read?

Generally, adding a headline is like creating a breath of fresh air in your section. While everybody else is intent on putting their business name in ultralarge type, you'll actually be providing people with a reason to read your ad.

Here's some great examples of Yellow Pages headlines that will help your ad stand out:

"7 reasons to call Jim's Widgets first."

"DON'T call anyone for Widgets until you read this."

"6 reasons why I'm the best Widget supplier on this page."

"4 things that are different about Jim's Widgets."

"Advice for those looking for Widgets."

"Warning...don't buy Widgets until you've read this."

Each of these headlines can be applied to any business in any section and each one has been proven to blow the other ads off the page.

It's also important to remember that people are looking to buy—so treat them that way. You don't have to convince them that buying your type of product or service is a good idea. You need to persuade them to buy from *you*. Include a headline that reflects that idea.

One of the other important things to know about Yellow Pages advertising is that people are looking for key words.

Here's an example: Let's say you're after someone to retile your bathroom. You're looking for two words: "tiling" and "bathroom." If you see an ad with those two words somewhere in it, you'll call the number.

On the other hand, if the ad simply says, "All tiling jobs," you may not call. People need to be completely sure they're dialling someone who can provide what they want. If the ad doesn't specifically mention what you're looking for, there's a chance you'll pass it by.

Think about the words you're market is looking for. If you rent appliances, it pays to mention everything you rent in the ad, not just "all appliances." In large type, write "fridges, TVs, videos, washing machines" and so on. Include everything.

Remember, the objective is not necessarily to be the best ad on the page. It's just to get them to call. Including key words is a way to ensure that happens.

Finally, don't be wishy-washy with your ad. *Tell* people what you want them to do. There's nothing wrong with saying in big bold letters, "Call George right now and organize a free consultation today."

Actually, it's 100 percent recommended that you include something like that.

There are three things that make a call to action work. First, you need to tell them when to act. As a general rule, *now* is the best time. Other options are "today," "immediately," or in rare cases "next time you..."

Second, you need to tell them precisely how to communicate with you: Either "drop in," "call," or "fax." In the Yellow Pages, the aim is to get them to phone you, and then drop in.

Third, you need to tell them what they are contacting you for: an appointment, a quote, more information, a free consultation, or a tour of the showroom.

Combined, your call to action might run like this: "Call now and ask to be sent a complimentary information package."

You might also like to include an offer as part of your call to action. For example, a free design consultation or a free voucher for a second dog wash when they have their first one (new customers only).

REFERRAL STRATEGIES

A referral strategy is a way of introducing new customers to your business at a low acquisition cost. Basically, it's a way of getting your existing customers to promote your business for you—a way of getting them to introduce their family, friends, and colleagues to your product or service.

There are a number of elements that, when combined, make up a successful referral strategy, from finding the right type of customer, to the strategy that best suits your type of business. There is one thing you need to understand above all else, and that's:

SERVICE. Your service must be extraordinary. Having good or even great service just won't do. If you want people to refer their friends, then make sure your service is first rate.

Once you're satisfied that your service is up to scratch, there are two key elements to consider:

1. What you want the people to do. You need to ask the customers to give you a referral. Now you may just ask them for names and phone numbers, or you may wish to get them to call people on your behalf. To get them to do anything for you, you need to consider the second element.

2. Your offer. If you don't give people a good reason, a "What's in it for me?," your strategy will fail. Of course, it stands to reason that the more difficult you make item one, the more attractive you need to make item two. If people really have to go out of their way to get a referral for you, you'd better make sure your offer is worthwhile. To find out if it is, ask yourself this: "Would I refer someone for that reason?"

So now you need to work out how you're going to get the referrals. One of the easiest ways is to use direct mail.

Here's what you do.

Send a mailing to your customers, starting the letter something like this: "Hi there. Just wanted to write and say thanks—thanks for choosing [business name]." After the preamble, get to the point: "We're aware that many of our customers come from referrals, that is, happy customers recommending that their friends visit us."

Then ask for the referral directly: "If you know people who are currently in the market, I ask that you give them one of the referral cards I've included. Thanks [name] and I look forward to seeing you again soon."

In your PS, offer a sweetener: "By the way, if one of your friends brings a card in and buys anytime in the next 21 days, I'll mail you a small gift—a voucher for a *free* massage." If the incentive is exciting, you'll find that referrals will flow in.

Best of all, it's generally very easy to get the incentive for free. In the example above, it would be simple to call the local masseur and ask for a couple of hundred free vouchers. Any switched-on masseur would understand the lifetime value of a new client.

To make the strategy even more effective, it's a good idea to follow up the letters with a phone call. Use questions such as, "Who was the first person you thought of handing a card to?"

HOST/BENEFICIARY

A host/beneficiary is when you and another business go into a loose partnership and help each other make extra profits. For example, a hairdresser might offer a free cut and style to the database of a beauty salon. The hairdresser gets new clients, the beauty salon gets more customer loyalty as the clients appreciate the *gift* from the beauty salon owner.

Host/beneficiary is ideal when you have a specific group of people you want to advertise to and there are other noncompetitive businesses already dealing with them.

Here's another perfect example: corporate training organizations. They know who their target market is (businesses that need help with customer service and sales) and the businesses that deal with them (stationery suppliers, computer shops, etc.). A host/beneficiary could work—they could get the stationery supplier to send the business owner a gift (a free one-hour needs analysis with a qualified trainer).

On the other hand, host/beneficiary strategies are probably inappropriate for a fast-food outlet—the market is probably too broad (anyone looking for a quick, cheap meal at lunchtime), and it's hardly worth going to the trouble and expense of setting up a host/beneficiary. You may as well just put an ad in the paper, as there's no specific business that would make a good host!

Remember, host beneficiaries work best because potential customers think the offer is a gift from the other business. They believe the business has gone out of its way to find this offer and pass it on. Because of that, they feel some obligation to take up the offer.

The way to market this to the database is via direct mail. Now, the letter must look like it's been written by the host business and therefore needs to be printed on that business's letterhead. The letter could look something like this:

Do you have any expensive jewelry you no longer wear?
Here's how to make every piece fashionable again...

Dear [name],

I've recently come across an excellent idea.

I'm not sure about you, but I've got lots of jewelry that I no longer wear. Either it doesn't fit my finger, or it's gone out of style. I mean, these rings still have immense sentimental value—they just aren't fashionable anymore.

That's why remaking is such a great idea.

Here's how it works: You take your existing jewelry, extract the raw materials (gold, silver, gems), and create something completely new. Instead of purchasing a brand new piece, you modernize what you already have.

The results can be truly startling, as the before-and-after shots I've included illustrate.

Of course, you may be happy with the style—it could be the fit that's a problem. With resizing, it's easily taken care of. For less than you'd think, your ring can be reshaped to fit your finger perfectly.

And best of all...

I've arranged a free assessment for you. This is a 15-minute analysis with one of this city's finest jewelers, John Harris of Melissa's Jewelers. Mention you're a customer of Manhattan Cosmetics and John will clean and polish your ring for free. Then, after careful examination, he will explain the possibilities.

You'll be amazed—the most archaic-looking piece can be turned into something sophisticated and dazzling.

This assessment comes with no obligation. It's simply an opportunity to see how easily your old, unused jewelry can be transformed.

Phone John now at 234 5678, or simply drop in.

Julie Smith

Manhattan Cosmetics

P.S. If you have your ring remade in the next 28 days, you'll receive a special bonus—a $50 voucher to spend at Manhattan Cosmetics.

27. The 80:20 Rule

There's a classic rule in business: 80 percent of your business comes from 20 percent of your customers. There's a converse law as well: 80 percent of your headaches come from 20 percent of your customers.

Let me explain how this works. In business you have four types of customers: "A" Class, "B" Class, "C" Class, and "D" Class. Your A-Class customers are the ones who always pay on time and never haggle on price. They refer good quality customers to you and they come back on a regular basis. Your B-Class customers are those who you're working on getting up to A-Class status. Your C- and D-Class customers are the ones who are constantly complaining. They try to get the price down all the time, they place unrealistic pressures on your time, and, worst of all, they always let their bills get to 60- or 90-days overdue.

So the 80:20 rule of business is simply this: Your A class customers, those most regular and loyal patrons, are the ones who are providing 80 percent of your income.

Understanding that this is the case, you need to do two things with your customer base. You need to shower your top customers with attention and first-rate service, and spend a lot less time chasing after the 20 percent of customers who form the 80 percent of your complainants. There are people out there who appreciate good service and are more than happy to pay a fair price for it. There are also people who have nothing better to do than work out ways to create misery and ill feeling.

I remember visiting a print shop once. While I was there, another customer came in. It turned out that the printer had made a mess of his job. Naturally, the customer was upset, but he continued to berate the printer for 20 minutes, asking ridiculous questions like, "Are you trying to get things wrong?" and "How can I be 100 percent sure this won't happen next time?" Within one minute the printer had offered to not charge for the work (which had already been fixed and done properly) and do the next job free as well. I thought that was being more than generous.

But no, that wasn't enough for this customer. For the moment, he was important and people had to listen to him. He was taking advantage for all he was worth. After ripping through the printer for 20 minutes, he asked if he could see the boss—he wanted to get stuck into someone else now.

If I were that printer, I would have asked the gentleman to leave and never come back. Sure, the printer made a mistake, but this guy was a customer you would wish on your competition.

While the printer was wasting time trying to satisfy this idiot, he was neglecting *me*, one of his most regular and best paying customers. I wasn't completely miffed, because I could empathize, but other customers would be.

Dedicate your time to chasing after customers who will comprise your top 20 percent. They are worth a little more time and energy. Effectively, you can afford to *sack* your C- and D-Class customers—you'll probably be doing your business a favor.

Imagine how loyal and pleased your top customers would be if you spent 80 percent of your time looking after their every need. Often, business owners get it the wrong way around—they spend all their time trying to make the perpetually unhappy and unimpressed customers happy, and get complacent with the satisfied ones.

Part 2

∎ Business Principles

28. Acquisition Cost

The true purpose of advertising is to *buy* customers. Before I go any further, I should explain what I mean by *buying customers*.

When you place an advertisement, or send out a marketing letter or brochure, it costs you money. You are, in effect, making an investment. This, hopefully, results in a number of people responding to your advertisement. Think of it as your return on investment. Your acquisition cost is then the cost of the advertisement divided by the number of people who respond.

So let's have a look at how this works.

Imagine you've placed an advertisement in your local paper that costs you $200. You then get twenty responses to your ad and out of those twenty people, ten actually purchase something from you. To work out your acquisition cost, you divide $200 by ten paying customers, which means each paying customer has *cost* you $20. In other words, it cost you $20 to *buy* each customer.

Now that you understand how to work out your acquisition cost, you've probably already started to see its importance. To gauge the effectiveness of your advertising campaigns, you need to know how much each new customer is costing you. You can then work out which campaigns are worth continuing and which should be modified or forgotten altogether.

So it makes sense that to understand your acquisition cost you need to know two things: How much the ad costs, and how many sales you made as a result of that ad. The first figure is relatively simple to ascertain. The paper itself will be able to tell you how much your ad costs. But the second figure may require more effort. This is why you need to test and measure—remember what I said about this earlier?

Having told you all this, I should point out that many people still make mistakes when they calculate their acquisition costs. They know how much the ad costs, but they make the mistake of dividing that figure by the number of leads they get, rather than the actual number of paying customers.

It's easier to work out how many people respond to your ad rather than working out how many actually converted into paying customers. But this creates a problem, as you can't truly know how effective an ad is unless you know the return you're getting from it.

One of the interesting things you'll discover when you start to test and measure is that some forms of marketing may bring a lot of inquiries. However, this doesn't mean they are necessarily effective. Another form of marketing may generate fewer leads but result in more sales. This is because the different marketing mediums you use will often target a different type of prospect.

You'll also find that the ad you've previously received a good response from actually generates fewer paying customers. This is because you haven't qualified it well enough. For example, an ad that says, "Call for your free real estate information kit" will probably attract more time wasters than an ad that says, "Call now for information on how we can help you sell your home."

While the first ad might get more calls initially, your acquisition cost will probably be higher. Not only are you paying for the ad now, but you also need to include the cost of producing and mailing out the information kits.

The key to advertising is to lower the acquisition cost, but many people don't think outside the box when it comes to marketing. They think that making an offer will cut too far into their profit margins. Instead, they prefer to offer less and therefore run less effective ads.

One such client I worked with was a bakery. The owner of this bakery was running an ad in the local paper each week at a cost of $395 a week. He was averaging about 10 customers per week as a result of this ad. Therefore his acquisition cost was $39.50 per customer.

The interesting statistic here was that each customer spent about $5.00 when she came in. Of that $5.00, his actual profit after all costs were taken into account was about $2.35. So he was actually losing $37.15 per customer. That's the sort of marketing you'd wish your opposition were doing!

I sat down with him and convinced him he needed to make a stronger offer. I told him he needed to offer everyone who brought the ad in a free chocolate éclair. His reaction was priceless. "But Brad, I can't do that. My store will be full of people looking for a freebie."

"What, a store full of people?" I replied. "That would be hard to take."

His hard cost on producing the éclairs was about 30 cents. Not much of an outlay. So reluctantly he agreed.

The big day finally came and the ad ran. It was the same size and cost the same as the one that had been averaging 10 sales. I didn't get a chance to talk to him on the day the ad came out because he was too busy. He'd been right about one thing: His store was full of people. Interestingly, when we worked out the number of people who'd come in for their free éclair and then brought something else, we discovered that he'd actually had 247 paying customers as a result of the ad.

Now think about this carefully. A $395 ad plus 30 cents per éclair means his total outlay for the campaign was $469.10. But it brought in 247 customers, meaning his acquisition cost was now only $1.90 per customer. A huge savings over the previous cost of $39.50.

Best of all, the average expenditure of those who came in was $4.55. Less hard costs, he actually made a profit from this, possibly for the first time ever.

So how does this apply to you? Knowing your acquisition costs will allow you to market in a profitable way. When you know you're making a profit from each ad you place, how many ads can you afford to run? As many as you can.

29. Lifetime Value

To fully understand the concept of profitable advertising and marketing, you need to understand the concept of *lifetime value*.

Let me explain what I mean by lifetime value.

Let's imagine you place an advertisement in the newspaper and it costs you $100. Let's also assume that this advertisement brings you one response. The customer then spends $10 with you. Now spending $100 to make a $10 sale would not seem very profitable, but if that customer came back to you five times over the course of the next 12 months and spent around $25 each time, then all of a sudden the ad has started to pay for itself and you've started to make a small profit.

Then imagine that the customer stays with you for a further three years. Now that single $100 advertisement has, all of a sudden, resulted in $300 or $400 worth of profit for you.

You see, it's not only the money you make from the initial sale. It's the amount of money that you're going to make from that one customer over a period of years.

To calculate the lifetime value of a customer, you really need to work out how much that one customer will spend with you, on average, over the course of twelve months. And then, on average, if the customer stays with you for a period of five years.

Some will stay with you longer, others will move away from the area or no longer need your product or service, but in the average business you would expect the customer to stay with you for approximately five years.

The other thing you need to consider with lifetime value is how many friends that one customer is going to refer to you over the course of those five years. Your first ad may run at a loss, but if that customer keeps on coming back on a regular basis and refers friends to you, then you have had a very profitable advertising campaign. You therefore not only calculate the lifetime value of the one customer that the advertisement brought to you, but also the lifetime value of the friends referred to your business.

Keep this in mind with your advertising. It's not just the people who come from the first ad but how much profit you're going to make from them over the course of the next five years as well as how much you make from the other people that they refer.

It's all about wallet share rather than market share. A lot of business owners go out looking for market share; they look to get the largest slice of the potential target market for their product or service.

What I prefer to look at is wallet share—the amount of money I make from each customer who responds to my advertisement, not just from the first sale but over a period of time.

When you take the focus away from market share and start looking at wallet share, and when you truly understand the concept of lifetime value, it's then that you start to make a true profit from your advertising.

30. Lead Generation

So let's look at marketing as a whole.

Marketing is made up of five key areas, five things you will need to consider if your marketing is going to be profitable and your business is going to be successful.

The first thing you need to look at is your lead generation. By lead generation I mean the number of leads or inquiries that you get from all the advertising you are currently doing.

Lead generation is not about the actual customers you sell to. That comes later in your conversion rate. What you need to consider is how many people are responding to the marketing that you are doing at the moment.

In some industries a response is when someone telephones from an advertisement. In retail stores it might be people walking in through the door. But lead generation focuses only on those customers or potential customers who are contacting you for the first time.

There are many ways to generate leads—Yellow Pages, newspaper advertising, radio commercials, direct mail, television advertising, and strategies like referrals, flyers, post office box drops—whatever it is that you do to get a response and to generate leads.

Now this is one of the most important things to measure. You need to know how many leads you are getting on average each week to be able to know whether or not your advertising is effective.

Imagine trying to test advertisements without knowing how many inquiries you are getting prior to changing your ad. Let's say, for example, you have been running an ad for a period of four or five months and then decide to change that advertisement, believing it's not working anymore. Now, how can you tell if a new advertisement is working better than the previous one unless you have tested both?

One of the mistakes that I see business owners making time and time again is relying on only one or two forms of lead generation. They advertise only in a couple of different areas. What they don't consider is the number of potential leads they could be missing out on. What happens if the newspaper ad that was bringing you calls year after year all of a sudden stops working? If instead of looking in the newspaper, people begin looking on the Internet for those products or services?

So you need to understand that you can't put all your eggs into one basket. For any business I would recommend using a minimum of eight different forms of lead generation—more if possible. The thing is that you need to be contacting as many potential customers as possible. But as I have just mentioned, lead generation is just one of the five key areas of business when it comes to marketing. Let's have a look at some of the others.

31. Conversion Rates

I've made more money for my clients in this one area than I have with any advertisement I've written or strategy I've developed. The major reason for this is that this is the one area of marketing where people fall down more than anywhere else.

The most successful small- to medium-sized businesses in the world excel in the area of conversion rates. You can't ever hope to be successful without paying attention to this aspect of your business.

So what do I mean when I say *conversion rates*?

We just spoke about lead generation, the number of inquiries you get from all of your advertising, but getting inquiries is only part of the battle. You need to actually sell to the people who your advertising brings in.

Conversion rates are the difference between those people who contact you as a result of your advertising and those who actually buy. It's the percentage difference between the two. If your advertising brings in 100 inquiries per week and you sell to 30 of those people who inquire, then your conversion rate is 30 percent.

Let's have a look at why your conversion rates are so important.

I've had many clients who've come to me claiming that they need better ads. When I've asked them what their conversion rate is, the common response is, "We're really good at that area of our business, Brad. We average about 70 to 80 percent." I'd then say, "Really? Do you mind if we test that for a few weeks?" In almost every instance my clients have come back with egg on their face, telling me that the conversion rate they thought was 80 percent was really only 20 or 30 percent.

Now this is a good thing, and it's a good thing for one simple reason. You can't double 70 or 80 percent, but you can double or triple 20 or 30 percent. If a 30 percent conversion rate is giving them their current turnover, then doubling it will double their turnover!

However, you need to understand that there is often more than one type of conversion rate in any given business. For example, if you had sales reps who followed up direct mail letters to get appointments, the number of appointments per hundred letters sent out would give you one conversion rate. But you also want to know how many of those people they get an appointment with actually end up buying. Getting an appointment is one conversion rate, but the sales from those appointments are another.

If you test and measure your conversion rates, you'll normally discover a few interesting facts. First, it will never be as high as you thought it was. This is because it's easy to forget those people who came in, had a quick look around, and then ducked back out through the door. Second, it will teach you what you need to work on.

Take for example the situation we just mentioned regarding sales reps following up letters to make appointments. Now if you found that for every 100 letters they sent out, they were getting 10 appointments and then making on average 8 sales from these appointments. This would give you some interesting insights into what needs to be improved.

In this case, your conversion rate from your direct mail letters is 10 percent, but your sales from appointment conversion rate is 85 percent. In this case you don't need to improve what they're doing during the appointment, as 85 percent is excellent. What you need to do is get more appointments for them.

Now it could be that you simply need to send out more letters, or you may need to work on the telephone script they use to follow up those letters. You just need to test a few new letters to try and get a better response. Whatever it is, at least you know where to start looking.

The chances are, however, that once you make your team members aware of what the conversion rate is, they'll fix it themselves by trying a little harder in that area. I remember I worked with a gift store once that also sold cigarettes. The majority of people who came in through the door came to purchase cigarettes. Not only didn't they buy any gifts, they didn't even look at them.

I suggested to the storeowner that she start to measure exactly what her conversion rate of total customers to gift customers was. I got her to hire a door counter that could keep track of exactly how many people came into the store. She then got her team members to work out at the end of each day how many gift sales they'd made. After two weeks of testing and measuring, her conversion rate came back at just 6.5 percent!

I then got her to explain this to her team. She placed that figure on a whiteboard in the staff break room, with a weekly goal underneath. The goal for the first week was an increase from 6.5 percent to 7 percent. The team members all agreed that this was achievable, and they went about improving it.

At the end of the first week the conversion rate had gone from 6.5 to 18.7 percent! All the team members had done differently was to ask the people purchasing cigarettes if they'd seen the new products they had in store. It was a simple strategy but one that made this store many thousands of dollars in extra profits over the next 12 months.

But you need to test and measure your conversion rates all the time. Not just for a week here and there, but all the time. It's not hard. You just get your salespeople to keep a running tally of how many prospects they speak to and then how many actually make a purchase. You then need to analyze these figures on a weekly basis.

This is important because you can find out who is doing well, and who isn't. You can also tell if someone is starting to slacken off and find out what's causing it before it starts to affect your sales.

So, let's have a look at just some of the ways you can increase your conversion rates.

Sales Scripts

These are absolutely essential, no matter what business you're in. The easiest way to put together a sales script is to record what your top salespeople say during the sales process. Write down exactly what they say, and then get the rest of your team members to use the script every time they sell. Every customer is different, but the objective is always the same: Match the product to the buyer. You should have scripts for everything—from answering the phone to saying goodbye.

I remember working with one client whose team members had a terrible time selling to people who phoned in from their advertisements. They would answer the phone in a friendly voice, and say, "Can I help you?" They could never quite close the sale. Their conversion rate was consistently around 15 to 18 percent.

So I got them to change the words they used at the start of the conversation to give them a chance to get their sales pitch across. People would simply call up and ask the price. They'd then hang up and call the next business to compare.

I got the team to start answering the phone with the lines, "Thanks for your call. Just so I can help you best, is it alright if I ask you a few questions?" Sales went through the roof. They'd ask the prospects a series of questions about what they wanted the product for, how they were going to use it, how often they'd be using it, and people started to buy.

Another line I often use with retail clients is, "Hi. Have you been to our store before?" If the person answers, "No," they would continue with, "Just so I can help you best, is it alright if I take a moment to explain how our store works?" If they answered, "Yes," they'd go on with, "Great, can I just take a moment of your time to show you some of the new lines we've just gotten in?" Sure beats the old, tired, "Hi. Can I help you?" line.

Scripts are very important to your conversion rate. If you change what you say to each customer, how can you expect to be consistent? It's vitally important that you test and measure a variety of scripts to find the most effective one for you and your product.

You'll probably get sick of hearing it after a while but your customers won't, particularly if they haven't heard it before. Even regular customers won't notice that you're using virtually the same pitch that you used the last time they were in your store. Remember that you're the only person who hears it day in and day out. To your customers it's as new and effective as the first time you used it.

Print a Benefits/Testimonials List

This is a sheet that you can give to people who come to look at your products or store. It can contain the four most important things about your product or the seven reasons yours is a better choice for them. But you must make sure you use it each time.

Alternately, print testimonials on it—that is, direct quotes from your past customers about how good you are. A mix of both can work very well. The benefit of using testimonials is that your prospects will find it reassuring that other people have dealt with you and are happy with the results. By doing this, you're almost getting your past customers to do your selling for you. If you don't have any testimonials, ask your past customers to provide you with them. Some may not want to, but you only need a handful that are happy to help, and you're well on the way.

This can be a great way to close the sale. If your prospects seem interested but aren't quite ready to commit, having a list of testimonials from past clients can often tip them over the edge. Of course, a benefit sheet can do the same thing, but you need to make sure you list only the benefits and not the features of your product.

Demonstrations

If you can demonstrate the product firsthand, do it. Because many people are highly visual, they like to see how things work. This also gives them a chance to experience the product before they buy. If you can't demonstrate it, think of a way you can do something similar—what about before and after photos? Or what about giving people samples to try? If you're in the food or beverage industry, taste tests may be another option.

Videos are another effective way to demonstrate your product. Because most people tend to learn through seeing rather than hearing, showing them how something works is far more effective than trying to explain it to them. If you can't communicate the benefits of your product to your prospect, how can you expect to sell it? By demonstrating how your product works and what it can do for the consumer, your conversion rate is certain to increase.

On-Hold Messages

Putting people on hold can either annoy the heck out of them or encourage them to buy. If you have to put people on hold, why not take the opportunity to tell them all about your business—why it's so good, what you sell, why they should buy *today*.

Many businesses use basic, annoying, on-hold music. The reason they don't give more thought to it is quite simple: Their own company has never put them on hold before. You can also have a local radio station played to clients as they wait, but why waste such an excellent marketing opportunity?

On-hold messages give you the chance to tell your prospects about other products or services they may not know about. If you offer a guarantee or have a Unique Selling Proposition, this is your chance to let people know about it. This is great for professional people such as lawyers or accountants, and retail stores that get a lot of phone inquiries. In fact, almost any type of business can make use of this sales aid.

These are just a few of the ideas that you can use to improve your sales. Remember, there's no point having a great ad that gets lots of calls, if in the end you can't convert.

32. Number of Customers

No business in the world can get more customers. I have many clients coming to me claiming they want more customers, not understanding that it is almost an impossibility.

Let me clarify what I mean by that.

You can't get more customers. It just doesn't happen. What you can do, however, is increase the number of leads you get from your current advertising, and then improve your conversion rate. This will ultimately lead to more customers.

This is what a lot of businesspeople don't understand. It doesn't come down to the number of customers you have; it comes down to the two key areas prior to that—the number of inquiries that you get, and the conversion rate from inquiry to customer. This is why testing and measuring is so important. It is crucial that you know how many inquiries you are getting each and every week. And it's just as important to know how many of those you actually convert into paying customers.

Businesses that focus only on the number of customers they have miss the point. By working on the other two areas that lead to more customers, you can then get an increase in the number of customers that you are dealing with.

One of the other things that you need to consider (other than the number of customers you are dealing with) is how many you can actually handle.

On a number of occasions in the past I have seen business owners who believe that they need more customers. So they go and invest substantial amounts of money getting more prospects to come in. They didn't realize that they were getting sufficient prospects in the first place; it's just that their conversion rate was not high enough.

What then happens is they generate more leads and they get even more people coming in for the first time, but they don't have enough team members to handle them. If the infrastructure is not in place, then a business can quite often do more harm than good by getting a large number of inquiries.

The thing you need to remember is that if people come into your store, they expect to be served. If you generate too many inquiries and you don't have enough team members to service those people, they will walk around your store for a while, then leave in disgust. Chances are you will never get those people to come back.

To simply run advertisements that get more customers coming into your store is the fastest way to destroy your business. This is why testing and measuring is so crucial and why I spend so much time talking about it.

You need to know you can handle the extra customers before you go spending money on promotions to get them to come in. Once you know how many customers you can handle, then you'll know whether it's worthwhile or not advertising to generate more leads.

If you find your capacity is inadequate, that gives you the chance to evaluate whether or not it is worthwhile employing more team members or shifting to larger premises. Of course, there are other ways to handle it. Maybe you can have a direct mail system or a phone order system where people don't actually have to come in. It just means you need to put in a little more thought and a bit more time and effort.

I once worked with an office supplier who rented reasonably sized premises. Then he experienced an increased number of inquiries. People would come in and look around but his store could only handle so many people. From time to time he would run advertisements that would get the store packed. People couldn't actually get in, let alone get served. As a result, he was actually losing business as a result of these ads.

So what I suggested was the possibility of his working from home in a mail order business where he didn't need to hold stock. He would simply sell by ordering stock from suppliers when he'd received orders himself. He was hesitant to do this at first but eventually agreed to give it a try.

We put a catalog and order form system into place, and within a few short months he had increased his turnover marginally. More importantly, he had increased his profit margin substantially.

He no longer had the high overheads of rent, wages, electricity, and all the other things that come with a storefront. His business never needed to have a storefront and when he realized this and made the change, his business grew substantially.

33. Number of Transactions

One of the hardest things for business owners to grasp is the importance of marketing to their past customers. I've seen people time and time again pour money into advertising to get new people to come in and then never spending a cent on getting them to come back. What they don't understand is that getting new customers can sometimes drive a business broke.

We've all heard the statistics that 8 out of every 10 new business will fail in their first five years. Of those that survive, 4 out of 5 will then fail in the five years after that. Now, there are many reasons why this happens, but one of them is simply that they get too many customers.

What's that, I hear you say? You thought you were supposed to get new customers! Well yes, you do want to get new customers, but only if they come back and buy from you at least five times.

Each time you market to a new customer it costs you money. As we've already mentioned, this is what we call your acquisition cost. But what many people don't realize is that their acquisition cost is often greater than the amount of money a customer will spend on a first-time sale. In fact, the average business needs to bring a customer back at least five times before it begins to make a profit from him.

Let me give you an example to show you what I mean.

Let's imagine the owners of a cafe spends $300 per week on advertising. Now let's say they get thirty new customers as a result of their ads. Their acquisition cost per customer is $10.

Now if they sell a sandwich and a drink to each customer to the value of $5, and of that, $2.50 was what it cost them to make the sandwich and supply the drink. They've actually lost $7.50 per customer. Now if those customers don't come back, they've actually lost $225 on that campaign! If they continued to market in this way and not get people coming back, they'd lose $11,700 per year on advertising. How long could they keep that up before they were forced to close the doors?

You need to understand the importance of getting your past customers to come back. Amazingly, business owners will, on average, spend six times more advertising for new customers than they will to get past customers to come back. The really surprising thing about it is it's far easier to get someone who has already purchased from you to buy again than it is to convince someone to buy from you for the first time.

Just because people have purchased from you once doesn't mean that they will continue to keep coming back. In fact, if you're not keeping in contact with your past customers at least once every three months, they're no longer your past customers.

They'll start to respond to your competition's advertising and you'll have to work twice as hard to get them back. But it doesn't need to be hard work to keep them coming in. There are a number of cost-effective ways you can use to keep them coming back. Let's take a look at a few of the easier ways you can consider.

Offer Service Contracts

If you're constantly servicing the customer's products, you'll know when they need replacing. You'll also have the direct opportunity to sell them accessories, or get referrals.

This is especially applicable when your product requires a healthy amount of attention to keep running properly and new models only come out every few years or so.

Make the service contracts very attractively priced—it's as much an investment in your future earnings as a service. If they keep coming back to you, you'll know exactly when they may be in need of an updated model.

Continue to form a strong relationship with clients during the service period and make sure they are happy. It'll certainly pay off when they come to buy the new model.

Send Out a Newsletter

Sending them a news-style leaflet every couple of months can really make people feel as though they are part of your business. This is absolutely essential in cases where people only buy once every three months or more.

You must keep in regular contact and a newsletter is an ideal way—not only can you advertise any product you want, but you can also include tips, articles, and more. Some businesspeople even include extracts of their own poetry!

If you include enough good information, people will read it and, more importantly, they will buy. You don't need to make it too sales oriented. Just letting people know about anything new is usually enough. But having said that, you should always include an offer or two to get people coming back in.

Run a Frequent Buyers Program/VIP Card

The classic method of getting customers to come back: Give them a card that gets stamped every time they buy. Again, this is great for businesses with a product or service that people buy regularly, more than every four weeks or so.

You may want to offer every sixth purchase free, or a special gift on the tenth purchase. Work out the number and what you can afford, but make it generous. If it's a pathetic offer, people will be completely uninterested.

The card makes people feel like they are working towards something. Even if they can go somewhere else and get the product or service cheaper, they probably won't—getting it cheaper isn't as much fun as handing in a completed card and getting something free.

Collect a Database

This should be something you are already doing. If it isn't, you must start *right now.*

There isn't really a business on the planet that proves an exception to the rule: collect names at all costs.

All you need to do is say, "I'd like to add you to my mailing list—can you fill this out?" Alternately, you could say, "We regularly mail out special offers to our customers—just fill this out and you'll receive them too." You can also run a contest or just go through your invoices.

Once you have a database, there are an infinite number of things you can do with it. It gives you the power to contact your customers and sell to them direct.

You can even categorize them so you're only mailing to the people you know will probably buy.

Reminder System

This is where you remind your customers of things they need to remember, such as when they need their car serviced again or when they need to send their mother flowers for her birthday.

This works brilliantly for mechanics, dentists, and other businesses that take care of the things we tend to forget.

For example, people will actually appreciate a note in the mail that says, "Just a reminder—it's been four months since your last car service. You really should come back within two weeks. I'll call you shortly to arrange a time."

Florists can use the idea too: By getting a list of their mother's birthday, their spouse's mother's birthday, and everyone in between, they can make many more sales. Every time a special occasion crops up, they can call and say, "I notice it's your Mom's birthday—would you like me to send her a $35 bouquet?"

Direct Mail Regular Offers

This is where you send your customers letters in the mail advertising particular deals on certain items. Practically every business should be doing this. Of course, it depends on whether you have a list of customer names or not.

You should mail your customers an outline of special offers. You can pick products or services they have never tried or alternately a package deal on something they have.

You'll find you get tons of people coming back just by doing this. If you don't get them the first time, make sure you mail them again. If they still haven't responded after three mailings, it may be time to call it a day and wipe them off your list.

It doesn't really matter which method of keeping in contact you use. The main thing is that you keep your customers coming back. A good past-customer strategy is like money in the bank. It's the difference between a successful business and an also-ran.

34. Average Dollar Sale

The fourth key to marketing any business is the average dollar sale that is made per purchase. By that I mean how much your customers spend with you each time they come into your store.

Now, some customers may spend a lot and others not much at all, but what I look for is an across-the-board average expenditure.

The reason this is important is that it allows you to calculate how effective a campaign is likely to be. Whether it be a past-customer direct mail campaign or you're looking to attract new customers through a print ad, you'll know roughly how many responses you'll need to make a campaign work.

But this is only part of the benefit of knowing your average dollar sale. Once you know what the figure is, you can then start to increase it. Imagine what would happen if you managed to increase your average dollar sale by just 10 percent over the next 12 months, and by 10 percent every year after that.

Your advertising expense would be the same, as would your overheads, but your profits would increase substantially.

I once worked with the owners of a hardware store that was not doing particularly well in their area. They had a good customer base and their ads were bringing a very good response, but they weren't selling anywhere near as many products as they could have been. They asked me to help them out and I was only too happy to oblige.

I went into their paint department and had a meeting with their team members. I got them to put in place a checklist of all the things that people might need if they were painting their houses. When they'd finished, the list was quite impressive. They had drop cloths, thinners, paint stirrers, brushes and rollers, aprons, and undercoats—absolutely everything you'd need to paint your house.

So, then I asked them how many of those things they sold to each customer who walked in the door. The silence was embarrassing. I told them they had to use the checklist with everyone who bought paint from them over the next two weeks. When we checked the results at the end of that time, their profits had gone through the roof. We then did a similar thing with every other department in the store.

But selling more of your own products is just the start. With a bit of thought and effort, you can make a killing selling other peoples' services. Let me explain what I mean.

Let's imagine for a moment that you're a mechanic. Now, if some of your customers had dents in their cars, you could arrange a deal with the owners of a body shop who would pay you a commission on any customers you sent to them. Or if you were an electrical retailer who sold television sets, you could also sell television antennas to your clients. You wouldn't actually have to stock the antennas; you'd simply place an order for your clients and take a commission on top. With a little bit of forethought and planning, you can make money in ways you'd never have thought possible.

So let's look at a few more strategies for increasing your average dollar sale.

Use a Questionnaire

If you're unsure of any additional products or services that you could sell, a simple questionnaire can be very effective. This is particularly useful when you sell one main product and want to find out what other products your customers are interested in.

A business that sells stationery may find that its customers all have laser printers and currently buy cartridges from somewhere else. You could ask your customers what would encourage them to start buying the cartridges from you

Use this to ask your customers what they would like you to include with your existing service.

Rearrange Store Layout/Merchandising

Changing your store layout can be an effective way to increase your average dollar sale.

A pharmacy is a good example of the type of business that should apply this idea. A pharmacy could put medicine cups on the same shelves as the cough mixture, or cotton balls next to ointments and creams. Products that are likely to be used together should be stocked together.

Point of Sale (POS) Material

These take the form of shelf talkers and bin labels and are normally available from suppliers. Again, these are excellent for businesses that have a large range of goods, but also for businesses that sell accessories to support the main purchase.

It can be very effective to have a cocktail shaker display on the counter of a liquor store or a cool drink display at a gym. Ideally, the POS display should be of something that the customer would normally forget but probably does need.

If your current supplier isn't providing you with the "silent salesperson shelf talkers," then call and request that they do. If you're making up your own point-of-sale signs, remember to focus on the benefits of the product. And include a list of accessories that are commonly purchased with that item. It can help boost sales.

Impulse Buys

Place impulse items like chocolates or magazines at cash registers to tempt people as they wait. Great for high volume businesses: supermarkets, newsstands, and small food outlets.

A more creative application would be a toy store with candy at the front counter or close to the entrance.

The longer they wait, the greater chance of their weakening. Impulse buys can also be placed throughout the store. For example, flashlights next to batteries, mops with buckets, paint brushes with paint, etc.

Create Package Deals

An excellent way to move more items is to offer them at a discounted rate to customers who buy them as part of a package deal. This can be applied by most businesses, but especially those with a high volume of customers like supermarkets, pharmacies, and newsstands.

Imagine a newsstand that sold three popular women's magazines for the price of two. Many ladies would take up the offer.

Simply package up a number of associated products and sell them at a price that is less than they would cost individually. You can use this to get rid of slow-moving items by including them as part of the deal.

Be a bit creative with the way you increase your average dollar sale. What takes some time to put together now can make you a lot of money further down the track.

35. Turnover—Gross Revenues

Now you might wonder what turnover has to do with writing advertisements, and I'll admit, not too much. But you should understand the lack of importance that turnover has in your business.

What's that, I hear you say? Turnover not important?

Well, it's not as important as most people think. Turnover is the most highly overrated figure in any business. Often I hear people say, "'Oh, I had a turnover of $10 million last year." Well, that's great if you actually made a profit, but if your expenses outweighed your turnover, this figure is irrelevant.

The figure you need to be most diligent about is your profit. It is much better to have a turnover of $300,000 with a profit of $200,000 than a turnover of $1 million and a profit of $100,000.

But back to how this is relevant to your advertisements.

When you're about to advertise a product or service, you need to ask yourself, "Will this ad increase my profits?" not, "Will this ad increase my turnover?" Also, when it comes to testing and measuring the success of your ads, look at how much money you made after expenses, not how much extra was put into the till. Business is only about making money for you, the business owner, not about bringing money in that has to go out in wages, goods, and other expenses.

Put your focus into this and you'll soon start to see *real* results from your advertising.

36. Margins

Just as turnover is overrated, margin or gross profit is one of the most important figures in your business. However, a common mistake that is made is to confuse margins with markup.

They are two completely separate figures. Markup is a calculation on the cost price of your goods. So if something costs you $1.00 and you mark it up 100 percent it will make the retail price $2.00, giving you a margin or gross profit of 50 percent.

So let me show you how this all works.

If your product costs you $250 to buy and you mark it up by 100 percent, you will now be selling it for $500. Simple enough so far. But where people make mistakes is in confusing markup and margins. Someone with the markup we've just described might now go and advertise their goods at 50 percent off. They think, "Well, I just marked it up 100 percent, so if I discount it by 50 percent I'll still be making 50 percent." But this is not the case. Your margin is only 50 percent, not 100 percent!

So, if you now go and sell your goods at 50 percent off, you'll be giving away *all* of your profit. In fact, you'll be giving away more than just your profit, because your margin will not have really even been 50 percent. You have to allow for wages, bills, and other expenses. So if you mark a product up by 100 percent, and then discount it by 50 percent, you're actually giving money away!

It's all well and good to have a high turnover and to be selling high-priced items, but it's pointless if you're not taking money home at the end of the day. It all comes down to profit margins.

So before you go discounting your products, understand the difference between margins and markup. A big discount might bring a good response but it can also drive your business broke. Better to give away added value or to package up a number of products, but never, ever, give away your margins. Remember, you're running a business, not a promotion.

37. Profits

Finally we come to the end result of all the work and calculations you've just done.

Put simply:

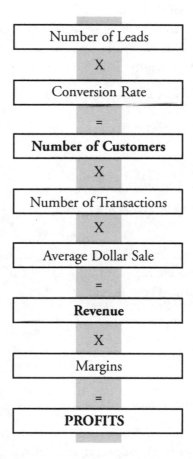

Profits are by far the *only* significant score your business comes up with, not to mention the prime reason for running the ads you're about to run.

So, why stress this point?

Two reasons: First, you cannot improve your profits without working on the *variables* that lead to it, namely the five points mentioned in bold above.

Each of these factors leads to a result: your profit.

Far too often people want more profit without realizing what it consists of. So go to work on the five variables and the profit will take care of itself.

The second reason to make a point about the importance of profit: As an accountant I was taught to focus on reducing costs and therefore improving your bottom line. Truth is that there are five areas to focus on, not just one. You see, margins will only get you so far. In other words, you can reduce your costs only so far before things start to fall apart. Let's guess and say that by really focusing on costs, you were able to reduce them by 15 percent. Great result—or is it?

You see, the formula says *margin*, not costs.

Put bluntly, you can make a whole lot more by focusing on the top side— leads, conversion, transactions, and average dollar sale—than you ever can by working just on your costs.

So, make sure you focus on profits, not turnover. Profits, not how many people you employ. And profits, not anything else that you pretend means that you're succeeding.

Remember, without profit you've just worked very hard for no return. Oh yes, to all the believers in the dot.com world, you can get market share and grow with a profit, if you know what you're doing.

Remember, *profit* is *king*.

38. Purpose

I'd like to take a moment now to tell you a bit of a story.

You may be tempted to laugh at what I'm about to tell you, but it actually did happen. The tragic part is it's happening every day in businesses all around the world. This is a story of a conversation I had with a client of mine. The business was a hardware store owner that specialized in plumbing and the selling of plumbing equipment and tools.

I was talking to the owner, John, and I mentioned that I had noticed he had an advertisement in Saturday's paper. The advertisement didn't say much; it simply had his name at the top like a headline and a few bullet points underneath.

I said, "John, do you get many calls from you advertisement?" He replied, "No, not really. None that we notice." I responded, "Well, why are you running it then?" To which he replied, "Well, you've got to advertise just to keep the name out there, I suppose. I hadn't really thought about it. The ad has been going in every week for a couple of years now, and I just saw no reason to change it."

Needless to say, this is one of the first things that I addressed when I started working with John. Anytime you run an advertisement, you need to understand what the purpose of the advertisement is! Now, you might say it's obvious—to make more sales and to bring more customers in—but that's a broad definition. You run advertisements for various reasons and you need to be exactly clear on why you are actually running them.

For example, you may run advertisements in the paper to get people to cut out a coupon and mail it to you in order to enter a contest. You might be doing this more as a means of building a database of potential customers that you can mail to at a future date than to make direct sales.

Another reason for running a campaign might be to create store traffic. In this instance, you might advertise a lower-priced item than the one you are actually trying to sell. The idea is that you advertise it just to get people through the door, and when they come, you work on upselling them to a higher model or a more expensive product.

With other advertisements you would be looking to make direct sales by advertising the product at the price you want to sell it and getting people to come in and actually make the purchase.

Alternatively, you could be introducing a new service to your past customers. You might simply be mailing out to let them know you are doing something new or that you have a new product or a new model. In this situation, you are trying to get them to come back to you again, rather than getting new customers coming through the door.

These are just a few examples. It's important that you have it really clear in your mind what the purpose of your advertisement is. How could you otherwise expect to know if the campaign has been effective?

It's a good idea if, before you start writing your advertisements or your direct mail campaigns, you actually sit down and work out what you are hoping to achieve. When you are clear on this, you start writing the campaign, and only then can you start writing your ads.

Once you have completed your ad, you then go back through it and make sure the advertisement is working towards that purpose. If you want people to phone in, does it clearly state that? Does the advertisement actually encourage people to take that course of action? If you want your past customers coming back for a special offer, then consider: Is that offer effective enough?

Once you are clear on the purpose and you have gone through and made sure your advertisement is following those lines and leading people to that outcome, then you need to put that purpose up on the wall. Stick it somewhere where you can see it.

When the campaign has finished, go back to your purpose and make sure that the campaign has given you the outcome you were after. If it hasn't, then you know not to run that campaign again in the future. You'll know you need to address certain areas and, more importantly, you'll know which areas to address if you haven't achieved the results you were aiming for in your ad campaign.

39. Break Even

What I'm about to teach you is the fastest way to drive your business broke. This is the one simple way to lose thousands of dollars in advertising and put enormous pressure on the cashflow of your business.

Don't work out the breakeven point for your campaign.

There it is. Simple, isn't it? So simple in fact, that thousands of business owners do it month after month, year after year, until their businesses go broke.

What they fail to understand is that there's more to advertising than getting a few people to walk in through the door. It's about making your advertising profitable. If you're not making money from your ads, you shouldn't be running them.

It's essential that you work out your costs up front, otherwise you'll have no idea what you need to achieve in order for the campaign to be worthwhile. You may find out after doing the analysis that the campaign has so little chance of success that you need to go back to the drawing board altogether.

So let's have a look at how you go about working out your breakeven point on any campaign.

The analysis needs to be done for the whole campaign. First, work out your total fixed costs. After you've worked out your total fixed costs (for the campaign), you then work out your profit (your average dollar sale minus your variable costs). This gives you enough information to work out how many responses you need in order to break even.

Divide this number by the total number of letters you are planning to send out or the cost of the advertisement you're about to place. This will give you a percentage response rate. As a very rough guide (every case is different) anything over five percent for direct mail is stretching it. If you need a higher response, you might need to rethink it.

The very best flyers and direct mail letters to untargeted lists achieve a response rate of around 10 percent. These are rare results. If you need higher than that to break even, reassess whether these strategies are the best way to go. The same applies to print advertising. Work out how many sales you need to make and whether that's an achievable amount based on your previous experience.

Without knowing this figure, you can't possibly hope to know whether your advertising is working for or against you. If you run a direct mail campaign that needs a 45 percent response rate to break even, you'll start to go backwards at a very rapid rate.

But there's another reason for calculating your breakeven point. It's simply so you can see how much true profit you're making from each campaign. Maybe you work out that your press advertising is more cost effective than your direct mail, or that television is making you more money than radio. Whatever it is, you can't make a value judgment until you work out what each campaign needs to achieve to be profitable.

I worked with a real estate agent once who was advertising on television and radio. He found he was getting slightly more inquiries from radio, but it was costing him substantially more in advertising rates. We worked out that the breakeven point was higher, and that he actually got more sales from his television ads than he did from radio. In fact, his radio ads were costing him money, while his TV ads were making him money, even though radio produced more inquiries. It was more cost effective to advertise on television.

So clearly, you need to work out your breakeven point on each campaign you run.

To assist you, I've included an example of a breakeven analysis sheet for a direct mail campaign. Now you'll need to change some things for press advertising and other types of campaigns, but the basic ideas are the same for all.

Break-Even Analysis

Hard Costs

Production	$	....
Paper	$	....
Printing	$	....
Delivery	$	....
Other	$	....
1. Total Fixed Cost	$	....

2. Average $$$ Sale	$	....

Variable Costs

Wages	$	....
Electricity	$	....
Telephone	$	....
Rent	$	....
Brochures	$	....
Other	$	....
3. Total Variable	$	....

Delivery Costs

Cost of Goods Sold	$ ....
Taxes	$ ....
Transportation	$ ....
Packaging	$ ....
Other	$ ....
4. Total Delivery	$....................

5. Net Profit [2/(3+4)] $ ....

6. Response Needed to Break Even (1/5) $ ....

40. Return on Investment

You'll no doubt recall that earlier in this book I mentioned that advertising is an investment. Well, just as with any other investment, you need to ensure that you're getting a worthwhile return on your money.

It's crucial that your ads are making you money. If they're not, then change what you're doing.

There are basically three different return-on-investment scenarios: You make a profit, you break even, or you take a loss. Obviously we'd prefer to avoid the last one, but sometimes an initial loss can still be profitable in the long term.

So let's look closely at what you need to consider in relation to your return on investment.

You have a number of things to consider. First, how much is your total investment in the ad you're running? Then you need to work out your profit on each sale you make. Now, I don't mean how many dollars you put in the till. You need to work out how much your stock costs you, your wages, power bills, phone bills, etc.

Also, consider the lifetime value of your customer as we mentioned before. Also the lifetime value of the referrals those new customers might give you. It's common that one form of advertising might bring you only a handful of customers, but if your referral system is a good one, you might end up with many clients from that one ad.

So, considering all this, remember that average businesses need to sell to customers three to four times on average before they make a profit from them. If this is the case with your business, you might lose money on the initial sale but in the long term make quite a tidy profit from your new clients. You just need to ensure that you keep them coming back.

But what if after all the calculations you find that you're losing more than you're making, even after considering the long-term profits?

You need to change your ad to bring you more customers, or find a more cost-effective method of getting them in as clients. Sometimes the cheapest form of marketing is not the most cost effective. Imagine you are running two marketing campaigns. The first one is a newspaper campaign that costs you $1785 per week. It brings you, on average, five new customers who each spend $1980 per year with you on average. Out of that, 40 percent of the money they spend is profit. That means that this campaign is making you about $2175 profit per ad each year.

Now imagine that your other campaign is direct mail. You invest $577 per week on this campaign but it brings you on average only one new customer every two weeks. These customers tend to spend less and your testing and measuring shows that on average, customers generated from a direct mail campaign spend only $950 per year. This means that your direct mail campaigns actually lose you about $387 per week (again assuming that 40 percent of what they spend is profit).

So you need to consider a number of factors before you can really work out if your campaign is giving you a worthwhile return for your dollar. If your marketing and your business are to be successful, you need to put in the effort and find out what your returns really are.

41. Only the Numbers Can Tell

There's one thing that most unsuccessful businesses have in common: They don't know their real *numbers*. They base their decisions on instinct, guesswork, and other nondescript factors.

When it comes to advertising, only the numbers can tell. The number of calls you get, the number of sales you make, the number of dollars in your pocket when all the expenses have been paid and your time considered.

There are so many business owners who are confused—they seem to be working hard and doing well, yet there's never any money left over at the end of the day. That's because they haven't worked out their real numbers.

When you apply this idea to advertising, things start to make a lot more sense.

Let's take an example. Bill runs an ad. It costs him $300. He gets fifty calls, thirty of which turn into sales. In his mind the phone has been ringing off the hook and he's been masterful at turning these calls into sales. The thing is, he's still not doing well and there's nothing left after expenses.

Why? Let's work it out.

Each sale was around $10, $2.50 of which was profit (by profit we mean that the item itself costs Bill $7.50 to buy). He made thirty sales, which gives him $75. So far, it's cost him $300 to make $75 and he hasn't even paid himself a wage, paid for the ad, covered employee expenses, or paid anything else!

That's a minor example, but many businesses operate this way all the time. They base their opinion on how they're doing on the wrong factors. Remember, only the numbers can tell.

Many business owners look for positive signs just to give themselves some hope that things are picking up. That's fine, except it often encourages them to ignore the bigger picture. At the end of the day if you're not making more money than you're spending, your business is just another expense, like having a mortgage or putting your child through private school.

Unfortunately there isn't an income to support this expensive drain on your funds. So ultimately the bank ends up subsidising your business and you end up in lots of trouble with the bank!

You need to work out the real numbers for each ad you run. Taking the example above, Bill would need to pull in 120 customers just to pay for the ad. If you're talking about local paper advertising, that's probably not realistic. Perhaps he needs to advertise a higher-priced product, find a way to increase his margins, or look at alternative ways of advertising (flyers, another paper, classifieds, etc.).

Getting lots of calls or seeing lots of customers doesn't mean anything if you're not making any money at the end of the day. You might end up paying money to work yourself into the ground!

42. Don't Discount

If this is not the number-one principle of business, it probably should be. If you don't get anything else out of this book, understand this one rule: *don't discount*!

What's the point of having a recommended retail price, if you don't use it? Besides, why shouldn't people pay your full retail price?

Discounting creates a perception in the marketplace that you are cheap, that the price you have on your stock or service is too high because you always offer a discount, or that you don't value you product or services.

It also affects your business long term. When you discount, you encourage price shoppers, not loyal customers.

A far better way to do business is to add value rather than discount. Offering things like free delivery or throwing in extras like slow-moving stock that you have trouble selling anyway is far preferable to discounting.

The trick is to offer products or services that have a high-perceived value in the mind of the consumer, while having a low hard-dollar cost for you, the business owner. Offering anything is better than cutting your prices. It could even be a fact sheet or a book with a relevant section on the particular product or service you are selling to your client.

Now having said all that, I know exactly what many of you are thinking: "But my competitors cut their prices. I won't be able to compete unless I drop mine." Well, that sort of thinking is quite simply a load of garbage.

Let me show you why.

If you sell a product valued at $10, you need to sell 100,000 to make a million dollars. But if you sell a product valued at $100,000 you only need to sell 10 to make a million. Now this might seem like an extreme example, but I use it to emphasize a point. If you're in business to make money, you should be doing more with less. Making more money with less effort.

Rather than discounting your prices, you should be raising them. What you need to understand is that you can increase your prices, lose some customers, and actually make more money than you were previously. If, for example, your current margin is 20 percent and you increase your prices by 10 percent, you can have a 33 percent decline in sales and still achieve the same gross profit!

So, discounting should be the last thing on your mind. Besides, you'll probably only lose C- and D-class customers anyway. You know the ones: Those who complain the most, want the world, and then never pay on time. You're better off without them.

The introduction of scripts into your business will assist with negating the price focus greatly. If you train your team to ask these magic questions, "Just so I can help you best," or "Is it okay if I ask you a couple of quick questions?," you'll find that the drop-off rate of customers is much less than you'd expect it to be.

These lines give you and your team the opportunity to ask lots of rapport-building questions that take the focus off the price and put it back onto service and giving your customers a solution to their problems. When you ask either/or questions, people then start making a decision as to which color they are going to have, not the price. Try it in your business; it works time and time again.

43. Add Value

Most businesses think the best way to attract customers is to discount. As we discussed in the last section, that's a misconception.

Adding value is a simple concept. It means that customers will get more for their money. Rather than giving them the same for less, you give them more for the same price.

So what's the difference and why is it smarter to add value? Simple—you can generally add a lot of value for a small outlay. Put another way, the perceived value of what you give the customer may be high but the hard cost to you will generally be low.

This is definitely preferable to discounting. When you slash prices, you are giving away exactly the amount you say you are. If you're taking off $15, that's $15 that you're not getting.

When you throw in something with a perceived value of $15 (that is, the item normally sells for $15) it's costing you far less. Perhaps the hard cost on the item is as low as $5. If you were to give a full $15, you could give something away valued at $45, assuming your margin was universal.

Let's consider the example of a mechanic. Imagine if a mechanic offered you $20 off your next service. That'd be pretty good and maybe even enough incentive for you to make a booking then and there. The problem is, the $20 is half the profit margin on the service. If the mechanic does this for every customer, he'll cut his takings by 50 percent.

Instead of the discount, the mechanic could choose to add value. Here's how: He could throw in a free wheel alignment (value $25, but negligible cost to the mechanic—he's already got the equipment) a 1-liter container of premium oil (value $7.95, but only $2 hard cost), a two-for-one voucher for a car detailer (value $35, but free to the mechanic, if the car detailer wants to promote himself), an engine clean (value $20 but negligible to the mechanic—he's got the equipment), and a free engine performance test and print out (again, free to the mechanic, but $15 value).

He's just managed to add around $100 value, at a hard cost of $2 plus 10 minutes of time. That beats a $20 discount any day. Of course, it requires a little more creativity than the straight discount.

In the end, the added value offer will bring you more customers and cost you less. It may also introduce customers to other aspects of your service. So before you reach for the markdown pen, think about adding more value.

> **Part 3**

▌Writing Successful Ads

44. Target—Offer—Copy

I remember a few years ago watching one of my new copywriters staring blankly at his computer screen. He had spent what seemed like an eternity trying to write an advertisement.

He'd start typing, stop and delete it, get up and walk around, come back and sit down again, and start all over. You see, nothing was working for him; he just could not seem to get into the swing of it. When I asked him what his problem was, he pointed out that he had writer's block. He explained he had already written an ad for one of his clients but the results weren't that good.

He had been disappointed with the results, and the client thought he could have done better.

So I asked to see the advertisement that he had originally done. As I looked over it, I was not surprised to see that the copy itself was quite good. The reason why I employed this guy was because he was a good writer.

I pointed out that the problem was not in the copy he had written. In fact, it was exceptionally good. The problem was that it was poorly targeted. The copy was fine, but it was the strategy that was at fault. The ad was for a client who worked on souped-up sports cars, pretty much aimed at the rev head sector.

Now, he got across the benefits and he had a good offer, but the problem was that he had been running it in the early general news section of the paper. He then tried running it in the business pages, assuming that men would read the newspapers, so that would be where he would get his best response.

But what he hadn't allowed for was the fact that the sort of people who would buy these services were more likely to read the sports pages. I suggested that he call his client and simply recommend that he run the advertisement in the following week's sports pages, and to measure the results from there.

The client was hesitant at first but then agreed to try it. The results were outstanding, the advertisement quadrupled its response from the previous best week, and the client was delighted. You see, the mistake that had been made was placing too much emphasis on the copy. What my young copywriter hadn't realized was that *what* is written is the least important of the three key components that go to make up a successful advertisement.

By far the most important component is the target, the person whom the advertisement is aimed at.

Interestingly, I find from the advertisements that I have written that the offer is five times more effective than the actual wording of the advertisement. The best-written ad in the world, given a poor offer and poor targeting, cannot expect to get a response. Yet the most poorly written advertisement that has a good offer, and is very well targeted, can get a very good response.

You need to be really clear on who your target is.

One of the easiest ways to target your advertisement is simply to target those specific people with your headline. For example, if you were advertising a product that would be used by women over the age of 35, you simply place a headline which says "Attention, women over 35." Immediately, all those people who aren't women over the age of 35 will read further or pass over your ad, but you didn't want them reading it anyway.

For all those women who are over 35, you have immediately grabbed their attention. This is something that is speaking directly to them. But it's a common mistake for people to spend too much time trying to work out what to put into their copy rather than just getting in there and saying what they have to say.

But the advertisement will still fail if the offer is not strong enough. The offer needs to inspire people to take action. Maybe its something that they get for nothing, or maybe it's just a sensational discount. Whatever it is, it needs to be good enough to get people to take action. But we will talk more about that later.

Of course, one of the easiest ways to overcome writers block is to simply look at the product or the service that you are about to write about. Just sit down and work out what it is about that product that makes it special. Why is it that people want to buy it?

Then you can look at why your product is better than your competition's—not that you criticize your competition, but that you simply talk about the benefits of yours over some of the others that are available in the marketplace. And then you would have a sensational offer, something that would get people to act quickly.

Understanding that the target is ten times more important than the copy, and that the offer is five times more important than the copy, then that is the ratio of the time you should spend on creating the advertisement.

The only things you need to consider are how to target your advertisement to the people that you are trying to reach, what offer will make them respond, and last, what is the best way to communicate that to them through your copy?

45. Guarantees

If you don't have a guarantee in your ads, you're ignoring what can be the most powerful weapon in your marketing arsenal. When people see a guarantee, it gives them a definite reason to deal with you: They can be *certain* that they will get exactly what they're after.

You see, most business owners mistakenly think that people care only about price. Don't get me wrong—price is a factor, but only a minor one. First and absolutely foremost, customers want *something*. If they have to pay more to get that something, then they will. They may not be pleased about paying more, but they will hand over the cash at the end of the day.

Let's say you're looking for a moving company. You've had some real shoddy operators in the past—people who've looked like they've been in the local bar for two hours before they come around and others who didn't seem to mind breaking the occasional glass table or denting the odd priceless antique.

You're feeling wary. You look through the Yellow Pages. There are heaps to choose from, some with prices as low as $32 an hour. You like the idea of paying less, but you can almost be sure that these "cheapies" will break your stuff before they even get it into the truck. The chances of them having comprehensive insurance at that rate is minimal. They'll probably swear in front of your kids and look like they just got out of jail. You're not eager to go through that experience again.

Then you see another ad. It doesn't say much, and it doesn't offer a price, but it does have something that catches your eye: a guarantee. It reads, "We will be very gentle with your possessions. We will quote up front and stick to it. We will be polite and presentable at all times, and we will make your move enjoyable. If at the end of the day you're not satisfied we've done everything we promised, we won't charge you."

That blows you away—someone has had the courage to answer every fear you had. And if they don't work out, you get the move for *free*! That wins you over and you book that company.

As it happens, the movers turn out to be everything they promise and 50 percent more expensive than any other quote you've had. You're not too worried, though. Everything went without a hitch, and anyway, how often do you move? And what price can you put on your treasured possessions? Why not get the best and make it easy for yourself?

If you can see the logic in this scenario, you don't need any convincing when it comes to the benefits of guarantees. For a moment, think about every fear customers have when dealing with businesses like yours. Now imagine if you could guarantee that these fears will not become a reality if the customer decides to deal with you. How much more business would that win you? It would be more than worth the 10 minutes it takes to write a guarantee.

In case you're wondering, guarantees *don't* attract scammers, or at least not in large numbers. The extra customers your guarantee attracts will more than cover the few dregs who come in to take advantage in an unscrupulous way. You'll just have to trust me on that one.

A guarantee means that you have a unique point of difference and it can mean that people will pay higher prices to deal with you. Try it and find out!

Most people think about guarantees in the wrong way. I couldn't count the number of clients who have said to me, "I can't put that guarantee in my ad—people will rip me off."

Think about this: 99.8 percent of the population is honest—the remaining 0.2 percent probably can't afford your product anyway. Cater to the majority.

Consider this: The process people have to go through to ask for their money back is an excruciating and socially uncomfortable one. It takes confidence, assertiveness, and self-assurance. As callous as it sounds, most of the population lack these qualities and don't have the guts to ask for a refund—even when you openly express you're willing to give one.

Once you get over the fear that people will rip you off, new possibilities open up. A bold guarantee says to people, "these guys must be good." It takes away the risk associated with the purchase and gives people confidence in you.

But a word of caution: Resist the temptation to simply say "Satisfaction Guaranteed" or "Complete happiness or your money back." These phrases mean nothing to people, as they've heard them so many times.

Try this: "You'll be astounded by our professionalism and dazzled by our efficiency. If you're not, we'll refund your money and pay for you to see one of our competitors."

If you're frightened by the prospect of including a guarantee like this in your ad, good. It means it's effective; it makes you think.

Importantly, your guarantee needs to address the biggest frustration your customers experience when dealing with your industry. Let me give you a brilliant example. The problem with going to the hairdresser is you never quite know how it will turn out—sometimes the hairdresser takes off too much and everybody laughs at you, sometimes she takes off too little and nobody notices. Here's how one hairdresser addressed this frustration.

Her guarantee read, "We'll cut your hair exactly the way you want it cut and you'll be delighted with the final result. If you're not, we'll refund your money twice over and pay for one of our competitors to fix it." This guarantee brought hundreds of people in, yet no one ever took her up on it. The reason was simple. After spending twenty minutes developing a relationship with the hairdresser, it was almost socially impossible for the customer to turn around and say, "I don't like the job you've done. I want twice my money back and for you to pay for me to see someone else."

That's the beauty of a guarantee. Very few people will ever claim it. Another great example of this was a music store I had as a client. The store owners told me they wanted to sell instruments to more young people, in the 7- to 10-year-old bracket. But parents were concerned that they would end up paying hundreds of dollars for the instrument and lessons, only to find out that their children couldn't play.

So I helped them design a guarantee that said, "We guarantee that after just four weeks, your child will be playing well, or we'll take back the instrument and give you a 100 percent refund."

At first they were apprehensive about offering such a guarantee. "But Brad, it can take weeks for some kids to even get started and many give up after just a few months." But what they didn't realize was that while the guarantee sounded great and addressed the concerns of the parents, nobody would ever take advantage of it. The guarantee was only for a four-week period, and the novelty of the new guitar or organ would not have worn off by then. Because the child would still be enthusiastic, what parent would be heartless enough to say, "Sorry Tommy, but you're hopeless. I'm taking your guitar back." No one I've ever met.

So, put some thought into your guarantee. What can you offer as a guarantee that sounds great, but one that people will almost never act on? Come up with the answer to this question and your sales will go through the roof.

46. Frustrations

Guarantees are designed to reduce buyer resistance. One of the most effective ways of doing this is to address a frustration.

Let me explain to you what I mean by that.

A few years ago, a well-known bank took the initiative of guaranteeing that the customers would never wait more than five minutes to be served by a teller. The reason for this was quite simple: One of the major frustrations people had when dealing with banks is standing in line for extended periods of time. So the bank addressed this frustration in its guarantee and business immediately increased. The bank owners understood that no one really went to the bank to stand in a line for a long period of time.

This can be applied to a number of businesses. What is it that is frustrating your customers? For example, what if you had a takeout food store and guaranteed that people wouldn't be waiting any longer than a few minutes for their meals? You'd be addressing one of the major frustrations that people have with takeout food, particularly if you owned a lunch store that catered to people who had only limited lunch breaks.

So if you had a guarantee that addresses that frustration, you will immediately appeal to those people who were put off by the fact that other stores didn't offer that guarantee.

It's not only with guarantees that you can look at these frustrations; you can also address them through the copy of your advertisement. What you need to consider is what it is that is frustrating your customers and what it is that frustrates the industry in general.

By mentioning this in your copy and explaining to people that you understand, you're building empathy. You are talking their language; you understand what they are going through. They will, therefore, relate to you, and they will purchase from you.

For example, imagine if you had a car cleaning product. One of the frustrations associated with a car cleaning product is the streaking that occurs after it's used. People wash their cars using a cleaning product that leaves streaks once hosed off and dried. But if you explain in your copy that you understand this frustration and that's why you've designed your product so it will not streak. Right away you are appealing to those people who were frustrated by those products that don't offer this benefit.

Before you write any advertisement, consider the things that frustrate people about your product or service. Make a list of them and then go through and identify how you can address them. This will be one of the major selling tools in your advertisement.

As soon as you get people on your side and have built rapport with them, your sales will automatically increase.

47. Tell the Full Story

If there's an interesting story to tell about your company, product, or service, then it can be very beneficial to tell it through advertising. People like to read stories; they don't like to read ads. So if you can make your advertisement as interesting as possible by telling an interesting story, you have a far greater chance of getting it read.

If that story leads the client to eventually buy, your advertising is going to be far more successful. To give you an example, Sears designed an advertisement to address the perception that the store was too expensive. Sears told the story of how the company made only five percent profit, explaining the costs that were involved in bringing the customers quality service and those sorts of things. The campaign worked brilliantly for Sears. Immediately the company had managed to overcome the problem of people perceiving Sears as being expensive. People realized they were just paying for extra quality.

So what is it with your business? What can you write in your advertisement that overcomes objections and leads people to a greater understanding of the way things operate?

An advertisement that tells the full story has the benefit of letting people in behind the scenes, of making them feel part of your company. If you go to great lengths to produce something of the highest possible quality, then you need to tell people that. Also, if you go the extra mile with service, explain that as well.

This works particularly well if you can use a real-life story. For example, you could tell a story about how customers who were having particular challenges came to your company and you worked with them to overcome that problem. Explain how you went out of your way to assist them and how happy they were with the results.

Another great idea is to let each department, or the people working in those departments, tell their stories. Get them to talk about how proud they are of the quality of work they do—everyone from your accountant right down to the person who sweeps the floor.

It's also a good idea to explain exactly how your system works. If you own a men's clothing store, you might like to explain that when people come in, the first thing you do is to sit down and talk to them about their lifestyles, about problems they have with clothing, whether they perspire a lot, or whether they feel cold. You sit down and go through a series of questions with them before you decide on what would suit them best. Then you start talking to them about color schemes and the sorts of cuts that will highlight their best features, and so on.

By explaining how your system works and how you are different, it gives you a greater chance of success and a greater chance of people wanting to become involved with you.

48. Advertorial

If you can master this form of advertising, you virtually have a license to print money. You see, the idea behind an advertorial is to try and make your ad look like it's an editorial. Let me explain why this is important.

Let's think about newspapers, or more specifically the term *newspaper*. Understand this: Newspapers are paper that news stories are printed on. They are not called ad papers. People buy newspapers to read the news. Sure, some look at the ads, some do buy them for the classifieds and those sorts of things, but on the whole, most people buy newspapers for the articles they contain. Therefore, it makes sense that if you can make your ad look like an article, there is a greater chance it'll be read. So how do you go about that? First, you need to use an article-style headline. What I mean by this is the sort of headlines that journalists would use at the start of a story.

One of the easiest ways to master this skill is simply to read the newspaper headlines that journalists have written in the paper you are looking to advertise in. You then copy their style. You would also want to use the same typefaces as the newspaper uses. Quite often the headlines are printed in a different typeface than the body or article.

You need to be aware that your advertisement can't look exactly like an editorial. Sometimes it can, but a lot of newspapers require the word *advertisement* to appear across the top. This is so the public knows the difference between what is an editorial and what is an ad. Having said that, placing the word *advertisement* across the top, particularly if you can have it all in capitals and in a small font size, shouldn't really make a difference to the response you'd get to your ad—many people won't actually notice it there anyway.

Part of the reason why advertorials work so well is due to people's perceptions about advertising. People tend to believe what journalists write; yet they are very skeptical about things written in advertisements.

If you are going to take out a full-page ad in the newspaper, then you want to make it look like an editorial as much as possible. You could run a couple of smaller ads on the page to make it look like the standard newspaper layout, but you want to run the vast majority of your advertisement in the style of an editorial. Simply breaking up the page with a couple of articles about your product and service, with a couple of advertisements and photos scattered in between, will make people less likely to just skip right over the top and they will scan every headline that you have on that page to see if there are any articles of interest.

One other thing to keep in mind with advertorials is that sometimes you can get the newspaper to run the editorial for you. What you are doing is supplying them with an advertisement and then supplying them with an editorial that you would like placed above that advertisement. It's normally better to have it placed directly above—you want people to read through the editorial—then once they're excited about your business, they can see your advertisement to get your contact details. It's also possible then in the advertisement to make an offer. This is something you wouldn't do in the editorial.

So, talk with your advertising rep about this. See if you can supply the publication with an editorial that goes directly above the ad. Possibly you might offer to pay 50 percent of the editorial price, which is the amount of space that your editorial takes up. If possible, try and get the publication to run it free for you. Either way, if you can master the art of making your advertisement look and read like a newspaper article, you will be well on the way to effective advertising.

MARKETING FRANCHISES A BOOM INDUSTRY

by Amy Fleming

A Queensland-based sales and marketing company has begun to franchise its operations to service the ever-increasing number of small-to-medium-sized businesses desperately seeking a competitive edge in the marketplace.

Recognized as one of Australia's leading marketing firms, *ACTION International* is currently offering a limited number of franchises throughout the state of Queensland.

Founder of the company, and international chairman Mr. Brad Sugars, explains that franchising was the only way to service this ever-growing market. *"There are literally thousands of small- and medium-sized businesses screaming out for this sort of service,"* explains Sugars. *"Our franchise owners are out there meeting the demand."*

According to Sugars each franchise owner is fully trained in the skills of business and marketing consulting, with full ongoing support provided by the state's Master Licensee Trevor Mayhew, an ex-*ACTION International* franchise owner. *"We're not necessarily looking for people*

who have worked in marketing in the past,"* said Sugars. *"We're looking for people who have owned their own businesses, or previously worked in a sales or management position."*

The initial investment for an *ACTION International* franchise is just $71,500, which includes all training, products, a marketing fund to be reinvested into each franchise business, and, of course, full ongoing support. The ongoing franchise fees have also been set at the lower end of the scale. While the marketing levy is a fairly standard 5 percent plus GST, the yearly renewal fees are fixed at just $19,800 p.a., making this one of the most attractive franchises in the market.

"We're only looking to sell a handful of franchises throughout Queensland this year," explained Sugars. *"We've already sold 15, so anyone who's looking to invest in this opportunity needs to act fast."*

People who would like to find out more about this exciting business need to call Trevor Mayhew at (07) 3891 7579. Office hours are 9:00 a.m. to 5:00 p.m. Monday to Friday, with appointments available for suitable applicants.

Get your phone ringing off the hook. After weeks of running standard ads with a moderate response, we placed this advertorial and were inundated with inquiries.

49. Sell Service

After you've bought a product or service more than once, you begin to realize that all operators in that industry are not the same.

Let's think about mechanics—consider the wide variety of service you get from one operator to another. Some are shifty and you can be certain they'll change a spark plug and charge you $600 for it. Others take the time to explain exactly what they're doing, find cheaper parts, offer you a courtesy car, and give you a coffee and muffin while you wait.

If you were looking for a mechanic for the first time, you wouldn't realize this. You might go to the Yellow Pages, phone up a few, find the closest and the cheapest, and go there. In your mind, they're all the same, so why pay more?

The fact is, almost everyone has dealt with more than one mechanic and almost everyone has been ripped off by at least one. People will take more time to search out someone they believe will give them better service and they'll be more likely to pay more for it.

When we say *sell service*, we mean promote that you offer better service than the next guy. That doesn't just mean adding the words *good service* to your next ad—you have to be much, much, much more specific than that.

Let's go back to the example of our mechanic. Imagine if a mechanic ran an ad that said this: "We'll show you exactly why your car needs fixing, explain how much the part costs us and how much profit we're making, give you an exact quote, and call you immediately for your approval if we need to do any extra work. When you come in, you'll receive a muffin and a cappuccino while you wait, as well as a courtesy car to get you around and we'll back the whole job up with a satisfaction guarantee. Added to that, we'll be the most polite mechanics you've ever dealt with and we won't make you feel like an idiot. If you're not satisfied with our service, we'll give you a $10 voucher to see one of competitors."

That's incredibly bold but it would certainly stick out. Forget about good service—these guys offer *awesome* service, and they absolutely tell you why and how. It barely matters what they charge or where they are. It'd be worth paying them a visit if you didn't have a good mechanic that you trusted.

Think about how this applies to your business. How can you offer better service and how can you explain it in your ads so that potential customers understand exactly what you do differently and how it will make their lives easier?

It may be that you already give far better service than your competition but you've never bothered to explain it in your ads or on the phone when customers call to inquire.

Or perhaps everybody does the same thing but nobody actually explains what they do. For example, maybe every car detailer sprays the inside of the car with scented rose oil to make it smell sweet. The thing is, customers probably don't know that and would be impressed if you told them.

People *will* pay more for good service, as long as they know exactly what you do differently and how it will improve their buying experience.

50. Offers

The number one reason why ads fail is this: *They don't have an offer*! I can't emphasize that strongly enough. If you don't make an offer for people to take up, your ad will fall into the category of either image advertising or name, rank, and serial number advertising. It will be a donation rather than an ad.

Image advertising is the type of advertising that uses lots of white space and snazzy or classy graphics. For example, the whole ad will be white except for a little bit of text in the middle that says "James House of Clothing." Our instant reaction is, "Wow, that must be an upmarket place." Sometimes this is the case with things like perfumes, luxury cars, and other upmarket products. But it doesn't give people a reason to buy. For most small businesses, it's not viable and you're just being egotistical if you try it.

One approach that is *never* appropriate is the "name, rank, and serial number" method. That's where your name goes at the top, bullet points about what you sell go in the middle, and your details go at the bottom. These ads *don't* work—in fact, I'd go as far as to say I've never seen one even come close to making a profit. Generally, you'll take a terrible loss.

This approach dates back to the earliest days of advertising (and I'm talking about the 1800s here). Back then, it was quite OK to just put down your name and details—how else would people find out where a business was, or that it even existed? Nowadays there are so many competitors that you *must* give reasons for people to see you and not the guy down the road. That's a *fact*!

One good reason for people to come to your business is the quality of your offer. This is a straight-out "You come in and we'll give you something extra special" appeal. For example, call us and book a roof inspection and we'll give a $300 voucher towards a full restoration. Or, "A free pair of sports socks with every pair of shoes."

Generally, your offer needs to be something rather generous, or it won't work. I've seen people try things like "Present this ad for a 5 percent discount." This kind of offer motivates nobody to do anything. Your offer has to make people sit up and take notice; it must knock them out of the sleepy haze most people walk around in.

Let's look at some basic guidelines when conceiving your offer.

First, put a time limit on it—you have to inspire urgency. If customers know they can get it any time, then why would they bother doing anything today? They'll turn to the next page in the newspaper, start reading the comics, and forget about you.

Your offer should last only a week, or until a particular date. Of course, it depends on the product. If it's something small and consumable, the time period should be short. For something that takes a little more consideration (like a house or car) extend the period for three weeks or so.

Second, your offer should be in limited quantities and, better yet, specific numbers. For example, "We have forty-six pairs of sports sock to give away before the end of the week." You can also try this: "The first thirteen customers who put down a deposit for their new homes will receive the patio free."

Third, the offer should be meaningful to the customers and the extra bonus should be something that they want. Think about it seriously. If your offer isn't generous enough, you may as well not have one.

If you have a rock-solid offer, you can base your entire ad around it. The headline can be a quick summation of your offer and the text can explain it in more depth and offer a couple of extra benefits when dealing with you. This approach can make advertising very simple indeed.

An ad without an offer is a waste of time. It has no pull, no selling power, and no urgency. Ads without offers tend to get this sort of response from the reader: "Yeah, sounds good but I'll think about it later."

And you know what? They never do. They throw the paper or magazine away and forget all about you. When they decide to buy a week or two later, they go to the Yellow Pages and call one of your competitors.

You've succeeded in encouraging people to buy the type of product or service you sell. Unfortunately, they went and bought it from someone else.

You see, the readers of your ad are just like fish; if you hook them but don't reel them onto the boat, they swim away, free to be caught by any other fisherman.

An offer *claims* your prospects. It gives them a reason to buy from *you*, and to do it *now*.

Sure, they could go somewhere else, or wait until next month, but they'd miss out on the special deal you're offering.

An ad with an offer gets people thinking. It makes them want to take action. After all, that's all your ad really is, a catalyst for action. If it doesn't make people want to do anything, it has failed and falls into that nebulous category of *image building*, or pointless advertising.

When people see an offer, they tend to think, "Well, I was thinking about getting one of those anyway—and this mob is offering a special deal this week. I may as well get it now."

So let's give some consideration to what you could offer.

The best offers seem incredibly generous yet have a low hard-dollar cost. For example, a top image consultant who normally charges $600 an hour might offer a free 15-minute introductory consultation—while it's only 15 minutes to her, it's $150 value to the prospect.

Or what about a restaurant that offers two free soft drinks with every meal. Hard cost: about 15 cents. Perceived value: $4.

Bradley J. Sugars

It's also important to remember that you're in the business of buying customers. Once you get them in through the door, it's easy to keep them for life (assuming your service and product are up to scratch). Think long term.

TYPES OF OFFERS

Here are some possible offers that would be worth considering:

The Added Value with Soft-Dollar Cost

Soft-dollar cost refers to products, services, or added extras that you can combine with your standard product to make it more attractive and increase its perceived value, but doesn't add much, if anything, to your costs.

For this strategy to be effective, the added extra must have a high-perceived value. In other words, your customers must see the added benefit as being great value.

The Package Offer

Package products and services together to create a more marketable combination. There is a higher perceived value when products or services are packaged together. Your customers will want to buy more, simply because of the extra products they get when buying a product they already want.

One of the best examples of a great package is computer equipment. Buy the hardware and receive the software free. This type of offer is very attractive to potential customers.

Discounts versus Bonus Offers

More often than not, discounting will cost you profits. A far better way of clearing stock and generating extra trade is to have a "2 for the price of 1" sale. Or try "buy one of these and get one of these *free*." The other way of putting this is every tenth purchase free, or when you spend $100, we'll give you $20 off your next purchase.

Valued-at Offer

If you are including a free item in your ad, make sure you value it. For example: Call now for your *free* consultation, normally valued at $75. This positions your time, product, or service much more than a simple giveaway that people won't value or appreciate.

Time-Limited Offers

Place a time limit on your offer. It will dramatically increase the response rate because it gives people a reason to respond right now. Place urgency in your offer. "For a short time only." "Call before such and such." "Only while stocks last." These will all create a sense of urgency in your consumer's mind.

Guarantee Offers

Using a guarantee offer is a great way to boost the response to your ad. People will be far more willing to part with their money if you take the risk out of their buying decision. The better the guarantee you make, the higher your response will be.

Free Offers

Giving away something absolutely free (no catches whatsoever) is often a brilliant way to build a loyal customer base. Offer a so-called bribe to get them in through the door initially, then great service and products to encourage them to come back. This type of offer can reduce your cost per lead dramatically.

51. Make Your Service a Product

If you operate a service-based business, there can be a real benefit in turning it into a package and selling it for an attractive price.

Here's a good example. Let's say you own a hairdressing salon. You could sell a package called "Good Hair Year" (as opposed to bad hair day—get it?). For $99, people get five visits, a treatment and scalp massage every time and a voucher for a facial on their first visit. You could go further with it, depending on what your profit margins allow.

The same applies to any service business. You can make a package and sell it to your customers.

Generally, it's good to give the package a name and sell it for a price that is less than the value of the individual components themselves. You want people to think, "Well, I'm probably going to be coming back anyway—I may as well save some dollars."

The advantage to you is obvious. If you sell them advance service, you've got a commitment from them that they will be loyal. If you treat them well, they could easily turn into customers for life.

It also makes your cashflow and schedule easier to plan. Imagine if you sold all your appointments in advance: You'd know how much money you've got and how much you have to do.

You might also try to get some vouchers from related businesses to throw in with the package. For example, the hairdresser could get a free minifacial voucher from a local beauty salon, a wardrobe planning session voucher from a fashion store, and so on. You can then say something like this: "Includes $134 worth of vouchers." That can really up the value of your package.

You should think of it as a sample bag. Remember when you used to go to the show and get those overpriced show bags? I remember studying the newspaper beforehand, working out which show bags were the best value. Some $5 bags apparently had $65 worth of value—they'd be the first ones I'd get.

In fact, the sample bag idea isn't as childish as it seems. There's nothing wrong with putting the vouchers and goodies in a bag, or for a bit more class, a basket. You could throw in some chocolates or a bottle of wine, depending on who your customers are.

You can advertise the package offer in your next ad, or alternately, simply sell it to your customers at the end of their appointment. You'll be surprised at how many you sell by saying, "Are you happy with our service today? Great. Can I show you a way to save $45 and get $78 worth of bonuses?"

52. Image

For many small businesses, image is not really a major concern. It's the kind of thing those pony-tailed ad execs in New York like to wax lyrical about. Sure, it matters for David Jones and Elizabeth Arden, but it's something less of a worry for Jim's Butchery down the road. That's probably being a little hasty. Image *does* matter regardless of how big you are or what you sell. But you'll get twice the exposure from people using your product than you would from image advertising.

First, we have to work out what we mean when we say *image*. The first thing most people tend to think about is a snazzy upmarket store or an exclusive perfume. We're not talking about that at all. Image simply means the way you are perceived by your customers.

Let's consider our butcher friend, Jim.

People may see him as the local clown, the friendly butcher who always lights up their day with a joke. Or perhaps they regard him as the backyard boy, the guy who uses rusty knives to chop up slightly off meat on the hood of his delivery van.

Either way, the image can always be traced back to the actions of the business owner. If his ads look like they were created by a 5-year-old using crayon and the store is in such a mess that it resembles a slaughterhouse, people would reasonably conclude that Jim is a sloppy operator. That would be his image.

On the other hand, if his ads look professional and his shop is always neat and as clean as an operating theater, people will feel more confident about dealing with him.

Your image is created by every action and everything that customers see. It is the sum total of your personality, your advertising, your flyers, your store's appearance, the attitude of your staff, your location, and everything else you can think of.

So how is this information useful? Simple. Once you realize that you actually *do* have an image and that it *does* have an impact on your sales figures, you then have the power to create a different image.

Consider how you'd like to be perceived by your customers. Would you like to be seen as a professional operator with friendly help and a rock-solid history of top-rate customer service? If so, you need to work out what you have to change in order to create that perception.

Maybe you need to clean your store, remove all old stock, improve the look of your ads, update your logo, remove that terrible spray paint graffiti on the side of your premises, and so on. Granted, all of these things cost money, but there is a clear value in spending it.

A better image can bring you more sales, better customers, and allow you to charge higher prices. People will not pay top dollar to see a bottom-of-the-line business. Even if your service is up to scratch, you have to make sure that every other aspect of your business supports your image of quality.

Of course, there are times when you don't want to have the best image. Imagine if you're in a business that's aimed at lower-income earners. You don't want to look like your store is ultraexpensive, as this will frighten your target market away and not really attract people who shop at the upper end of the price scale.

Your image needs to match your customers. If you sell high-priced items then look classy if you sell more "middle of the road," then look professional but not exclusive. If you're selling at the lower end of the market, then look affordable. By portraying the right image, you'll position yourself for success.

53. Being Specific

Let me pose a simple question. What sounds more impressive?

More than 20 varieties of Nike shoes in stock.

OR

23 varieties of Nike shoes in stock.

Research shows that the second statement will always attract more people than the first. It's more memorable, more believable, and more interesting. This has been proved over and over again.

Think about Baskin-Robbins. Can you remember how many flavors they have in store? If you've got a sweet tooth, you'll almost certainly remember that they have 32 different flavors of ice cream.

And what about Kentucky Fried Chicken? How many herbs and spices do they use on their special chicken? The answer is, of course, 11. That's a lot more impressive than "more than 10," or "lots."

When people see a specific number, they tend to think, "Well, that must be true." It's important to choose a number that is not even, and not a multiple of 5 or 10. Even if you offer exactly 20 types of computer printer cartridges, you'd be better of saying 19.

How can you apply this idea to your business? Think about what you offer. Chances are there is something you could put a number on. For example, a hairdresser could say that her staff has 67 years of combined experience. She could even turn this into a slogan: "Marie's Hairdressing—where we've been cutting hair for 67 years."

Being specific also extends to explaining exactly what you do and how you do it. Let's consider car detailing. Instead of just saying, "We clean your car top to bottom," why not list every single thing you do?

The beauty is that every other car detailer may do exactly the same thing, but because people didn't realize how precisely and intricately you perform your job, they'll be surprised and impressed.

There's a famous example from the United States. A beer manufacturer broke the mold of beer commercials (girls in bikinis, the beach, etc.), by explaining in very precise detail how the beer was made.

No detail was spared and the text wasn't "dumbed down" for the reader. It was the actual instructions on how to make this kind of beer. It was so impressive that sales of the beer skyrocketed. Beer drinkers thought, "If they go to that much trouble, it must taste good."

The funny thing was that the process outlined in the ad was almost identical to that used by every other brewer. Because no one knew that, the ad worked wonderfully and the beer started to taste better in the minds of the drinkers. Amazing but true!

54. Boredom

There's an age-old adage in marketing: "You can bore people into doing anything, especially not giving you their money."

In this life, people want a sense of fulfilment. If they can't get that, they'll settle for some entertainment. The last thing they want is to be bored and understimulated. Boredom is an anathema to the human race and only second to grief in the unwanted emotions stakes.

So what does all this mean? Simple. It means that your ad should be *exciting*, or at the very least, lively.

Now let's not lose sight of the big picture here. That happens too often in advertising: Ad writers aim for entertainment but forget to sell the product. How many times have you said, "That's a great ad; I love that one," but completely forgot what it was for.

That means it was a *bad* ad.

These ads tend to win awards and the praise of ad executives, but they won't win any favor with your accountant. If you come up with one of these ads, you're essentially just paying the newspaper, radio, or TV station to promote a funny message to the world. That's very charitable, but it won't help your business.

You need to avoid a completely sterile and boring ad without going over the top. The best rule to follow is this: Create an offer that is truly exciting, then get excited, and then write your ad.

Forget about being funny or clever. Perhaps you're the greatest jokester you know. Even so, forget the laughs. Chances are, nobody else will get your sense of humor and if they do, they'll have a chuckle and then read the comics for some *real* entertainment.

You need to combine the excitement with the selling message. Use words that genuinely get people excited, like "Not to be repeated," "Exclusive," "Nothing like this has been seen, or will be seen again," or "We're stupid for offering this, but we need to get your attention."

Just go a little bit further than you'd normally go. Even if you're normally a very calm and serene person, it pays to be a little like Crazy Freddy when writing your ad. By the way, Crazy Freddy owns a restaurant called Crazy Freddy's Restaurant. Every fourth meal is free—that's right, every fourth person gets a free meal. You don't know until the end of the meal, so there's no way to rig it. This deal does get people excited and it creates a bit of extra fun in the lives of Freddy's regular customers.

Think about this: How can you create more excitement? It probably has a little to do with the way you write your ads and a *lot* to do with what you're advertising.

55. Cheat

Remember when you were at school? Your work had to be your own, and if you were caught looking at someone else's answers during an exam, you could be failed right on the spot.

We've been taught that there's something basically dishonorable about copying someone else's idea. This is an idea that most of us carry over into our adult lives and almost always into our businesses.

Let's say there's a competitor who's doing something that is working particularly well. Perhaps it's a restaurant offering half-price drinks on Tuesday and two-for-one meals on Wednesday.

Most business owners would think, "Hmm, that's a good idea. How can I come up with a great idea like that?" For some reason, they believe that the idea has already been done and they must invent something new.

This is a fallacy, pure and simple. If someone else is doing something that works, there is absolutely no reason why you shouldn't steal the idea, lock, stock, and barrel. Who cares if you're being a rip-off merchant? I'd rather be a rich rip-off merchant than a broke original.

You can copy the idea down to the finest detail. You can advertise basically the same way (although you should change words to avoid any copyright problems) and use the same prices. If the main reason people are dealing with your competitor is because of the idea, there's no reason why they wouldn't switch to you if you're offering the same thing.

Some business owners have an ethical problem with this concept and that's understandable. The reality is, the competitor may be doing well with his idea, and your stealing it will diminish it's power. That could put the competitor back to square one.

I guess all business owners empathize with each other, so some of us would be reluctant to knowingly damage the business of another, competitor or otherwise.

The fact is, all is fair in love, war, and business, and I don't see a problem with looking after your own interests first.

Some people might feel strange about stealing an idea and worry that customers will see them as unoriginal, or copycats. The truth is, customers aren't paying all that much attention. They don't care what you do, just as long as they're benefiting from it.

You shouldn't steal ideas only from your competitors. Find good ideas in other industries and copy them too. Every time you see a good marketing idea, or respond to an ad, ask yourself, "How can I apply these ideas to my business?"

56. Advertise Something People Want

I guess the title of this section must seem almost ridiculously simple. In fact, you perceive it as completely inane and obvious. Stick around, because you'll discover that there's a lot more to this than you think.

A major reason why ads fail is this: People are just not interested in what you're offering. You can follow every other rule in this book and write the best ad in the whole world, but if people don't want what you're selling, they're not going to buy as a reward for your writing such a good ad.

Let's consider hardware stores. Right now, there are huge chain stores opening everywhere. These megawarehouse stores offer everything you could want in the one place: ample parking, staff members who know what they're doing, and even a guarantee that you won't find a better price anywhere.

If you own a local hardware store, you'd have to be pretty worried. How can you mix it with these big guys? Your ad might read, "Come to Jim's Hardware and see a smaller line, pay higher prices, wait longer to get served, and find it difficult to park."

That's a pretty cynical viewpoint but you won't make any serious change in your business unless you face up to the most important question: "Is my business truly viable and for how long?"

Let's think about convenience stores. These days, supermarkets are generally open until 9 p.m. most nights. Again, supermarkets have lower prices (by far), a much bigger range, better parking, and more. The only call for a convenience store is when you urgently need something at around 11:30 at night. That means the convenience store has to stay open even later just to capitalize on a very small market.

More depressing still, service stations are stocking more and more lines, meaning that anything you can get at a convenience store, you can probably get at a service station for less (and you can get it while you fill up your car).

That makes for a no-win situation. The convenience stores are selling less, which means they have to charge more, giving customers even less reason to shop there.

There is no magical answer or special trick here: Customers naturally want things to be easier, cheaper, and faster. If there are people out there offering that, they'll probably beat you. That's just the facts of life.

The other situation is where people invent things that they need, and expect everybody will beat a path to their doors.

The most extreme case I ever dealt with was this: the $800 iron. Now, I'm not much for housework, but the most I'd ever pay for an iron would be around $50, absolutely tops. This lady had invented a super-duper iron that cut your ironing time in half. She'd worked out that to stay in business, she had to sell the irons for $815.

Safe to say, there weren't many takers. Actually, she'd sold exactly none when I first met her. She asked me to write an ad for her. I declined.

Let me recap. A lot of ads fail for a very simple reason: They're trying to sell something nobody wants. Like a daily cream that prevents you from getting a rare strain of tinea, or a special driving course that helps you drive at the speed limit, or a four-volume book on the life and times of some no-name forties movie star.

Sadly, this is where so many business people go wrong. They advertise what they can make, rather than making what they can advertise. In other words, they don't tailor their products and services to the marketplace.

Change the formula of your cream so that it cures all tinea, alter your driving course to cater to people who like to drive over the speed limit, and condense your four-volume biography into a three-page summary (or better still, throw it out and reconsider completely).

If there isn't a market for your product, the best advertising in the world can't help you out. You can't sell the unsellable.

On the other hand, a product that everybody wants (like a cream that gives you blemish-free, clear, beautiful skin in seven days) barely needs advertising. It will take off by itself.

As a check, ask yourself the following questions before you advertise:

What section of the general public is most likely to buy this product?

Is this a large number of people?

Can they afford it?

Can I communicate the benefits of this product/service to these people in an ad?

The answers to these questions may force you to reconsider.

If you discover that you're beating your head against a brick wall, take heart. There are ways around it. Maybe you need to package your product with others, or sell it to others who have easier access to your target market.

57. Give More Than They Expect

One of the easiest ways to increase the response to your advertising is by giving people in your target market more than they expected to get from the advertisement.

To give you an example of how this might work, imagine you are running an advertisement for a hardware store and you were talking about gardening. You might be trying to sell hose fittings and those sorts of things. Imagine if your advertisement had an editorial component that gave free hints or tips on what plants are currently in season, or some hints and tips on trimming and pruning. Giving people little extras like that will encourage them to read your ad. It will also help establish you as an expert in their minds, which means they are more likely to come and see you.

Giving sensational offers is another way to really increase the response to your ad, but you need to put some thought into this because the offer doesn't generally have to come from your business. You can arrange it with another business.

You could also use other things to tempt your target market. You can use such things as consultations. This can be particularly effective for people like accountants, attorneys, or bookkeepers, as well as those who sell software.

You can also exceed your customers' expectations by entering them into a competition every time they purchase. It could be a competition to win a vacation or something similar.

So put a lot of thought into your business and be creative. It doesn't need to cost you a lot of money, but the results in the end can be quite exceptional.

58. Copy—The Words You Use

As I mentioned earlier, your copy is not as important as the target market or the offer that you make. Having said that, it doesn't mean that your copy is not important; it's just not as important as the others.

Understanding that the headline is the advertisement for your ad, you need to understand the significance of the first one to two paragraphs. Your headline draws people into your advertisement, but that's as far as it goes. Your copy then needs to get people excited and get them to the point where they are ready to purchase, or ready to call or come in—whatever the action is you want them to take.

The first couple of paragraphs really need to expand on the benefits that you've mentioned in the headline. The first 50 or 60 words are crucial. You can have the best headline in the world, but then if you lose the reader's interest in the first few lines, your advertisement will not be successful.

So how do you get your readers excited in the first 50 to 60 words? Well, the only way to really do this is to explain the benefits to them and give them your reasons why they should read on. If you show a lot of benefits in the first couple of paragraphs, then the reader will be excited enough to read further. Your copy needs to have enthusiasm, it needs to be upbeat, and to move at a fast tempo. You need to have brief sentences that get the readers drawn in and gives them the impression it's not hard to read. It needs to be the sort of thing that you can really fly through.

Your copy needs to do a number of things. First, it needs to build dissatisfaction in your clients' minds. What I mean by this is that you want to build up dissatisfaction with where they are in their lives. It's not that we want to have them dissatisfied with the ad or what they are reading, just their position in life.

When you can build dissatisfaction, you get to the point where the readers want to change. You then need to give them a vision of what life could be like.

If you can explain to them how much better life would be if they, say, lost that weight and managed to keep it off, you are well on the way to getting them to take action.

So, the formula is to build their dissatisfaction, then show them what life could be like. Create the vision.

Throughout your copy you also need to be building rapport. Now, by *rapport* I mean you need to show that you understand the situation that the readers are in, and that you are willing to get in and help them. But this needs to be done in an enthusiastic and upbeat way.

Your copy needs to have a plan; it needs to work in an ordered manner. First, to get the readers interested, to build their dissatisfaction further, create the vision and then give them the first steps that they need to take in order to achieve that vision.

If you don't plan your advertisement, then it becomes disjointed, so you need to have a flow. Once you've drawn the readers in and you've gotten them excited, you need to take them through the process that ultimately leads to the purchase (or to get them to call or respond to your ad). Unless you have a clear goal in mind, unless you write your copy with a lot of enthusiasm, you will never achieve this.

59. Focus on Benefits

Now this is one area of advertising that people have a lot of trouble coming to grips with. For a lot of people, when they write their copy, they just ramble on with no clear direction. They seemingly have no formula or purpose.

I have seen many ads where people have just spoken about how long they have been in business, through how many generations the business has been handed down, and so on. None of these things really interest the reader; none of them give a clear benefit.

Readers should see the benefit immediately—the headline draws them in, the first couple of paragraphs then explain the benefit.

It then has to show them the benefit of actually taking action, of actually contacting your business. The easiest way to do this is to write down all the benefits that people will receive from your product or your service. List them, then sort that list out in some form of order. You can do this by figuring out what the key benefit is to the members of your target market, what the one thing is they are really after, that one thing your product or service will give them.

Once you have that, you can look at the second most important benefit, and so on. Once you have put them in order, you'll have a formula for writing your ad. The number-one key benefit should be mentioned in the first paragraph. You then go on in your copy to mention the second most important, then the third and fourth. If you have a great list of them, you'll need to list them in bullet-point form.

Now, your major one or two benefits you'll explain in full paragraphs, but the subsequent benefits you'll list as bullet points so people can quickly scan through them. It's not a good idea to leave any of the benefits out simply because they won't fit into your ad. If that's the case, just buy a bigger ad. The bullets are just one way to overcome this. So your focus has to be completely on the benefits for their users, never on the benefits to you. You have to communicate what your product and service will do for them; what will make their lives easier or better.

Focus on their key basic desires: people needing to feel loved, wanted or accepted in certain social groups. Explain how your product or service will help them achieve this, explaining to them that their lives will be better if they buy your product.

When you stop rambling and start focusing on the benefits, you'll see a remarkable improvement in the response you get to your ads.

60. Write as You Speak

I often laugh when I read the advertising literature that comes to me in the mail. It almost always starts off with "Dear Sir" or "Dear Brad" and then goes on with, "I am writing to you in relation to a new service, which…"

The reason I find it so amusing is because it's so sterile and emotionless. As I have just mentioned, your advertising copy needs to have enthusiasm, and terms like "Dear Sir" and "In relation to" certainly don't have any enthusiasm. They're absolutely cold. They are just not written in the language that people speak.

Most people tend to learn to read at an early age. They first learn at school and they actually learn by reading the words out loud. Once they become skilled at that, they are taught to read the words to themselves. In other words, to say the words in their mind and not verbally. When people are reading your advertisement, they're saying the words in their minds.

So it's very important if you are to communicate effectively with them that the wording of your ad is the same as what you would say to them if you were speaking with them face-to-face.

Advertising is really just a form of one-on-one communication. If you were talking to someone face-to-face, you wouldn't use terms like, "In relation to" or "Dear Sir." Honestly, can you imagine going up to someone and saying, "Oh, dear Brad, I would just like to talk with you in relation to a new product or service we have." You simply wouldn't say it. What you are far more likely to say is, "Hi, Brad, how's it going? Is it OK if I take a moment of your time? I want to talk with you about this new product that we have to offer."

See how the two convey completely different emotions? One is written in the way you would speak, while the other is written in the way we were taught to write at school.

Your advertising isn't meant to be boring and sterile; it's meant to be enthusiastic; it's meant to be interesting. It doesn't really matter where you put the periods, or how grammatically correct you are. It's all about making it interesting for the person to read and to convey a simple message. Your copy should be written in a conversational tone and it should be fun. It should be fun for you to write, and it should be fun for the reader to read.

One of the simplest ways to learn these skills is simply to write your copy and then to read it out loud. Better still, get someone else to read it back to you. When you listen to the copy being read out loud, if there is anything that you would not normally say face-to-face, change it.

Imagine being paid to wake up to this view... *Every Morning!*

Let's get a few things clear before we go any further... I'm a straight shooter who tells it like it is. I don't exaggerate or make false promises, I just stick to the facts. You've probably worked out by now that I don't like wasting my time, so I'll let you know right up front that if you haven't got $1.1 million to invest, you may as well stop reading now...

Good I see you're still with me. Well now that *you've identified yourself as a smart investor*, let's get down to business.

I'd like to offer you the chance to buy **a rapidly growing business**, right here in the magnificent Gold Coast Hinterland. Your investment can really be broken down into 2 parts...

Part One – is the land and property you'll be investing in. It's approximately 5 acres of prime land that's been independently valued at $750,000. It comes complete with a duplex home that would suit a family, plus a granny flat or alternately a renter that would have no trouble fetching $150 per week.

I should point out that when I say prime land, I mean **PRIME LAND**, with great soil plus long permanent creek front.

Part Two – is the business. You're probably wondering by now what the business is. Simply put – it's a Dog Boarding Kennel. Now before you say 'that wouldn't interest me', or 'I don't even like dogs', there are a few things you should know.

Firstly, you don't need to know much about dogs, or even like them much for that matter. My wife was not particularly fond of dogs yet she's loved every minute of the 8 years we've been here. The other thing you need to know, is how much money this business makes. It's an absolutely solid income, and it's set to get even better.

Turnover of the business is close to $100,000pa and conservatively could be expected to **rise at least 40% in the next 12 months.** In fact, the business is in its strongest ever growth phase, with profits **rising by 20-30% every year for the past 3 years.** Best of all, the business is basically all profit. You would be hard pressed to have more than $30,000 expenses each year!!!

Now if you're anything like me, you'd rather stick to the facts of what the business is doing now, and not what its potential is. But there are a few things you need to know, and keep in mind when looking over these figures.

One of our major competitors is being re-zoned, meaning **the turnover of the business has the potential to double in the near future.** More importantly, council regulations do not favour the establishment of similar businesses in the area. This basically means that as more and more of our competitors sell their land to developers, the number of potential clients will grow dramatically.

There is also space to build a cattery, which would definitely make good money, and income from worm farm owners who rent space on the property has the potential to **make you $300+ per month.**

So why am I looking to sell the business you ask? Well it's time for my wife and I to retire. I've loved every minute I've spent here. The magnificent lifestyle, sensational climate and great people you get to meet through the business has made my time here very enjoyable. But I've been doing this for a long time now, and the time's come for me to move on.

So now it's your turn. This is your chance to own a rapidly growing business that would suit an investor, couple or partnership arrangement.

This opportunity won't last long, so I suggest that you call me **TODAY** on **(07) 2345 6789**. And maybe you could be getting paid to wake up to this every morning.

Another way to get a handle on this is to do a sales pitch into a tape recorder and then to transcribe that into your ad. An ad is just a sales pitch in writing anyway, so by pretending that you are trying to sell to a customer and speaking into a tape recorder, you'll have the perfect language for your advertisement.

If you want your advertisements to be truly effective and communicate your message to the reader, simply write as you speak. Forget about the grammar and everything that you learned at school. You simply write it in a conversational tone. Grasping this one concept will make a huge difference in the response that you get from your ads.

Straight shooting: The easy flowing, honest, straight-to-the-point style of copy used in this ad virtually guarantees a genuine, qualified lead.

61. Write in the Present Tense

There's something about the present tense that makes your writing more exciting, and as a result makes people more receptive to taking action (remember our section on boredom).

Here's a quick refresher (in case you've completely blocked out everything you learned in English class).

The present tense means you are writing as if the event is taking place right now. The past tense is where you're writing as though it happened previously, and the future tense means that it will happen.

For example:

Present Tense: I walk to the shop.

Past Tense: I walked to the shop.

Future Tense: I will walk to the shop.

When writing your next ad, think about this. Go through with a pen and mark everything that is in a tense other than the present tense.

Instead of saying, "You will get a special bonus," write, "You get a special bonus." Apply this idea throughout and check out the difference—your writing takes on an immediacy that it lacked before. By the way, this last sentence is in the present tense—did you notice?

62. Radio Station WII-FM

Now it might shock some people to know this, but the people who are reading your ad are not interested in you. People choose to read things that are of interest to them, or that they will get a benefit from. So in effect, what people are looking for in your ad is the WIIFM, which simply stands for "What's In It For Me."

Never start you advertisement off with how long you have been in business, because that is one of the least important issues for them. Readers are only interested in the things that they will get out of it.

So how do you fix your ads if you have been making this mistake? Well, the first thing to do when you finish writing the copy is to sit down and go through it and take out any "I" or "We" statements—focus instead on the benefits to the customer.

When you are reading through your ad, check to make sure it's appealing to the WIIFM factor. You need to imagine that you are the prospect. Just sit down and picture what you would want to read, what it is that you are after, what are the benefits that you are looking for. Think about it as you, you, you. When you read through it, ask yourself, "Does this really communicate to me; does this talk to me, the prospect, or them, the business owners?"

Once you work out what you want and what you'd be looking for in your ad, it's just a simple process of relating that through your copy. But to be effective in this area, you must focus on them. Remember always that people who read your ad will respond only if you explain what's in it for them.

People's favorite radio station will always be WII-FM.

63. KISS

KISS is nothing erotic, nor is it in any way romantic. KISS stands for "Keep It Simple Stupid."

That's a pretty blunt way of saying, "Make your ad easy to follow and easy to respond to." Don't add anything that you don't have to.

People pay only part attention when reading ads—they don't want to have to think. Your ad should lead them straight from A (not caring) to B (definitely wanting to buy whatever product or service you're trying to advertise to your target market).

Some business owners try to do too much in one ad. First, they try to convince their prospects that they need what it is that the business owner's selling. Perhaps it's a product or service that most people have never even considered buying before. Then, the business owner tries to encourage the person to take action.

That's generally one step too many. The ads that work best essentially say, "You already want this. Here's a way to get it faster, cheaper, etc." The ads that generally don't work essentially say, "You've never heard of this before, and you don't know that you want it, but read these 300 words to get convinced, then read the reasons why you should buy it from us."

The best ads are always the simplest ones. For example: "What are you doing for lunch today? If you've got $3, you can come in to Jim's Bakery and walk out with a pie, chips, and can of Coke—we're opposite Big W."

Here's a good example of one that won't work: "Insure your lawn mower: Did you know that most lawn mowers break down after only two years of use? Now you can insure yours against theft or breaking down."

KISS also means that you should use short sentences, short words, and no jargon or technospeak. Remember, people are only half-interested to begin with, and they'll switch off as soon as you start making things difficult to understand.

Just imagine you were speaking to fidgety children with a million other things going through their heads. You wouldn't start by saying, "You know how blah, well blah blah and that can mean blah blah but sometimes blah blah and anyway, two out of three blah blah."

You'd be better off simply saying, "You need this. I can give it to you if you do this." The simpler your offer, wording, and sentence structure are, the better.

Also, there should be a clear, logical flow throughout your ad. It should have a beginning, a middle, and an end. Each sentence should flow into the next one and they should all lead to the ultimate point: "You should do X NOW."

64. AIDA

For many people, writing ads is a hit and miss affair. Now I have already mentioned that you have to test and measure to find out what works, but a way to get a head start on writing the ideal advertisement is to know a simple formula. Most successful ads all follow just one simple formula. It's basically the science of writing ads that sell. Now, there are many different formulas for writing ads, but the one we are about to discuss is one of the oldest and one of the best. It's called AIDA.

AIDA stands for Attention—Interest—Desire—Action. Let's have a look at how it works. Firstly, the A for attention is critical. You could write the best copy in the world, but if you haven't grabbed the readers' attention in the first place, it will never be read. The attention is absolutely crucial; fail to do this effectively and your advertisement will flop.

Once you've gotten their attention, you need to keep them interested in the rest of the advertisement. One of the most effective ways to do this is by talking about the benefits—remember WIIFM?

Another basic way to keep their interest is by telling them why they should be interested. Explain to them what they are going to get from continuing on with your ad. If you have a special offer, then allude to it and expand on it.

Now that they are interested, you need to build on their desire. You do that by playing on emotions. The basic emotions that you may wish to target will be the fact that they will be more loved or accepted in their social group if they buy your product or service, that they will have more respect from their peers, or they will have improved self-esteem. Just fulfilling basic needs is the easiest way to capture your readers.

Desire is all-important, and this is the stage where you start to look at frustrations that they've had in the past and the dissatisfaction that they are feeling now. Desire is then building the vision of what life could be like if they buy your product or service.

Now it's time to get them to take action. This comes at the end of the ad. You need to tell them exactly what they need to do to fulfill that desire.

It is also important that you make it easy. It needs to be step-by-step. Don't assume that people understand that they need to cut the coupon out and send it in. Explain it very clearly.

If you focus on this simple formula, your ad will be incredibly successful.

65. Credibility

In this world, the message is often less important than who is delivering it and why. If people believe that the person knows what he is talking about, they'll listen with more interest and be willing to set their own preconceptions aside, even if it conflicts with their egos.

Although I tend to despise ads that simply say, "Mal's Plumbing, 34 years' experience, reasonable rates," there is something to be said for experience and the inferences people draw from it.

Instead of just "34 years' experience," why not find a new, more interesting way to put that message across? For example, you could say, "Mal took on his first apprenticeship in 1965, and started his own plumbing business in 1967. He has fixed more 26,000 drains and has dealt with more than 13,600 customers. He knows plumbing and drainage better than anyone."

If the ad also includes a photo of Mal with a caption and a list of the various plumbing associations he belongs to, your reader would associate high credibility with Mal and his business.

All of this adds up to more trust and more willingness to pay higher prices. You'd expect someone who started plumbing in 1965 to be able to fix your leaky tap. He would probably also be able to do it faster and in a way that might prevent the problem from recurring.

The trick is being more specific than just "34 years' experience." You could go further than to just list the plumbing associations Mal belongs to. For example, you could say "Mal is a member of The Master Plumbers Association. To become a member, he had to pass 7 different written exams and 11 practical tests. Only one in four plumbers pass these rigid tests the first time—Mal did. He is also an accredited fitter and turner, meaning he has studied fitting and turning for three years and been examined by a master craftsman."

Now, Mal is being set up as some kind of superplumber, not just a guy who's been clearing blocked drains all his life. Generally, it pays to draw your potential customers a map, rather than expecting them to infer things for themselves.

Setting up this kind of credibility can also help you achieve better customer relationships. When people call to speak to Mal after reading this ad, they'll be under the impression they're talking to the god of plumbing.

The truth is, there are dozens of plumbers in the area who can claim close to the same experience, but they will appear to be backyard boys when up against Mal.

Tell people specifically why you know what you're talking about, and customers will flock to you—everybody loves an expert.

66. Admit a Flaw

We've all heard the saying "too good to be true." The thing is, we subconsciously consider this notion every time something seems to be too perfect or too generous.

If you really want people to believe what you're saying, admit a flaw here and there.

If it's all gloss and sheen, people tend to think that you're trying too hard to impress and that some elements of what you're saying must be lies, if not the whole lot.

Here's a great example: "This piano sounds pretty much as good as one twice the price. I've been amazed by the sound actually. It's beautiful to play too and it looks great. I've been a little disappointed by the lack of a warranty though. Even so, it's a hell of a bargain."

Customers tend to think, "Well, if this salesperson is telling us that something is wrong with this piano, everything else they're saying must be true." Of course, nobody consciously processes it like that, but that's the end result.

The basic logic is this: It's in the interest of the piano salesman to highlight something negative, which infers that he must be completely honest.

This is a brilliant technique if you're making some fairly lofty claims about what you do, or what you sell. It's a great idea to follow anything that sounds "too good to be true" with an "of course" statement.

An "of course" statement goes something like this: "This is truly one of the most powerful cars I've ever driven. You hit the accelerator and it takes off like an airplane. I reckon it would beat a Ferrari on an airstrip. Of course, it doesn't handle as well as a Ferrari."

Right away you've established credibility. After almost losing it completely with the outlandish Ferrari comparison, you reel it back in by admitting a flaw.

This is an easy technique to incorporate into your advertising. It allows you to make big claims and promises, and then qualify them with a flaw. It works almost every time and in every situation. It gives people the impression that you're "on the level" with them.

Surprisingly, admitting a flaw will rarely do your sales appeal any damage. People will generally uncover any shortcomings anyway. If you try to dodge them, it will only make them more suspicious.

If you preempt the customer and say, "Of course, it won't do x, y, and z," it encourages the customer to think, "Oh well, I can live without x, y, and z—at least it does a, b, and c."

67. Salesmanship in Print

Many years ago a young copywriter by the name of John Kennedy coined the phrase "Salesmanship in print." He did this when applying for a position with the Lord and Thomas advertising agency. It's a term that has remained with us ever since, simply because no one has been able to put it better, or more succinctly.

To explain this further, you have to imagine that two hundred people read your advertisement. In effect, it's like having your salespeople talk to two hundred people one-on-one. Advertisements are like having an extended sales team, but you need to understand that your ad is selling one-on-one.

So considering that you are writing your advertisement to make sales, it's easy to understand that you are not writing your ad to make people laugh, or to tell them about you or your store. Your ad is simply designed to sell.

Many people get caught up in the belief that they need to have humorous advertising, something that will make people laugh. But it simply doesn't work that way.

So remember, advertising is all about selling. You need to write this on a large piece of paper and stick it on your wall.

68. Make Sure You Use a Headline

Running an advertisement without a headline is like leaving the "open" sign off the front of your store.

Your headline is effectively the "open" sign for your advertisement. It's the thing that says, "Hi. We've got something worthwhile here. Come and see what it is."

People reading a newspaper will skim through the headlines and stop at the one that seems most intriguing, the one that interests them the most. It's the same with advertisement headlines.

You see, a headline is basically your advertisement for your ad. Headlines by themselves will not normally make a sale, but what they are doing is selling the readers on the idea that they should read your ad further. Many ad agencies and creative copy writers have made the mistake of trying to be too clever and not placing headlines at the top of the advertisement. In fact, I have seen what would be a very effective headline quite often appear halfway through the copy.

The problem is that people didn't read this far!

Your headline needs to grab the reader's attention and to promise a benefit. You need to understand that your company name is not a headline. The only people who get excited about seeing your company name at the top of your ad are you and (maybe) your mother.

Headlines are so important that you should write a couple and then leave the project overnight. This gives you a fresh outlook, just like the average reader would view it.

Pick the one that grabs your attention by offering benefits, and go with that. That's just one of the key steps to writing successful headlines. Let's look at a few of the others.

69. Use Your Product Name in the Headline If Possible

Now let me say right up front that this technique won't work for everybody, but I suggest if you can use it, you should. Simply use your product name in the headline to let people know exactly what it is that you are selling.

People who are in the market for a particular product or service will be attracted to any advertisement headline that mentions that product or service. You need to understand, though, that you only get one chance with your headline, and probably very few people are in the marketplace for your service or product at any one time.

If they are in the market for your product, then obviously by putting that product in the headline, you are immediately going to attract their attention. That's what they are looking for.

If you don't want to promote a specific brand name, try the idea of including the words "large line," explaining to people that you have a wide assortment of the types of products they are after. It can also be beneficial to include a price in your headline, but you do this only if you have the very best price.

If people are in the market specifically for your type of product, then the best way to get to them is to include that product in the headline.

70. 20 to 25 Percent of the Space of the Ad

With understanding the importance of your headline, you need to also understand that your headline needs to be big. If you read through any newspaper or magazine, you'll see that the headline is substantially bigger than the body copy.

Your advertisement headline needs to be the same. It needs to be very big. People skim through, reading just the headlines, so it needs to be big to make it easier for them to see it.

I have seen many people in the past trying to cut down on the cost of their advertisement by using a smaller headline. Wouldn't you rather pay an extra hundred dollars for an advertisement that someone is going to read? Seems like good solid economics to me. So, don't be stingy. Your advertisement needs to be as big as it needs to be. Your headline needs to be large to attract attention.

As a general rule of thumb, your headline should take up 20 to 25 percent of the total space within your advertisement. Any larger than 25 percent is wasted; anything less than 20 percent is too small. People won't see it.

It's also important that you don't run your headline on an angle. This is another mistake that I have seen many people make. People don't read at an angle; they read in a straight line, from top left to bottom right

If it's running in a newspaper, lay it out exactly the same as the newspaper's headlines. The same with a magazine. It needs to be easy to read.

71. Long Headlines Generally Work Better Than Short Ones

It's a common misconception among copywriters that headlines that are too long won't get read. Your headline needs to be as big as it needs to be, and I'm not talking size only—I'm talking about the number of words.

That doesn't mean that in your headline you should just ramble on; you still need to get quickly to the point. But a short headline that doesn't convey a message is pointless. It's foolish to think that a 7-word headline is going to work better than a 12-word headline if the 7-word message doesn't convey the point that you are trying to get across.

So one of the most effective ways of writing long headlines is to sit down and write exactly the way you would say it, with as many words as you possibly want to use. Do this with a number of headlines, then go back through them and remove any words that don't need to be there. Sometimes this means that you will need to find new ways of saying the same thing, but often when you go through your headlines a second time, there are words that just don't need to be there.

There is another thing to keep in mind with a long headline: It sometimes can look wordy; it can look chunky and difficult to read. One of the easiest ways to overcome this is to make the key words in the headline a larger point size. Take the key five or six words and make them bigger. Now these words should almost be able to tell the story by themselves.

72. Make the Headline Easier to Understand

If people are looking over advertisements quickly, and understanding that people skim the headlines, then your headline only gets one shot at them. Your headline needs to get the message across in a very simple and easy-to-understand manner. People need to be able to tell at a glance whether what you're saying is of interest to them and what the main benefit is in their buying from you.

Now a simple way to test whether or not your headline is conveying that message in a very quick and simple manner is to write out a couple of the headlines that you intend to use and then to get people to read them. But don't let them sit there and read them for an extended period of time.

Just flash them up in front of them and ask them what they understood by it. Any headlines where there is confusion and they can't repeat exactly what it is you're trying to get across need to be revamped. You keep redoing them until they tell at a very quick glance exactly what it is that you are selling.

It's important that you don't try to be clever and that you're not too vague or ambiguous in your headline. Remember, it's all about making sales.

73. Seven Reasons Why

This is one of the best headline starters you could use. It offers benefits and stimulates curiosity. It also makes writing your ad ridiculously easy. All you have to do is list the 7 reasons.

Importantly, it should be 7 reasons, not 5, 10 or 4. There's something about the number 7 that seems odd and specific.

People tend to think, "They've chosen 7, so there must be something interesting." It's just slightly out of the ordinary, which makes it ever so intriguing. That can be enough to hook them in.

Here are some examples of headlines starting with "7 reasons why:"

7 reasons why you should stop what you're doing and call JS Swimming Pools right now.

7 reasons why you should build a pool with JS Swimming Pools before June 31.

7 reasons why customers of JS Swimming Pools refer 2-3 friends.

7 reasons why you should make an appointment to see Madame Zelda this week.

7 reasons why no one has ever asked us for a refund.

7 reasons why your cat would rather be eating Feline's Friend.

74. Here's How—Here's Why

Another great headline starter is, "Here's how," or it's close relative, "Here's why."

These headlines stimulate immediate curiosity and generally provide a benefit to the reader. This starter also makes you, the writer, think about exactly what you are offering to the reader in return for reading the ad.

Here are some examples:

Here's how you can be the envy of every other kid at school.

Here's how to have a swimming pool this summer without spending more than $4000.

Here's why JS Swimming Pools have been building 3 pools a week for the last 2 years.

Here's why you should call JS Swimming Pools for a quote today.

Here's how to lose 10 kg in three weeks.

Here's how to make more money this year than ever before.

Here's how to make your thin friends green with envy.

Here's why people always think I'm 10 years younger.

Here's why you need to take your pet to the vet every six months.

Here's why you can't afford to miss Big Boy Menswear's opening sale.

75. How to—How You Can

These headline starters follow the same pattern as "Here's how." They create curiosity and promise a benefit for reading. You will discover how to do whatever the headline says.

Here are some good examples:

How to earn $780 a week, working from home and finishing in time to pick the kids up from school.

How to buy a swimming pool for half the price.

How you can lose 7–8 kg in one week and not feel hungry (and before you ask, yes—this will work for you!).

How you can escape all bank fees without losing any convenience.

76. You

The most important word you can use in your ad is *you*. People want to know what's in it for them—I can't stress this strongly enough.

Have you ever read (or written) one of those ads that says, "We've been in business for 12 years, we've got lots of experience, we do a better job than anyone else, we, we, we, we." It's like we, we, we all the way home.

The point is, the readers don't want to read *we*. They want to read *you*.

For example, "You'll discover the benefits of dealing with a truly experienced plumber. You'll get better service than ever, which will make your life so much easier. You won't have to wait either, because you'll be attended to less than 20 minutes after you call."

It certainly has a different feel than the first one. You'll find that *you-text* is a lot more grabbing than *we-text*. You're being completely clear and up front: There's a benefit to *you*, the reader, for reading this ad.

Next time you go to write an ad, count up the number of we's and the number of I's. It might surprise you how little you've been focusing on the reader and how much emphasis you've put on yourself.

Writing in "yous" forces you to think in terms of benefits. It makes you think, "Well, we've been in business a long time but how does that help our customers—what do they get out of it?"

You can't exactly write "you'll find out that we've been in business a long time." It's just absurd. You'll end up with something like, "You'll get your plumbing taken care of quickly—you can be confident of that because we've been doing this for 56 years."

Here's a classic story in the advertising business. A famous ad writer wrote a long ad—in fact, it was around 3000 words long, all in small print and taking up a full page in the *New York Times*. It was, and still is, a huge amount of text to include in an ad.

Another ad writer working in the ad agency reasonably asked, "What are you doing? Nobody will ever read that. Who the heck has got the time or the motivation to sit down and read your epic ad? That'll bomb, and bomb very, very badly."

The writer of the ad turned around calmly and said, "Yes, but you haven't seen the headline yet: "Everything We Know About YOU."

77. FREE

There's no doubt people like getting stuff for free. If you include the word *free* in your headline somewhere, it's more likely to be read. In fact, the most successful ads I've seen always have "free" sticking out boldly somewhere in the ad.

There are some caveats to that, however.

First, if you trick people into reading your ad using a massive FREE at the top, and then don't deliver on the promise, your ad will definitely fail. For example, I once read an ad headed with the word FREE. The word took up a third of the ad. Underneath it said, "Soft drink with every main meal over $30."

Needless to say, that was something of a letdown. It makes you feel cheated and misled, which in turn will make you even less likely to visit the restaurant, call the business, or whatever it is the ad is trying to encourage you to do.

If you use the word free in such a bold way, make sure that the offer is truly something remarkable, or else the whole thing will backfire and people will be turned off dealing with you (when they were neutral about buying from you before).

Second, if you are offering something completely *free* (that is, with no obligation to purchase anything else) be prepared for a surprise.

I remember running a promotion with a florist—we handed out flyers offering a free rose. No one came in. It was completely bewildering. It was only later that I worked it out. People are often too embarrassed to claim something free. It makes them uncomfortable.

It's strange but you have a better chance with a "free X when you buy a Y" appeal than you do with a "free X no strings attached" approach. People just don't expect to get anything for absolutely nothing.

Free is probably the most over-used word in marketing, so you need to remember to pull it out only when you've got something pretty amazing to give away, and only when it's tied in with something else. The offer has to be unbelievable but believable, if you get my drift.

Often you're better off going for a package deal: "Come in and get A, B, and C for just $X." People don't feel embarrassed asking for "one of those $X deals." They just think they're capitalizing on a good price. The same doesn't always go for "free." Some people just feel weird saying, "Oh, and can I have my free donut with that steak dinner?"

78. Now

This is another great headline starter that works especially well in newspapers. It makes people think that there has been an innovation, or that something has changed or improved.

Here are some examples:

Now a swimming pool is affordable.

Now you can own a swimming pool without paying a cent until next year.

79. At Last and Announcing

These headline starters work in very much the same way as *now*. They're great for newspapers—people are reading the paper to see if there's anything new happening.

Here are some examples:

At last—an inground swimming pool for under $4000.

At last—a swimming pool builder who charges low prices all year round, even in summer.

Announcing—the lowest ever price on an inground swimming pool.

Announcing—the first inground swimming pool to win the AR Pezeley Award for Innovation.

Announcing—a proven way to make more sales with fewer staff.

Announcing—a brilliant new book on the healing powers of vinegar.

Announcing—a hairdresser who guarantees you'll be thrilled with your haircut.

80. DON'T

Don't surprisingly is one of the best headline starters you could use. Surprising perhaps because the aim of advertising is to tell people what to do, not what *not* to do.

Regardless, *don't* generally works a treat—it inspires fear and curiosity at the same time and, assuming that what comes after *don't* is interesting, it always makes for a hooky headline.

Here are some ways to use *don't*:

DON'T buy a swimming pool until you read this.

DON'T make these mistakes when designing your swimming pool.

DON'T buy any more beer until you read this.

DON'T commit to a loan before reading this.

DON'T turn the page before cutting this ad out.

81. Newsworthy

One technique you should consider when you're advertising in any news publication is the *newsworthy* headline. In fact, it makes sense that this approach should work well for you.

So how do you go about writing a newsworthy type of headline?

Well the easiest way is to read through the articles within the publication, and take note of the headline styles. Then write your own headlines in a similar style. Writing your standard *ad* type of headline will not give you the desired effect. You need to have the readers believe that they are reading something like an article.

Let me show you how this type of advertisement works.

Imagine you want to advertise new accounting computer software and you've got a number of quotes from people who used it and were impressed. The standard type of ad might have a headline something like this:

"Here's how you can improve your accounting systems..."

Now this headline would be fine if you wanted to run your standard type of ad, but if you want to use a *newsworthy* headline, you'd try something like this:

"New accounting software the best in the market, says industry expert."

See how this headline is more of a *news* type? It would have a good chance of getting read, as people who are in the market for new accounting software would probably read it and would believe it to be the best because an *industry expert* says it is.

Another form of advertising that uses a newsworthy approach is the press release. Now, press releases are not a true form of advertising in that you're not paying for the article to be printed. Rather, you're trying to convince the editor of a newspaper or magazine to print an article about you, your business, or your point of view on a particular subject. Why? Simply to get your business some free exposure.

Unlike a normal ad, you can't have a blatant selling message in your article. It needs to be more subtle than that.

There are probably many things you would like to say in order to promote your business. You need to remember that the media are not there as your free advertising vehicle. If it's not newsworthy, it won't get used. To give you an idea of what I mean, let's look at a store that imports rugs.

If the store owners were having a sale, they'd probably like to say something like, "Huge Sale: 70% off all rugs." The problem with this is that it sounds like an ad. There's no news angle.

If they were to approach it from a different angle, it would probably get exceptional coverage. For example, they could say, "The decline of overseas currencies is killing small business." They could go on to say that because of the decline in the dollar, cheap rugs are flooding the market. Because of this, they've had to reduce their top quality stock by up to 70 percent and, if the current trends keep up, many other local businesses could soon be feeling the pinch.

Notice how the second example approaches the same story from a more interesting angle. It also gives them a chance to tell readers that their stock is better and that the readers should beware of cheaper, inferior products, in a roundabout way. If your story doesn't have a news angle, it won't get published. You need to say something to your potential readers—that is, there must be a strong story line to get them interested.

Any selling message that you include in your press release must be subtle and not get in the way of the story. Remember that this kind of unpaid promotion is a great way for you to get your name in front of the public.

Try to find an important point of difference, unusual benefits for customers dealing with you, or some other newsworthy angle about your product. Keep in mind that *news* must be just that.

Writing a press release about a product that's been on the market for years won't work. It needs to contain something new and interesting. Let's consider a newsworthy point of difference. Stop and think for a moment about the things that make your business unusual. Then ask yourself if those differences are truly newsworthy. For example, if you want to promote a steak and seafood restaurant, you'd be hard pressed to stand out. But what if your steakhouse owners offered to drive their patrons home after they'd had too much to drink, in the customers' own cars? That would be worth promoting.

Finding the benefits to your business can also be challenging. Oh sure, you can probably think of dozens of benefits, but how many of those would make for good reading? In this situation you're probably best to go for a human-interest angle. For example, a real estate agent might have just sold 42 houses to one family over 78 years and 3 generations. If the family then spoke about the exceptional customer service that kept it coming back, you'd have a good chance of getting some free publicity.

Perhaps you can find some other newsworthy angles. Maybe you've just opened a new room in your restaurant where customers get a foot massage before they dine, or you have a famous author coming in to your store for book signings. Or you may have just been given a prestigious award. Perhaps one of your staff has done something amazing for a customer.

If something has happened that has genuine interest value, let people know about it. But remember, it must really be newsworthy as the following example demonstrates.

PRESS RELEASE   Date 00/00/00

Imported fashions cause stir in marketplace.

Local clothing agent and manufacturer, Zelma Creations, has just secured the rights to import two popular Australian labels, it was announced yesterday by Zelma Marketing Director, Michelle Jacobs.

"We're very excited. This is a real coup, not only for us but for New Zealand fashion in general," Jacobs said. "Zone 7 and Julia Crampton are two of the most exclusive designer labels to come out of Australia. There's already a buzz around the marketplace since word of our success leaked out."

Well known in the New Zealand fashion industry for innovative marketing, Jacobs puts the company's success down to well-developed strategies. "We've worked hard in recent times to be different," she said. "With the assistance of Australia's leading marketing company, Action International, we've begun to offer a number of revolutionary services to our clients."

Zelma Creations provides a number of unique services for its customers. "We help them with such areas of marketing as using point-of-sale material, store layout, and window displays," said Jacobs. "We actually employ someone to go to each store and train our customers in these areas."

One of their most successful strategies is that of closed-door sales. "These sales take place after hours," explained Jacobs. "Stores invite their clients to exclusive previews of the upcoming season's fashions." Speaking with Jacobs, you soon realize why Zelma Creations have become such a success. "Our philosophy is based on customer service," says Jacobs. "We believe that business is meant to be fun, and that a happy store is a successful store."

Zelma Creations can be contacted directly at (01) 234 5678.

Contact: Michelle Jacobs

Phone Number: (01) 234 5678

82. Loop

You probably already know that the headline is the most important part of your ad. In effect, it's the "ad for the ad," the bit that helps people decide whether they'll bother investing their time reading about you or not.

That probably puts the pressure on. I'll bet you're filled with thoughts like, "Don't you have to be an advertising genius to write a great headline?"

The simple answer is *no*. The complex answer is *no*, as long you're aware of one simple principle: the *looping* headline.

I'm about to tell you the seven things that make a headline loop.

No, that's a lie—but I did just illustrate what a *loop* is. You were reading on to see what the seven things were. I opened a loop—I posed a question in your mind that you had to read on to answer.

If your current headlines only state something, there's no curiosity value; there's no benefit for me to read on.

Consider these headlines: "Real grit," "Fantastic," "Take two at meal times." These headlines could be targeted at anyone and could be about almost anything. There's absolutely no reason why I would want to read on.

Imagine if I came up to you on the street and said, "Real grit." You'd think I was a crackpot. Good headlines communicate. They give you a clear idea of what the ad's about and create enough curiosity for you to read on.

A looping headline poses a question in the mind of the reader, a question that can be answered only by reading the rest of the ad. Most of the headline starters we've covered in previous chapters open a loop.

For example, "Here's how to buy a half-priced swimming pool" very clearly opens a loop. The question is posed: How do I buy a half price swimming pool? The same goes for "Seven reasons," "How to," "How you can," etc.

The key is curiosity. It's a more potent force than most people realize. When people read a headline that stimulates their natural curiosity, they start reading the ad almost in spite of themselves.

Think about it. If someone said, "Oh, I had a dream about you last night—wow, it was amazing!" Could you resist asking them to give you more details? Even if you were late for a meeting, or looking for a toilet, you'd probably still be willing to hang around to find out.

The same might happen if someone said, "Hey, I've found out how to quit my job forever and earn more working three days a week." You'd probably want her to elaborate. Applying this idea to headlines, the key is to make your headline make people want to read on. Obviously, the trick is to make the question that you pose in your headlines as interesting as possible.

The best headlines combine curiosity (looping), self-interest, and a news element all in one. For example, "How you can use this new device to clear up acne spots in two hours or less."

If you suffer from acne, you'd be desperate to read on. If you didn't, you probably wouldn't. That's fine, because the nonacne sufferers wouldn't buy anyway. You're immediately getting the intense interest of exactly the people who are most likely to buy your product.

The headline also loops because it says, "this new device." The first thing you ask yourself is, "What new device?" Of course, you'll need to read the ad to find out.

Here's another great one that loops: "The only real way to succeed in network marketing." If you were a network marketer (obviously the target market), you'd be itching to read this ad. If it promised you enough benefits and a decent offer, you'd probably respond.

That's a formula for successful ad writing. Combine a looping headline with great benefits and a good offer, and bingo—you have a winner. Think about that the next time you write an ad.

83. Curiosity

I've never told anyone this before. For years I have kept this secret to myself. It's the secret of how to write a headline that works, every time.

Feeling a bit curious? It's not surprising, as the opening lines were designed to create that effect. The opening line immediately arouses the emotion of curiosity. The same opening line that I started this section with could very easily be used as a headline for an advertisement. You see, curiosity headlines are designed to draw people into your ad. They create a great amount of interest and people can't resist reading on.

Often, the curiosity style of headline is very similar to the types that newspapers use for their headlines. You'll notice that newspaper headlines often contain just a few words to get the message across. One of the techniques that they use is to arouse curiosity.

The reason this works so effectively for both newspapers and advertisements is that most people like mystery. They like intrigue and they like gossip. They love to learn new things and they love to read about taboo subjects.

A very good curiosity headline will have people desperate to read on, but you must be cautious. You must be careful not to lie or mislead the reader. So if your curiosity headline is drawing people in, then your first paragraph should really continue on with that theme, but only as far as the first paragraph or two.

Then you must quickly move in and start to expand to get across the message, which is the sales pitch

Some people, as soon as they get to a sales message, will become disinterested, but it's safe to assume they weren't buyers in the first place. Start to talk about your product or service and tie that into your story. Then you'll be well on the way towards a sale.

So, what sort of headlines could be used to make people curious? Let's take a look at a few different styles.

Let's imagine for a moment that we are selling weight loss pills to people who are overweight. An effective curiosity headline could be, "How this one tiny tablet helped me marry the girl of my dreams." Or if you were selling an ergonomic chair, you could use a headline like, "Revolutionary chair helps man walk again."

So, read through newspapers and magazines and look at the style they use for their headlines. You'll very quickly get a feel for how a curiosity headline should be written. Once you have mastered this style of writing, you can expect to get a much higher readership for your ads.

84. Quick and Easy

If there's one thing that's indubitable about human nature, it's that people like things to be quick and easy. People don't like hassles or things that take up a lot of time. Lifestyles have become more hectic. People have less and less time to spend doing things and the world is moving at a much faster pace.

Therefore, anytime your headline promises the benefit of making something faster or easier, you will immediately appeal to those people who are busy and don't have much time in the day (which nowadays includes a large percentage of the population).

It does not only need to highlight the time that they'd save. A headline that promises to make a boring task faster, or a difficult task easier, would definitely pull a very powerful response.

It's all about giving solutions. If your product or service overcomes a problem, then you need to explain that in your headline. It might be that your store gives very fast service, or that you give very easy-to-understand advice that will provide a step-by-step solution to their problems. If that is the case, then you need to communicate that in your headline.

To give you an example of how effective this can be, consider a boring and time-consuming task like washing your car. Now, imagine that you had a product that made washing the car quicker and easier than ever before. Your headline could then read something like this: "It only takes seven minutes each week to keep your car in showroom condition."

Now if the people reading your ad are sick and tired of washing their cars (because it takes forever and leaves them with sore and tired arms), chances are they're not only going to read your ad; they'll be ready to call you then and there. You are offering a very easy solution to a task that they would rather not be doing.

Explain how your service is faster; how life will be easier when they start coming in and buying from you. It could be something like a drive-through supermarket, but imagine if you could phone your order ahead, then drive-through an undercover loading section, and be in and out in just a few minutes.

One of the keys to headlines that communicate something quick and easy is to include a time. What I mean by a time is this: "In and out in just six minutes." It's important to always try to include a definite time.

A headline that says, "Paint Your Entire House in Just Eleven Hours," will always work better than one that says, "Paint Your House in Less Than Half a Day" because it's far more specific.

Being vague by just saying "hours," "half a day," or "less than a week," isn't being specific enough. People will believe you've just made it up. If you can give a specific time, then you've got a much greater chance of success with your headlines.

85. Qualify the Reader

One of the things that you need your headline to do is to qualify your readers or your target market. By that I mean you want to only be attracting those people that you want to do business with.

If you're advertising a retirement village, then it's fairly pointless to have eleven- and twelve-year-old kids reading your ads. Your headline needs to qualify the right kind of people. In the past, I have seen a lot of headlines that don't qualify the right people up front.

So, lets have a look at how to write a qualifying headline.

Imagine you were writing an ad to sell luxury sports cars. Your headline could be, "Attention, anyone looking to buy a luxury sports car." Now most people understand how much a luxury sports car costs (they'd have a ballpark idea anyway), so it's going to be only those who have the money, or who are looking for that particular product, that are going to read the ad and ultimately respond.

Now this is far more effective than having a headline that simply said, "Attention anyone looking to buy a new car," for obvious reasons.

Maybe you might have a hair loss treatment product, in which case your headline could be, "Anyone suffering from hair loss." Now those people who aren't suffering from it are not going to read the ad, and you wouldn't want them to read it in the first place. So be very specific with your headline. The more specific you can be, the better the quality of response you'll receive.

86. Question Headlines

While being one of the most popular types of headlines, question headlines are also one of the most difficult to write effectively. It's a technique that should be used only by experienced writers—they should be used with caution by anyone who has not written many ads.

One of the major problems with question headlines is that you might well have the right product but simply ask the wrong question. To demonstrate what I mean, pretend for a moment that you are writing an ad for mobile phones. The phones you are selling have four key advantages over other models.

First, they have a clearer signal. Second, they don't drop out as much as other phones on the market do. Third, they can store more numbers than any other phone on the market and, finally, they are a lot lighter.

An inexperienced writer might write a headline such as, "Looking for a mobile phone with crystal clear sound?" In itself it's not a bad headline. But what if the people reading your ad say to themselves, "No, I'm not looking for a phone with crystal clear sound, but I would really like one that is lightweight."

Now they will skip your ad rather than reading on, even though your phone is lightweight, simply because you didn't ask them in the headline if they were looking for a lightweight phone.

So, is the answer to ask in your headline, "Looking for a mobile phone that's lightweight?" Well, maybe not. Possibly readers are after one that stores more numbers.

It's not a matter of your product being right for the people who are looking to buy. You're simply asking the wrong question. If you have three or four key advantages, you're far better off with a headline along these lines: "Why are more people turning to our mobile phones?"

A question headline is normally a closed question. And this is one of the challenges people have when writing them. In readers' minds they can simply give you a yes or no answer.

So the most effective form of question headline has an element of curiosity. The readers are intrigued, but you need to ask questions that are going to draw them in, not ones they can simply give a yes or no answer to.

Let me show you what I mean. Imagine you are advertising a baby-sitting service. Which of the two headlines below do you think would work the best?

1) Do you know the five most common problems with baby-sitting services?

or

2) Do you know these five most common problems with baby-sitting services?

Now if you suspected that the second one would be more effective, you are right. The wording indicates that you are about to teach them five different problems with baby-sitting services, whereas the first allowed them to subconsciously say yes or no.

The first headline doesn't really indicate that you are about to tell them the five problems, so the chances are that they will skip straight over the top of the ad.

Remember with your headlines to have an element of curiosity, and remember also to be as specific as possible—to let the readers know that you are about to give them some specific information. Any question headline where you can simply answer yes or no will not get a response.

87. Reader Group

When you're looking to place an advertisement in any publication, you need to work out who the members of your target market are, then which publication best reaches them. But you also need to consider a few other points.

With any publication there will be a number of different sections. For example, a daily paper will normally have an early general news section, a sports section, classified advertising, etc, etc. Some of these sections appear every day. Others, however, such as business or automotive sections, may appear only on certain days of the week.

So where and when do you advertise?

Well, you need to work out who are the various reader groups of the publication you're about to advertise in. You also need to know which editions they buy more regularly. If you're aiming at women aged 30 plus, you might advertise in Tuesday's Lifestyle section. If you're targeting males aged over 20, you might advertise in the sports pages. But there are sports sections in every edition of the paper, so if you wanted to advertise only once a week, which day would you choose?

You'd probably choose Monday's edition, as it will contain all the sports results from the weekend. But these examples are obvious. What if you're aiming at males and females aged 18 to 25, employed, with an average income of over $455 per week. Where would you advertise then? Which part of which edition of which publication?

Fortunately, you don't have to try to work it out for yourself. By simply asking the publication for its readership figures, you'll be able to make an educated decision by yourself.

You see, every publication will have these figures. They'll be based on surveys that will have been conducted by independent research companies. These companies interview a cross section of readers and then furnish the newspaper with a report of their findings. These surveys are normally done once every few years, although some publications may have them done more often.

So, before advertising in any print medium, make sure you identify your target market and find out which editions it mostly reads. By having this research at your fingertips, you can make a more educated decision on when and where to place your ads. But, remember to keep an open mind. Research can help only so much. To be sure you're getting the best results, test and measure different editions and different sections.

88. Use Words Your Audience Can Relate To

Understanding this one simple point has made me more money than I care to remember.

When I first started writing ads, I'd be frustrated by the fact that sometimes they worked but quite often they didn't. I got frustrated to the point where finally I sat down and analyzed the results, and it was only after doing this that I realized there was a certain type of person responding to my ads. The ads that weren't targeted weren't getting a result.

The reason: I was speaking in a language that some people could relate to but others couldn't.

Advertising is all about building rapport, empathy, and making people think that you are just like them—that you have the same values, the same beliefs, and experience the same frustrations. Any advertisement that can build those feelings will immediately earn the reader's trust. Once you have built that trust, you are well on the way to making a sale.

People won't buy from someone they don't trust, and they don't trust anyone who doesn't speak their language, which is why it is critical that you only use words your readers understand—the words they use themselves in everyday conversation.

This is why people trust their friends and associates. They're people who talk the same language as they do, people they've known for a period of time. So, your ad must be written the same way.

It comes back to the *who*—understanding the members of your target market. Now to write effectively in their words and their language, you need to listen to how they speak. Listen to the types of words they use, the phrases they use. Then write your advertisement in that language.

That could include slang words or swear words (although you should never go over the top with swear words, even if your target market does swear quite dramatically). In essence, write your ad just like you are having a conversation with the members of your target market.

This is doubly important when you are writing ads aimed at lower socioeconomic groups. If your ads are aimed at people with a low-educational standard, or limited vocabulary, then using big words will confuse them. If they don't understand your ad, they won't read on.

By going for longer, more complicated terminology and explanations, your ad can appeal only to that percentage of the population that has an extended vocabulary or a good understanding of the English language.

One of the easier ways to test your ad to make sure that you are going along the right track is to find someone who you believe is in your target market, someone who speaks the language of your customers. Get that person to read your ad out aloud, and any part that sounds unnatural and doesn't flow, go back, scrap it, and start again.

Once you've written something new, get him to read it again, and keep doing that until it flows and it's easier for him to read and understand. Once you have done that, your ad is ready to go.

89. Get to the Point—ASAP

It's important to remember that people are basically coming from a position of disinterest. They are not reading the paper for the advertising, and, more often than not, they consider the ads a distraction.

Have you ever opened up a glossy magazine, only to find that the first ten pages are full-page ads? I don't know about you, but that annoys me. In fact, I'm much less likely to look at those ads than others in the magazine.

It's funny, because those advertisers spend much more to get their ads right up front and they're probably the least read in the whole magazine.

The thing is, you really need to make your point quickly. People are not willing to hang around waiting for you to tell them what the good part is. It's not like a verbal conversation, where people won't walk away even if you're boring. There's nobody around and there are no manners to worry about, so readers will happily stop reading your ad if it doesn't grab them right away.

Some may disagree, but I think you should *expect* the marketplace to be cold, unfeeling, fickle, and uninterested. People often feel hostile towards marketing, and they resent its attempts to manipulate them.

Your ad has to say, "Wait a second. This is *really* worth reading and you'll *really* be pleased if you do."

Too many advertisers start by rambling on about nothing in particular. They feel the need to warm up. Here's a good example:

"Here at John Fashions we like to give great customer service. We've been in business since 1987, and we're still going strong. We believe that fashion is important, not just fun. With that in mind, we're opening a new store in the city, the biggest in Sydney—there'll be more than 1700 suits on display and the most ties anywhere in the southern hemisphere."

Did you notice the problem? The ad was written back to front. It started with the least important information and ended with the best part. The first three sentences could have been left out entirely.

If you need to warm up when writing your ads, don't be afraid to completely erase everything you say before you get to the best part. Hit your readers with everything up front, and then fill in the blanks later.

The above example could have started with

"John Fashion menswear store is about to open in Sydney City—more than 1700 suits on display and the biggest line of ties ever assembled."

90. Keep Your Sentences Short

The main thing to remember about writing ads is this: Grammar doesn't matter one bit. Neither does spelling really, although it's probably preferable to get everything spelled correctly.

Forget everything you learned about writing English at school (that shouldn't be too hard) and just write as you speak. Your sentences should be short, basic, and superpunchy. Here's an example of *not* doing that:

"Pursuant to last week's sale, we still have stock left over, leading to our decision to mark down our suits further still, which means even bigger savings for the customers who are quick to come and see us in our Parramatta store."

Not only is the grammar worse than anything an informal writer could come up with, it's downright long and confusing. Here's how it should be written:

"We didn't sell out—good suits still available. Even bigger discounts this week! Come in to our Parramatta store now."

It gets the same point across but much more clearly and in a decidedly more lively fashion. This "clipped" writing adds life and urgency to the ad, whereas the other sounds like an obituary.

Try to include one idea per sentence. Avoid the use of joining words such as *however, whereas,* and *because.*

It's strange, but I was once told to write everything so a 10-year-old could understand it. Having tried that idea out, I can only pass on the same information to you. You'd be surprised how many people out there have trouble reading anything mildly complex.

If the truth be known, educated people prefer to read short, simple sentences. When you read a short sentence, you don't have to think. The idea sinks right into your brain. Here are some examples:

The dog is brown.

Our sale ends Tuesday.

We guarantee to get things right.

Here are some examples of sentences that make you think. You have to keep in mind the first part and juxtapose it with the second.

Because we've recently had our factory burn down, our new store will not open for another two weeks.

If you compare our price with that of a larger warehouse, you'll find that on the whole, we're generally cheaper.

You get the idea. Short sentences are easy to read. They also give people a sense of speed and excitement.

The greatest misconception about advertising writing is that it takes skill. Some would even go further and suggest it takes some sort of artistic talent as well. Both are fallacies—in fact, being under some delusion that you're creating a masterpiece is more of a hindrance than a help to your ad. People aren't interested in your so-called art. They want to know what you can do for them.

Forget everything you've heard about advertising writers. The ones who claim to be "creative" are usually the ones who don't sell anything. The best advertising writers in history have been the men and women in the street, the ones in touch with common people.

The best ad writers understand that most people are basically selfish, uncultured, uneducated, lazy, greedy slobs—let's not mince words. People don't care about you and they don't care about your business. They have no time to clown around with you and very little interest in being educated by you.

You need to either promise them the world or scare the pants off them. It's the only way you'll hold their interest.

You need to speak in their language—small, easily understood words in short punchy sentences. People speak naturally. They use slang, contractions (it's, they're, etc.), and bad grammar. If you want to really relate to your readers, you need to do the same in your writing.

Just write it like you say it, and I mean that almost literally. If you'd say, "You'll get 25-years' warranty on your tank, so if things clog up, you're covered," when talking to people face-to-face, write it that way in your ad.

91. Call to Action

One of the basic mistakes I have seen time and time again in advertising is that the ad doesn't close the sale. Sure, the headline draws you in, the copy gets you excited, but the ad then fails to ask you to take action, or to get you to respond.

Remember, advertising is a form of sales, but instead of being a verbal sales pitch, it is a written sales pitch.

I have seen many salespeople who have the gift of the gab. They get people to the point where they are almost ready to buy. Then they simply don't ask for a sale, possibly because they have poor beliefs about money or a low self-esteem. Whatever it is, they simply don't manage to close the sale.

An advertisement without a call to action is exactly the same. People will not respond unless you have a really clear and very powerful call to action. So let's take a look at a few examples:

The first and easiest is to ask your prospect to call or to come into your store. People are very good at following instructions, so make it clear. Tell them to pick up the phone and dial your number now, or tell them to cut out the ad and bring it into your store within the next 24 hours. It's very important that you spell out exactly what they need to do.

Second, include an offer with your call to action. This is particularly effective if they are time-limited offers where you tell people to act now: Call within the next 24 hours; offer only available for the next seven days. These will get people to respond quickly.

Now, some people prefer to respond in different ways, and you need to be mindful of this as well. So test and measure your calls to action. Some may prefer to call you rather than come in and see you face-to-face. Some may prefer to mail in a coupon to get some free information before deciding to make an appointment.

Test a variety of different response devices to see which one your target market is most comfortable using, and then continue to use that time and time again.

The other thing that should be associated with your call to action is an outline of what will happen if people don't respond. Tell them what they'll miss out on; tell them how their lives will be affected if they don't act.

It's a matter of doing what it takes in order to get people to respond, and if you believe in your product or service, you shouldn't have a problem doing this.

Make people feel guilty or upset about the prospect of missing out on what you are offering.

92. Contact Details

One of the most embarrassing mistakes you can make in advertising is to forget to include your contact details in your ad.

I know this from personal experience. Yes, I once ran an advertisement that didn't include a phone number. People still managed to track me down, but how many sales did I miss out on simply because I didn't give anybody a way to respond.

This is something you need to check, and double-check, with every single ad that you write before you place it. Depending on the desired response, you need to include all your details. Let's look at some of the contact details you need to include.

First, a phone number (unless you want someone to just simply cut out a coupon and send it in). It's still a very good idea to make sure you have your phone number in there, possibly a fax number as well. If you spend a lot of time out and about, or if you have only a limited number of phone lines, including a mobile phone number can also be worthwhile.

As far as your address goes, if you want people to come into your store, you need to include your physical address. Sometimes it is a good idea to use a reference point.

For example, if there is a landmark nearby, explain that you are a couple of hundred yards up the street or across the road from it. But use something that people will find easy to locate.

If you want people to mail in a response, your mailing address obviously needs to be included.

One of the most important things to include these days is your e-mail address. It's something that many people fail to include in their advertisements.

You might even have your own Web page. If it's well written, well designed, and follows the ideas included in this book, then its address also needs to be included.

Your contact details need to be in the bottom right-hand corner of your advertisement—this is what's often referred to as the anchor point. People read from the top left corner to the bottom right hand corner, so as the eye scans over the ad, you want it to finish on your phone number or address. This is absolutely crucial because some people will still just skim it, no matter how well written it is.

They'll read the headline, a couple of paragraphs, and then the very next point their eye will go to is the bottom right-hand corner. If that includes your phone number, then there's a good chance they're going to call.

Many people have made the mistake of putting their logo there, but the trouble is, logos don't sell. People can't respond via your logo; they can only respond via your phone number.

You also need to include all your contact details on coupons, if you are including a coupon with your advertisement.

This is a point that is often forgotten by many business owners when they're running their ads. People will cut the coupon out; that's really what a coupon is designed for. But they might cut it out and put it in their handbags or wallets, or put it to one side. By the time they come back to respond to it, the advertisement they cut it out from is probably long gone.

So, if you don't have your contact details included on that coupon, guess what: There's nowhere for them to send it.

93. Use Testimonials

Over time, people have become skeptical about advertising. Many view it as blatant lying. It becomes harder and harder to convince people that you are telling the truth in your advertisement. The one easy way to overcome this is through the use of testimonials.

Testimonials are something that your past clients have said about you that indicates they are happy with your service or product. It just lets people know that your product really works.

Gathering testimonials from past customers to use in ads is very important. One of the easiest ways to get testimonials is just to ask. Ask people when they come in. Say, "Hi. You've been to our store before; you've been using our product for some time now. Would you mind providing a brief testimonial—just your thoughts on what our service is like or how the product is performing?"

People will be happy to do this; it's really just a matter of asking. Some will say no, but the vast majority that you approach, providing they've been dealing with you for a period of time, will be happy to give you a testimonial.

Testimonials shouldn't be overused; just use a handful of key ones—it should never be necessary to use a long list of them. Three or four are normally advisable, and don't use the whole testimonial, just the key sentences.

It's beneficial to include the name of the people who gave the testimonial and the area in which they live. You don't give exact addresses; people often don't want their addresses given out. What you do is state their names under the testimonial and the suburbs or the towns in which they live.

An effective way in which to use your testimonials is as a *pull quote*. What I mean by this is that in your advertisement you take out one quote (one testimonial that someone has supplied you) and place it in a larger font between a couple of columns of text. Then you put a line across the top and the bottom. It's just a couple of key words that people have said about your business.

Testimonials that overcome a nagging doubt in peoples' minds can be incredibly effective. People who are reading your ad are probably thinking as they go along, "Well I don't think this would work for me." If at that point they come across a testimonial from someone who addresses that specific issue, all of a sudden they're convinced. It's something that someone else has said about you; you haven't said it about yourself, so its far more credible.

The testimonials you don't use with your ads can be displayed around your store on walls, or you can include different ones with mail ads you send out. Don't use the same testimonials over and over again; rotate them because it adds credibility. It's not like you have had only one or two successful customers in the history of your business, so use a variety of testimonials.

It's a good idea to use testimonials at your point of sale. Display them prominently so people feel comfortable and satisfied about the purchase that they are about to make. It reinforces that buying from you is a good decision.

94. Include the Price

Now let me state right up front that this is not a good idea for everyone—it will work for only a few businesses. The businesses it will work for are only those that are very price competitive.

By that I mean that their prices are better than those of their competition. If your prices are better than your competition's, including the price in your ad is an absolute must.

This works very well because quite often people put off calling if they don't know what the price is. No one wants to call up and, halfway through your sales pitch, discover your product or service is well out of their price range.

By including the price, you can make it easier for these people to judge whether or not they can afford your product or service and whether it's worth looking into further.

People are 70 percent sold if they know what your price is and still contact you. They will normally have only a few niggling questions, a few things they want to clarify before they go ahead and buy.

It's also a good idea to list what people don't pay for if you've got extras. To give you an example, let's imagine we are selling an outdoor setting. In your advertisement you might state that the setting is being sold for just $169. In addition, they'll also get an umbrella, placemats, coasters, and a table cloth, valued at $74, absolutely free of charge.

This way people can see the true value of what they're getting. One of the mistakes that people make is that they list all the extras but don't list what those extras are valued at. You do.

Some people won't respond immediately to your ad—they'll take your ad and your price and start to price shop with your competitors. If you've got a fantastic deal, then this will blow your competitors out of the water. People will make you their last call, knowing that they are going to buy from you, because you have the best price (and extras).

If you are competitive on price, make sure you include that. Your competitors might not like it but as long as you are making sales, who really cares?

95. If It's On Sale, Show How Much I'm Saving

Have you ever noticed how some businesses are always having sales? 50 percent off, or 60 percent off. This seems to be the case with Persian rugs. But having something on sale in itself does not guarantee a response.

People want to know how much they're going to be saving by coming to your sale. This is the mistake that a lot of people make with their ads: They simply don't tell people. They just don't explain exactly how much it is they are saving.

People want to feel they've got a great deal. No one likes to feel ripped off. People like to boast to their friends how they haggled someone down, or how they bought something of great value at a greatly discounted price, or how they bought it at the regular price and got so many extras thrown in.

So in your ad you need to list your prices—not just the sales prices but what the regular price is and exactly how much they are saving.

This will definitely get the phones ringing off the hook and the people flooding through your door, providing there is a substantial saving there.

It doesn't matter what you are selling. Show people what the original price was, what the new price is, and exactly what it is they are saving. That way your ads are sure to get a better response.

96. Make Sure You Give All the Information

This is one area that could be called a trap for young players—people writing ads for the first time.

Quite often they will list their product; they'll list their price, and if it's on sale, how much customers will be saving. But they don't specifically explain what it is that people get.

Now, computer stores are very good at this. Look through the computer advertisements in any weekend paper and you'll see that they don't just advertise a computer for sale; they give all the specifications of that computer. What size the hard drive is, what speed it is, how many megs of RAM it's got—everything that the consumers need to know to be able to make their decisions.

If they didn't do this, they'd open themselves up to all sorts of problems. You see, when their customers, or potential customers, go to talk to your competitors to see what sort of deals they're offering, your competitors might cast doubt on exactly what they'll get when buying their product. They'll tell you that their competitors' products are inferior, that they don't include this, and they don't include that.

That may or may not be the case, but to overcome this you need to spell out absolutely everything they get—everything that's included with the package.

This is probably more important with technical or electrical products than it is for others. Make sure you include absolutely everything, because people get excited about the add-ons they get.

Quite often people will buy a product just to get the extras, not so much because they want the original product, but because they just want the other things you are offering.

This means including a lot of detail in your ad. The best way to do this is to list it in bullet-point form. By doing this people can quickly scan through, refer back, and see exactly what it is they are getting.

Sometimes you might like to keep a few things up your sleeve, things like a special bonus offer that people can find out about when they call up. That's fine. That's a really good tactic, but everything else should be spelled out. It's only the bonus that you keep up your sleeve.

97. Anticipate Questions

Anyone who's ever sold before understands that people ask a lot of questions before deciding whether to buy or not.

The benefit of selling face-to-face is that you get to address those questions individually and you get to overcome any objections.

Now, while you can't exactly do that with your advertising, you can anticipate some of the questions that people might ask and give those answers in the ad.

For example, if you are selling furniture, people might be wondering whether it comes in a color that will suit their homes. You can anticipate that question by mentioning in your ad that your furnishings come in a range of colors to suit every home.

By addressing a number of these anticipated questions in your advertisement, you're making the sales purchase easier when you get face-to-face with them.

Most of the questions will have already been answered by your ad, so there are only a few you will have to address when speaking to them. It's not only questions that you need to anticipate; you also need to consider potential objections.

If you can address them, you'll get a much higher response to your ad. Lets look at an example. Say you are selling a beauty treatment and that you are making certain claims about the treatment you're providing. People reading that advertisement might think to themselves, "I've heard it all before and it doesn't work."

If you believe that people may think this way, you need to address that in your ad. You can do this by saying, "I know that you're thinking you've heard it all before and it doesn't work, but this treatment does. We've tested it on over a hundred different skin types and have seen remarkable results."

So, anticipate questions and anticipate objections. Cover these in your ad. You will find the sales process becomes a lot easier, and your conversion rate will be higher.

98. Say What You're Going to Say, Say It, and Say What You've Said

If you can follow this rule when writing your ad, you're probably on the right track. It means that you have only one main idea and your whole intention is to hammer it home throughout the ad.

Your headline introduces your topic and gives the reader advance warning of what you're going to say. For example:

"How to save 25% on your long distance calls."

This headline sets it up nicely. Not only does it loop, but it tells people exactly what they're about to find out. It also selects the target market—people who never make long distance calls or don't own a phone will never read this ad, and that's fine.

Next, you need to say what you want to say, using simple, precise language and basic sentence construction. Here's an example:

"If you're with Telstra, you're wasting your money. You could be getting exactly the same service with GGTY Communications. We charge 25% less across the board and we do exactly the same thing."

That gets the point across. Now to ram it home, repeat it in a slightly different way. Here we go:

"That's right—our rates are much cheaper than Telstra's and you won't lose any of the convenience or service you're used to."

If your readers haven't gotten the point after that, they never will. You round out the ad by using a call to action. Here's what that looks like:

"If you'd like to start saving money today, call 1-800-999-5555 and ask to be switched over. In 30 seconds you could be on a new calling plan that costs you less. Call us right now."

This is a great example of an ad that had one point to make. As you can tell, it makes it well and would no doubt work extremely well. When you've read it, you'll know everything the company wants you to know: If you switch to that company, you'll save 25 percent and you won't lose any service.

Apply this idea to your advertising. Work out the one rock-solid selling point you'd like to promote, then bang it home. State it in your headline, back it up in your body copy, and then repeat it in a slightly different way.

Top the whole thing off with a call to action that restates the main benefit, and you'll have the most powerful ad you've ever written.

Part 4

▮ The Layout: Making It Sell

99. Layout

I have a good friend who works as a graphic artist. As with most people who work in marketing, I felt that I had a good eye for design and a natural flair in this area. I would look over his work and tell myself there's nothing to it. Anyone could do what he does.

I would sit down to design an advertisement and visualize how it should look. I would write the ad, get the photographs and logos together, then sit down in front of my computer ready to do it up.

Time and again I found that what I saw in my mind was not what came out on the page. My ads would always look "interesting." So, I would try a few tricks in an attempt to dress them up.

One of my favorites was to use a number of different fonts, or typefaces, as they're sometimes known. I would have the headline in one font, the subheadlines in another, the body copy in a completely different one, and the captions in a different one again.

I would have pictures set at an angle, and I would then try to wrap the text around them. Headlines and any shapes or objects (such as the myriad of background objects I would use) would sometimes be off-center and thrown about the page in such a way that you'd be forgiven for thinking I was having a seizure at the time I put it together.

Of course, if I had the option of color, this presented a whole new frontier in which I could make all of the fundamental mistakes ever made in graphic design.

I would then proudly sit back and gaze lovingly at the monstrosity I'd just created. I would show it to colleagues and friends who'd screw up their noses as if the advertisement had just released a foul-smelling, gaseous emission. They would sometimes try to offer some constructive criticism or an encouraging word, but more often than not they'd tell me that my layouts were repulsive. Not that they were being too harsh; in hindsight, they were only telling me what I should have already known.

Eventually I swallowed my pride and went back to Robbie and asked him to tell me where I was going wrong. His answer was quite surprising.

He explained that I was putting too much into my layouts. I was trying to be too clever. He pointed out that if I kept with the "Keep It Simple Stupid" theory, I would have more effective layouts. The points he shared with me were very valuable, so I'd like to share those with you now.

First, he pointed out that I should stop using so many different typefaces. For someone with no formal design training, I should never use any more than two. If I wanted to make any part of the text stand out, I should use bold, italics, or underline.

As for the photographs, I should stop placing them at an angle. Once again, unless you've had formal training in graphic design, you probably won't have a great idea of how to keep it all balanced. Keep your photos square to the page and align everything in blocks. That means that if you have two columns of text and you wish to place a photograph in the ad, make sure that the columns line up with each other. The columns should line up at the top and be the same length to give your ad balance.

You can then place your photograph above the text, or in the middle of it, providing it doesn't throw the columns out of alignment.

The background objects and clip art I'd been using had to go. They were making my layouts confusing and were starting to compete with the selling message. Of course, this is the last thing you want. The idea is not to create a work of art; it's simply to make sales.

As soon as I began to use the block style of designing ads, they began to produce better results. With everything "square" on the page, the layout itself had stopped getting in the way of the sale.

Robbie went on to explain that with the headline at the top of the page, subheadlines that told a story throughout the body copy, the only thing I had left to remember was to include my contact details at the bottom right-hand corner. The reason for this is that a person's natural reading style is top left to bottom right, the way you'd read any page of text.

The bottom right-hand corner is called the *anchor point*. The last thing you want to tell someone reading your ad is to pick up the phone and call you. Therefore you need to have your number in the bottom right-hand corner.

Robbie pointed out that as the human eye runs from top left to bottom right, the headline should always be above the body copy. Anytime a headline was placed in the middle of the copy or the middle of the ad, the eye had to read it and then travel backwards to read the rest of the ad. As this is unnatural, it should be avoided.

Your body copy should always be *justified*, not *rag left* or *rag right*. By that I mean the left- and right-hand edges of your copy should look neat and even. The letters at the end of each line should form a natural line down the page. Robbie explained to me that a number of tests had been conducted that had shown comprehension was significantly lower when a rag right or rag left setting had been used. As comprehension is vital, it's imperative that you justify your copy.

Finally, he told me that layout and design is not about being artistic. Ads are about communicating a sales message. It's about giving the reader information. Therefore, an ad that looks plain but gets the message across is far better than one that looks creative but gets poor results.

100. Font Size

In case you don't know, *font size* is the size of the type that you use in your ad. And it's measured in points.

You'll hear newspaper people and graphic designers talk about 12-point type, or 10-point type. Perhaps they'll say 12-point Times, or 9-point Arial—these are different sizes and styles of type.

Generally, you should select the size of type based on how much space you have to fill and how many words you want to fill it with.

As a general rule, you shouldn't go under 8-point type, or over about 13. Ten point is a good rule of thumb. Sometimes it depends on the target market you're going after. For example, older people may not be able to read small type easily and may choose not to read an ad for this reason.

By the same token, it can be quite exhausting to read large typefaces—your eyes have to travel so far to read a few lines of text. This is why 10- or 12-point type is so universal.

Research has been conducted on the effects of using different typefaces and sizes. It has its place, but probably moreso when it comes to designing textbooks.

If people want to read your ad, they'll do so regardless of the size of type you've used (within reason, of course). If they don't want to read it, they won't, even if you've followed all the guidelines to the letter.

The type size is a very minor consideration, but, to be safe, try to stick between 10- and 12-point Times New Roman. You can't really go wrong, especially if your offer, headline, and copy all work together.

101. Sans Serif or Serif

People who work in the printing or advertising industry will no doubt be familiar with the terms sans serif and serif. For those of you who are not, let me explain what they mean.

Sans serif and serif refer to different styles of fonts or typefaces, as they're sometimes called. Basically there is one key difference between the two different styles.

Serif refers to the little "feet" or lines at the bottom of each letter. For example, the text you're reading now is a serif font—the feet of each letter has a line under it. Sans serif fonts don't have these little feet. This sentence is written in a sans serif typeface. The word *sans* is French means *without*. So the easiest way to remember which is which is that serif fonts have feet, sans serif fonts don't.

Serif Font
Sans Serif Font

Now that you understand the difference between the two, let's have a look at the importance of "feet" versus "no feet."

The reason this book has been written using a serif font is simply because it's easier to read. This is because the little feet at the bottom of each letter form a natural line that the eye can easily follow. Were the entire book to be written in a sans serif font, you'd probably find that you lose your place a lot. Your eyes would become tired and you'd find it hard to concentrate.

Therefore, when writing any type of advertising material that has large blocks of text, you *must* use a serif font. As the point of writing the ad is to get people to read it, it makes sense that you'd use the font that's easiest to read.

San serif should only be used for headlines, subheadlines, pull quotes, or brief captions under photographs. Even then I'm reluctant to use it if I'm writing a longer headline. Sans serif fonts tend to have smooth lines which can be quite eye catching, which is why a lot of people use them for short headlines.

Explaining to people that they should never use sans serif fonts as body copy can be very frustrating. Why? Because often they have well-intentioned friends who wouldn't know a good ad from a pile of toilet paper and who tell them to use a sans serif font because it looks good. Of course, this is a load of garbage. Looking good has nothing to do with writing effective ads, whereas making sales does. If you want to design something that looks good, take a course in oil painting.

I remember one particular client I worked with who complained to me that her ad was not working. The client assured me it needed to be completely rewritten. As I looked over the ad, I was quite impressed with how she had worded it. The problem was not how it was written; it was the fact that the sans serif font she used was almost impossible to read.

I mentioned this to her, but she assured me there was nothing wrong with the font she'd chosen. She went on to explain that a graphic artist had chosen that font for her. At once I knew I had a real fight on my hands. Because she had consulted a graphic artist, she was sure she had the right typeface. It took me ages to convince her that the artist was looking at it from an artistic point of view and not according to how effectively it would sell.

We changed the typeface for the purpose of testing and measuring and immediately got a huge increase in the number of responses—from 0.4 percent to 5 percent. We hadn't changed the wording at all; we'd just made it easier to read. So the hard and fast rule is serif fonts for body copy, sans serif only for headlines and other small pieces of text.

102. All Capitals

All capitals is a "no-no," except very occasionally and for effect.

The paragraph I'm writing here is in lower case and is very easy to read. This is partly due to the large amounts of white space around each letter. The lower half of the letters all look the same, but the upper half are all quite different making them easy to distinguish.

THIS PARAGRAPH, HOWEVER, IS FAR MORE DIFFICULT TO READ. THE LETTERS FORM A LARGE RECTANGULAR BLOCK, WHICH CUTS DOWN ON THE WHITE SPACE AROUND THEM. AS WITH LOWER CASE, THE BOTTOM HALF OF THE LETTERS LOOKS SIMILAR, BUT THE PROBLEM IS, SO DO THE UPPER HALVES. THIS MEANS THAT YOUR EYE NEEDS TO WORK HARD TO DECIPHER ONE LETTER FROM ANOTHER, LET ALONE IDENTIFY WORDS OR FOLLOW THE FLOW OF WHAT'S BEING SAID.

I've been sent direct mail letters previously that have been set in all capitals and, after a few moments, I have thrown them away because they were so hard to read.

Never write your entire ad in all capitals. It's immensely difficult to read. There are no ups and downs for the reader's eye to follow, so the whole thing looks like one imposing block of text.

You can use all capitals when you want a word to STAND out.

It can be good to use all capitals in headlines, but only on individual words. For example, FREE and YOU are good words to choose. This is the same with your body copy. If you do choose to use all capitals in your headline, do so only if your headline is short, say two or three words at the most. Any more will not add impact; in fact, they can detract from the impact of your ad.

103. Italics

I remember reading letters that were sent to me by my grandmother many years ago. They were all handwritten—word processors were not commonplace at the time, and my grandmother may well have thought the term was somewhat naughty. In fact, had I mentioned word processors to her, she may have washed my mouth out with soap.

But back to the reason I mention these letters.

My grandmother's style of handwriting was to slant the words to the right. This made them in some ways easy to read, as they sloped in the direction I was reading.

Italics work the same way, but the problem with them is that people are not used to reading whole ads in italics. It could be argued that if you placed an ad in all italics on a newspaper page that didn't have italics, it would stand out. Indeed, it probably would. Anyone who took the time to read a few paragraphs would find that after a while they wouldn't be able to notice a difference in readability. In fact, this entire paragraph is in italics and as you'll have noticed, it's not that hard to read. Unfortunately, people are busy and because reading all italics feels a bit odd, chances are people will give up reading and move on.

Italics do stand out, but not to the same degree as all capitals, bold, or underline.

Once again, the key is not to overdo it. Never write your whole ad or a long passage in italics. Even if you are quoting somebody, it's better to separate the paragraph and put the quote in quotation marks.

Italics are best used for emphasis in the same way as bold or all capitals are.

104. Underline

Underlining text is great for effect but should never be used excessively.

As with all capitals, it does make words harder to read. It's a real turnoff when four or five lines are completely underlined. This can be a major deterrent for potential readers.

Part of the reason for this is that lower case letters like g, p, j, and q have little tails that hang below the line. These tails become somewhat obscured by the underline, making it difficult to decipher which is which. For example, <u>gpjqy</u>.

Use underline when you want to make your point, but only sparingly and never for more than a sentence at a time. The main benefit of underlining is it adds emphasis to a word or words, making them stand out. When you read words that are underlined, you get the idea that the <u>writer is really trying to make a point</u>.

You'll notice that in the last paragraph, rather than highlighting the entire sentence, I chose to underline just a key phrase. You should always <u>keep the line continuous</u>.

Underlining a word <u>somewhere</u> in a <u>sentence</u> and then another <u>further</u> on and <u>another</u> towards the <u>end</u> looks <u>ridiculous</u>, as <u>demonstrated</u> here.

Using underlining is an excellent way to break up a large, uninviting page of solid text. It makes the layout more fun and enjoyable to read.

Remember, if you use underlining too often, you'll wreck the effect completely. You must use it only in moderation and on only the most important parts.

105. Bold

I ran an interesting test in my office some time ago. I typed up a letter and gave it to my team members. The letter informed them of what was going on in the company and events we had coming up. In the middle of the letter I wrote a couple of sentences in bold inviting them to a morning meeting.

Often this technique is used to break up a long letter. Interestingly, out of the 32 people I gave it to, only 3 showed up at the meeting. When the other 29 were asked why they hadn't bothered to attend, they all replied they hadn't known it was happening. They had all read the letter, but had skipped over the bold paragraph and missed the message.

Interesting.

So why did this happen? Well, as I mentioned in the paragraph on using capital letters, it's got a lot to do with the amount of white space around the letters themselves. The problem with using bold is that there is a lack of white space around the letters, making them difficult to read. Words set in bold can sometimes have a "ghosting" effect where the letters appear to blend into each other.

This paragraph has been set entirely in bold to give you an example of how a lack of white around the black text can make reading hard work. In fact, were I to set a few chapters in bold, you'd probably end up with a headache trying to read them.

It's also worth noting that this book has been printed on reasonable quality stock (paper). Newspapers, in an attempt to keep costs down, use paper that is of a much lower quality. This is understandable, as they are designed to be read once and then thrown away.

The reason you need to keep this in mind is because the paper they use tends to be coarse and grainy. This causes the ink to bleed into the paper more, which means the limited white space you have around letters in bold is cut down even further. In fact, if you use a small point size, the letters can come out looking like an illegible black blob.

Use bold to highlight key points, but only sparingly, and on only the most important words. If you use bold the whole way through, you will be deterring readers from reading your ad.

106. Drop Capitals and Pull Quotes

A drop capital is the big first letter of a paragraph that seems to "drop" into the first few lines of text, like the "A" at the start of this sentence.

If your ad is lengthy (more than about 100 words), a drop capital can actually draw the reader in. Because the first letter is so large, it demands attention. So you should always use one, right? Well, not so fast. While it stands out, it can detract slightly from the overall readability of your first paragraph.

Why?

Well, because a drop capital drops down about three lines, your eye is drawn to the bottom of it. Your eye then needs to work its way back up to the next letter in the word. Often people I've spoken to about drop capitals complain that it takes a moment to work out what the first word is. The last thing you want to do is slow the reader down. As I've previously mentioned, your first paragraph is vital to the success of your ad. If you don't get the reader drawn into your ad, then you've lost the chance to sell.

But as with anything, it pays to test and measure to see if it brings a higher or lower response rate.

Another technique that I use is one that I'm fonder of. It's the use of *pull quotes*. A pull quote is where you take a quote out of the body copy of your ad, enlarge it, then place it to the side of, or in between, your columns of text. You would also normally place a single line above and below the quote.

Now you no doubt have seen this technique used in magazines and journals. They take an intriguing passage, or sometimes a controversial comment from the article, and then place it in very large type to attract attention. Chances are you've also found that you read the pull quote before you decided to read the article. If the quote is interesting enough, or arouses your curiosity, then you've probably gone on to read the entire article.

This same technique works in advertisements.

"Take an interesting passage from your body copy and place it in a pull quote."

If it gives readers the impression that they're about to learn an interesting fact about your industry, product, or service type, you've a good chance to at least get them to start reading. It's up to the rest of your copy to inspire them to call you.

A few last points about pull quotes: Use them only if you have two or more columns of text. I wouldn't bother for anything less, as a pull quote would then begin to compete with your headline. Finally, don't overdo it. One pull quote per advertisement is all you should ever use. With those points in mind, go forth and test it—I'm sure you'll be pleased with the results.

107. Photos

Before you read this next section, I want you to conduct an experiment.

Pick up the Yellow Pages and open it at any page. Observe what your eyes are drawn to. See what stands out. If you're like the rest of the human race, your eyes will be attracted to pictures of people, particularly their eyes.

The main reason to include a photo of yourself in any advertising you run is so your ad instantly becomes a beacon on the page.

Place a head-and-shoulders shot of yourself in the top right-hand corner of your ad, place a caption underneath it, and, while your name and title are fine, why not add a quote as well?

Place a caption under your ad. Try something like: George Harris (Manager). "I guarantee to make you $11,000 in your first week."

Importantly, make sure you are facing into your ad, not out at somebody else's. There's nothing worse than looking like you're more interested in the ad next to yours.

If you're going to use a photo of your product, select pictures of people actually using it. Not only does it attract the eye, but also it also helps people to imagine themselves with the product.

In addition, most products look incredibly boring by themselves and lack life.

Last, always be thinking in terms of what will sell—if words will sell better than pictures, use words.

Studies have shown that ads containing a picture that takes up between 25–75 percent of the total advertisement have greater readerships than those without one. Having said that, I believe your photograph should not take up too much space. While your picture may convey a sales message, I would prefer to use words to make the sale. Therefore, I would never have a picture taking up as much as 75 percent of my ad, but it does pay to keep pictures large.

108. Captions That Sell

Every photo or picture you include in your ad should have a caption, and that caption should make a strong selling point.

It's been shown that captions are close to the highest-read parts of print ads—after the headline. People look at photos (often before headlines), then want to know what the picture is of, or why it is there, and captions tell them.

The best captions are ones that have the main selling message in them. The photo illustrates the main benefit and the caption below tells readers exactly who's doing what, why they're doing it, and the precise way this action or product is improving their lives (inferring that the prospects could also be receiving the same benefit as the featured party).

For example, let's imagine you're advertising a lawn mower. Now if your lawn mower lasts longer than anybody else's, you could have a photograph of a large oval that's been freshly mown. You might also show some other lawn mowers that look broken down. You'd complete the picture with a caption underneath that reads, *"Long after other mowers have given up, the XYZ mower is still going strong."*

You'll notice that I've put this example caption in italics. I normally do this to make it stand out from the rest of the text around it.

Make sure every photo you include has a caption. To put in a photo and not a caption is a real waste.

Remember, the majority of people will generally see the elements of your ad in this order:

Headline

Photo

Caption

Text

If your caption doesn't grab them, they probably won't want to read your text. So spend some time on it and really make it sell. Make the caption capture the main point or benefit you're trying to get across.

109. Columns

Ever noticed how newspapers and magazines always use columns? This is for a good reason: People prefer to read this way.

There's something about columns that makes text easier and more appealing to read. Perhaps it's that the text doesn't seem as imposing, or perhaps it's just that there seems to be less to read.

The number of columns you use will depend on how wide your ad is. Generally, your columns will be around 5-8 cm wide. This is a rough guide and is also dependent on the length of your text. Smaller text means smaller columns. More text means more columns.

If you don't have the computer skills to create columns, tell the newspapers or magazines your requirements. They should be able to work it up for you in a flash. Remember, they do this kind of thing every day.

Make sure your columns are even in width—it's distracting and off-putting when you have one skinny column and one fat one. For some reason, this is likely to deter people from reading your ad.

Columns will definitely increase readership of your ad. If you're using more than 150 words, you should use them.

110. Subheads

Subheadlines have three major benefits:

1. They break up large blocks of text, making it easier to read. If your advertisement looks like one big chunk of text it can put people off. By using subheadlines, you can break your copy up and give it some space.

2. They allow someone skimming over your ad to read only the points that interest them.

3. They spark the readers' interests. If your headline doesn't get them in completely, you get a second chance with your subheadlines.

It is important that your subheadlines tell a story. They need to be able to convey your message to those people who are just browsing your ad. To test that your subheadlines do this effectively, give your ad to a number of people and tell them to only read the headline and subheadlines, and then to put the ad down. Then ask them what they think the ad is all about.

Of course, they won't know many of the details that are contained in your body copy, but they should at least have the roughest of ideas about the basic gist of the ad. Remember, never make your subheadlines too long—three to four words is as long as they should be. Also, always set them in bold. Why? Well, people are used to this format; therefore if they want to skim your subheads, you need to put them in the style they're looking for.

As a rule, your headline should set the main point, then each subheadline should fill in a different part of the story, with the last subhead instructing people to act right now.

Of course, if your text is short, subheadlines aren't really necessary. You should use them only when you need to break up a large amount of text. You'll find your readership will almost double.

111. Put Your Headline under Your Picture

Now some people will tell you to never, ever put a photograph at the top of your advertisement. In many cases I'd agree with them. But there are times when putting your headline under your picture can be very, very effective.

Someone once said a picture paints a thousand words, and sometimes it does. So if you have a photograph that generates interest and ties in with your headline, why wouldn't you put it above your headline?

This can be particularly effective if you have a very long headline and you're looking at ways to convey the same message while using fewer words.

To be effective, it has to be the style of picture that really creates interest. Your standard product or customer photo won't work in this type of ad. You really need something that draws readers in and gets them asking themselves, "What's this all about?" A headline that adds to this will then leave the prospect desperate to read on.

One of the more effective types of curiosity photo is one that really gets "in your face." By that I mean photos that are dramatic and really make the reader sit up and take notice. A picture that has real "shock" value with a strong headline underneath will normally get good readership. The final response you get depends on the other factors we've discussed.

To give you an example of how this works, imagine you were writing an advertisement for a company that manufactures elderly mobility aids such as walkers or motorized scooters. If you have a photograph of an elderly lady lying in the street, with a headline that said, "Would you let this happen to your Grandmother?" you would have a high-impact ad. Or you might try the same photo with a news headline like, "Australian Senior Citizens Lacking Care."

This type of ad also works well with a headline that uses a play on words. For example, you could have a photo of someone with a black eye, broken nose, and various other injuries, with a headline something like, "You should see the other guy."

But remember that no matter what type of photograph and headline you're going to use, the bottom line is that it has to sell. A dramatic photograph with a clever word play is wasted if it doesn't bring inquiries. Don't try to be too clever. The only reason you'd put your photograph above your headline is to draw more people into your ad. If you're not getting calls, you need to try a different style of advertisement.

112. Coupons

Coupons are a great way to measure the success of your campaign. If you're not getting coupons back, then your ad is not working. Because many people will only briefly look over your ad, you need to repeat your offer in the coupon.

This isn't absolutely true. Sometimes people will respond to your ad but forget to cut out the coupon. Other times people will just come in because they like the look of your business. They might not even be worried about taking up your special offer.

It's a good idea to put a dashed border around your coupon, as it encourages people to cut it out. So does a little pair of scissors icon—it sounds simplistic but it will work.

People will normally read the headline first, the subheadlines next, and then finally the coupon or PS. You can often get people to go back and read the copy by making a strong, clear offer in your coupon.

It's a good idea to include a headline on your coupon. This gives you a second bite at the cherry—people may be attracted by your first main headline, or they may get hooked by the second, smaller one on the coupon (either way, they'll be reading the ad).

Sometimes it's a good idea to put codes on coupons from different ads. This allows you to test and measure which ad is working.

I can't overstate the importance of testing your ads. The greatest business people and marketers are not necessarily the smartest or most innovative. Most simply understand the concept of testing and measuring.

When you are testing and measuring, there is no failure (except the failure to record your results and analyze them). Every step brings you closer to the right formula and the right approach.

If you approach your marketing expecting everything to work the first time, you'll be bitter and disappointed when you discover it doesn't. You may even give up before you should.

Remember this: Marketing may have certain rules, but it's still largely a matter of trial and error. You give it your best shot, and then find out for sure.

It's essential that you meticulously record every result. It's extra work, but you'll be glad when you have a marketing strategy that you know will produce results. That level of confidence only comes from testing and measuring.

113. Dashed Border

As we mentioned in the last section, a dashed border around a coupon can encourage people to cut it out. The same can be said for a small pair of scissors icon.

When you put a thick dashed border around your entire ad, the effect can be quite eye catching and startling. It won't necessarily make people want to cut your ad out but it will make it stand out on the page.

A dashed border means that the border around the ad is broken, or dotted. For example - - - - - - - -.

The reason it makes your ad stand out is simple. Most ads have a solid border around them or no border at all. The eye will naturally seek out anything that is different or eye-catching.

The other thing to consider is where your ad will be positioned on the page. You'll pay more for placing it on a right-hand page, but it's probably worth it. Right-hand pages get a much higher readership—people just find the right side of the page easier to look at.

You'll also pay more for being in the early part of the paper. Again, it's probably worth it, but it's something you need to experiment with.

Also, remember that having a dashed border won't help that much if your ad is small and jammed in with 40 other ads at the bottom of the page. People tend to just skip over gluts of little ads.

The paper is well within its rights to stick you down there—you've paid for them to run your ad and they have run it. Unfortunately, nobody will ever look at it. A dashed border will aid in increasing readership slightly, but the cause is already lost.

114. Reverse Print

I've got to admit that I have mixed feelings when it comes to the use of reverse print. By *reverse print* I mean printing white text on a black background (or light-colored text on any type of darker background). Why the mixed feelings, you ask? Let me explain.

Reverse text can be particularly effective when it comes to headlines. Having white writing on a black background can make your headline stand out. But you can also make mistakes with this technique.

It's a very popular way of "dressing up" an advertisement. For people with limited skill in graphic design, using reverse block can turn a boring ad into something a little more interesting. The problem comes not in the design of the ad, but the actual printing of the ad in the publication you choose.

When you use a reverse block headline in your ad, it looks great on your computer screen because it's surrounded by white space. Print it in a publication with a lot of black on the page and all of a sudden it begins to blend in. In some cases it blends in so much that you can quite easily miss the headline altogether.

One of the techniques for overcoming this is to have a lead-in line that has black writing on white space at the top of the ad, with a reverse block part of the way down, almost like a subheadline. The challenge with this is that it breaks up your ad. The top of the ad may be missed, with people thinking it's a different ad altogether.

By now you might be wondering why anyone would ever use reverse block in their ads. Well, simply because it can be very effective.

The easiest way to make sure your headline stands out from the crowd is to use a drop-shadow behind it. A drop-shadow is simply a light grey box that sits behind and slightly to the side of the black area the headline appears on. It looks like the black area is sitting up off the page and is casting a shadow.

Another way to stop your reverse block from being lost is to have a fine white area around it. This way it will always look like part of your ad.

There are a few other things that you need to remember when using this type of ad. First, make sure your headline is *big*. Now I don't mean a long headline; I mean you need to use a big font size. This is because when ink is printed on paper, it tends to "bleed" into the paper a bit. So if your lettering is too fine when printed on the page, some of the white writing may actually fill in with ink, making it very difficult to read.

To make it even more effective, always use a dark block that takes up a minimum of 25 percent of the total size of your advertisement. Yellow Pages ads in particular need to have a big reverse block. People see yellow writing on black sometimes in the Yellow Pages, but if your headline is to stand out from the rest, make sure the block you print on is big. If you can't make it big, don't use reverse colors.

So far I've spoken only about headlines in reverse block. This is because there are few other places I would recommend it's being used.

One of the other places you might use it in an ad is in a starburst. A starburst is a black (or dark-colored) star that normally has the word *special* printed on it. This can work very well, as it draws people's eyes to your offer or special, which will help you get a response. I would also use it to highlight the telephone number in the ad.

Often you don't need to go completely black. A medium gray will often give the same effect. What if your ad is not in black and white but to be printed in color instead? Well, then I'd tend to not recommend using the technique at all. White text on a red or blue background can really get lost, so it's normally best to steer clear of reverse block headlines in this instance.

If you decide not to go ahead with a reverse block but still want to make your headline stand out, why not try putting a shadow behind the letters? A light grey shadow can really make your headline stand out on the page. But as with everything, only testing and measuring will really teach you what works best.

115. Logos

It is not really my intention to try and tell you how to develop a logo. It is my intention rather to talk about the use of logos in advertisements—when and how to use them.

Logos, or logotypes, as they are sometimes known, are an identifying symbol for a product or service. There are three main types of logos. The first one is simply the name of the company or product set in a particular typeface, using a particular style. With this style of logo, the typeface chosen is normally an unusual or uncommon one.

The second type of logo is a picture or an image. For example, McDonald's has the "Golden Arches," as its logo is known. Nike has the famous "Swoosh" symbol, and Mercedes Benz has the three-pointed star. These logos are images and have no type or text. The final type of logo is a combination of the first two. They consist of the company or product name in a particular typeface, along with an image or illustration.

Now I said at the start of this section that it was not my intention to tell you how to design a logo. If you need one designed, then go and talk to a graphic designer. But I will mention this: If you are going to use a symbol or a graphic as all or part of your logo, then choose one that is relevant to your product or service.

I remember a computer consultant who had a horse as her logo. When I asked her why she used the horse, she explained that it was for no other reason than that she liked horses. Other people I spoke to about it asked if she was a horse trainer, or was she selling some software to help people gamble successfully on the horses. She would have been better off not using any symbol at all.

The other thing I would like to mention to anyone thinking about having a logo designed is to make sure that it's not too complicated. It should be a very simple image or picture that may in fact be nothing more than a few simple lines. This is important because if your image has too much detail, when you try to reduce it to fit into an ad, it will lose its definition, making it hard to identify. So it's vitally important that you keep it simple.

Now that we've covered that, let's look at how, when, and why you would use one in an advertisement.

One of the reasons for having a logo is that people generally like to buy familiar products. They like to purchase from companies they've at least heard of before, because it gives them a sense of quality, or at least of being able to trust the company they're about to deal with. For many people, this takes a lot of the perceived risk out of the purchase.

So, if people have seen your logo a number of times, they'll tend to feel that yours is an established and trustworthy company that they can feel confident dealing with.

Even if they've never dealt with you or your product before, they'll feel safer if they recognize your company. This recognition can come about through the consumers' seeing your logo on advertising material prior to making their purchasing decision.

Another benefit of having a logo in your advertisement is that it can add a sense of credibility or class to your ad. I've seen many occasions where I've tested an ad without a logo, and then the same ad with a logo, and noticed an increase in responses (albeit marginal) with the ad carrying the logo. It just makes your business look more professional.

Having looked at these benefits, keep in mind that the logo itself doesn't actually *sell* anything. It might make people feel a little bit more comfortable if they recognize your logo, and it can occasionally generate a few more responses, but the logo itself doesn't sell.

So given that it doesn't sell, it pays not to take up too much space with a logo. I've seen many instances where people have made it almost a feature of their ad. A big logo in the centre of the page is, I imagine, meant to get me excited. Well, it doesn't. The best way to use a logo in an ad is to place it in the bottom left-hand corner. This way it can look classy but it's not getting in the way of those things that do sell—the words.

Now some people will try to tell you that a logo is the be-all and end-all of marketing, and if you don't have a great logo, you don't have a great ad. People have said this to me on numerous occasions. My response is always the same: "Oh, so the logo is one of the most important parts of any ad. Tell me, how do they look in a radio commercial?" Now, normally at this point they make some stuttering and stammering noises.

While it may help with your ads, it's not crucial. I know many businesses that have a great response to their marketing, despite not having a logo. So don't get too carried away with the whole "corporate image" thing.

One last point on logos and then we'll move on: Never use your logo in an advertorial. Because an advertorial is designed to look like an editorial, you'll lose the effect if you include your logo. Why? Well, ads have logos and editorials don't, so the simple rule is when running an ad, place your logo in the bottom left-hand corner (not too big), and when running an advertorial, never use your logo.

116. Size

There's a lot more to working out a size than most people think. Usually, it's a case of, "How much can we afford?"

The question really should be, "How much do we want to make?" If the ad is good enough, it should make you money, not drain your funds.

If you don't have an ad that you know works, you need to guess. You need to think about how many responses you need to break even. That means, how many sales do you need to pay back the advertising cost?

Here's how you work it out.

First, you need to work out your average profit. To do this, measure the amount of profit in each sale, every day, for three days. Then, find the average. If you want to skip the hard work, estimate this figure.

Next, choose a standard ad size. If it's a newspaper you're thinking of advertising in, find out the price on an ad that is one-eighth of a page. If you're dealing with a magazine, get the price on a quarter-page ad.

Now, divide the ad cost by your average profit. This will give you the number of sales you'll need to pay for the ad.

Here's an example.

Let's say a hairdresser makes about $15 profit from each haircut. She takes out an ad that costs $270. This means that she needs 18 new customers from the ad. Anything less and the ad is costing her money.

Of course, it's not a hard-and-fast rule that you must break even on every ad. In the case of the hairdresser, she would probably be happy with nine new loyal customers. After each customer has been in twice, she will become profitable.

This is called lifetime value—the amount customers spend with you over the course of their lifetimes. In the case of a company with a high level of repeat business (hairdresser, restaurant, mechanic), it might be worth losing money the first time, just to gain a new customer. This customer may ultimately be worth thousands.

If you get out of "break-even" thinking and into "lifetime-value" mode, a whole new world of possibilities opens up. If you're confident you'll get these new customers back again, you can afford to offer something incredible and take a dead loss the first time they come in.

Once you've established whether you have to break even, or whether you can afford to rely on the lifetime value of the customer, you are then in a position to make a decision about size.

Let's look at a break-even situation first.

To decide how big your ad should be, you have to guess how many replies you're likely to get. This can be tricky, especially if you haven't had a lot of experience with advertising. In fact, even if you've advertised many times, it can still be tricky.

You can really rely only on what you've done before, what your competitors seem to get, and your instinct.

In the end it comes down to probability. Let's say you sell pizzas with a profit margin of $1.20. Taking out an ad that costs $1200 means you need 1000 new customers to pay for it. You need to judge whether that's likely to happen. If you ran an ad last year and got 5 replies, it looks pretty improbable.

In some cases you may realize that breaking even is nearly impossible, in which case you have to think about lifetime value, or advertising somewhere else.

The other thing to consider is this: Papers and magazines with high rates usually have high readership. It's not as if you're paying more for nothing. If you go with a cheaper paper, you're likely to get a lower response rate.

Once you've weighed all that, then consider how much space you actually need. How much text is in your ad? How big are the other ads on the page? Will you be seen if you go small? Do your pictures need to be a certain size?

If you need more space than you can reasonably afford, you may need to look at a different approach—that is, another creative approach. Perhaps you could take the picture out and trim some of the text.

Last, it's important to start small and work your way up. Do your ad big enough so it has a good chance of working but not so big that you'll go bankrupt if it bombs. Take all that into account and decide upon a size for your first ad.

117. Page

Think back to the last time you read a newspaper. As you turned the pages, which one did you look at first? The right-hand page or the left-hand page?

Well, if you're like most people, you would have looked at the right-hand page first. As you turn the page, you can see the right-hand page before you see the left-hand page, so your eye is drawn to whatever is on that page.

Part of the reason for this is that most stories don't run over two facing pages (pages that face each other) in newspapers. A novel, however, would be a different matter. Because the story runs onto the next page, you immediately turn the page and look for where the last sentence finished off. But because newspaper articles are all contained on the one page, with new articles normally being on new pages, it doesn't matter where you start reading.

It stands to reason that if you want your advertisement to be read, the perfect place for it would be on a right-hand page.

This is not some well-guarded advertising secret known only by a few. It's certainly well known by the newspapers themselves. Of course, if the right-hand pages are the best place to put your advertisement, it stands to reason that most people want a right-hand page. Not everyone reads the paper from cover to cover. Some people only skim through the first 14 to 16 pages, then stop reading. So not only do you want your ad on a right-hand page, but the closer it is to the front of the paper, the better.

Understanding this, newspapers charge more for these pages. They do this in the form of a loading, which is sometimes as much as 50 percent more than the normal price of running an ad.

You may be tempted to think, "Well, they can forget it. I'm not paying a loading." But the fact is that papers have been charging loading for years and customers have been happy to keep paying. Why? Well, obviously because they've found that the returns from these pages far outweigh the higher price. Therefore the rule is simple: Pay the loading and get the best position.

Now, if you're testing and measuring ads, you might like to test them in another part of the paper first. It's not advisable to pay a loading on a new ad that hasn't proven itself yet.

Another consideration is the target you're aiming for. If you're aiming at men between the ages of 20 and 45 with a certain income level and specific interests, then you might be better off running your ad in the sports pages, as many men read the papers back to front, starting with the sports pages.

If you were advertising business services, then you might place your advertisement in the business pages. It all depends on whom you're trying to target and how specific that target is.

118. Position

So now that we've paid a loading and gotten an early right-hand page, our next consideration is the position on the page that we want the ad to be placed on.

Now, we never, ever, want our ad to be placed in the gutter. The gutter is the left-hand edge of the right-hand page (or the right-hand edge of the left-hand page), where the two pages meet.

Ads placed in the gutter definitely get a lower response. They are more difficult to find, sometimes even when someone's specifically looking for them, let alone when you're hoping a potential client will stumble across them.

So, if you're not in the gutter, then you want to be on the edge of the page. Now we're on a right-hand page and we now know that we want our ad to appear on the very outside edge of that page.

The last thing we need to think about is whether or not our ad should be in the top right-hand corner, the middle, or the bottom. My preference is the top of the page, and for the same reason that we need to use a right-hand page.

As people turn the page, they'll look at the top to scan the headlines. We want our ad to catch their eyes as soon as possible. If I can't get this position, then I want the bottom right-hand corner because this is the anchor point of the ad. Because we read from the top left-hand corner of the page to the bottom right, it makes sense that this is the next best place to be.

One last thing: Keep in mind that you may find it difficult to get the exact spot on the exact page you're after. You can get your advertising rep to ask for the top right-hand corner, but there's no guarantee that you will be able to secure it. This is because members of the production team, who seldom listen to the advertising department, determine the layout. But still ask; they may be able to get it through for you. They will at least be able to guarantee that your ad doesn't end up in the gutter.

119. Run Vertical Ads

It's been my experience that vertical ads work better than horizontal ones. That means that tall and skinny works better than short and fat. There's no clear reason for this; you'll just need to accept it as the case. I've proven it personally time and time again.

One of the main reasons for this could be that newspapers naturally set their articles out this way. Because people have become used to this format with articles, they are more attracted to ads that are oriented the same way. Another reason might be that a tall skinny ad looks like less reading than a short fat ad that runs over more columns. Whatever the reason, it definitely makes a difference.

When designing your ad, make sure that it is about twice as high as it is wide. If you're getting the paper to produce it, ask for this specifically.

Newspapers sell space in column centimetres. One column centimeter is one column across by one centimeter down. A *10 × 2 means 10 cm down by 2 columns*. These are the terms the newspaper uses, therefore, if you're going to run an ad that's two columns wide, you need to make it at least *5 centimeters* high.

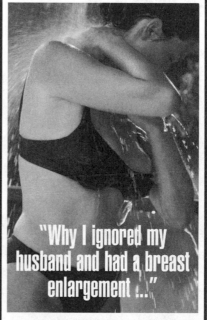

120. Full-Page Ads

The important thing to remember when considering a full-page ad is that double the size doesn't always mean double the business.

In fact, I can't remember a case where doubling the size of the ad from a half page to a full page meant that the phone rang twice as much, or the sales figures went up by 100 percent.

Research suggests that a half-page ad will get 74 percent of the inquiries that a full-page ad will, assuming everything else remains constant (headline, photo, position, etc.).

Research also suggests that one-third of a newspaper page will achieve 62 percent of the response of a full-page ad, and a quarter-page advertisement will get around 68 percent. I always find that fascinating—a quarter-page ad will actually get a higher response than a third-page ad. It has a lot to do with the vertical versus horizontal question we spoke about before.

So what does this mean?

Simple. You're better off placing two half-page ads, rather than one full-page ad, assuming that the cost of either option is around the same (generally, it won't be but it will depend on the publication).

You need to sit down and work out the figures using the above ratios as a rough guide. If it turns out that you will make more profit (percentage wise) by running a quarter-page ad as opposed to a full-page ad, then you might be better off booking four ads in different sections, or four ads in different papers, or alternately, four ads over four weeks.

This is an important consideration, because the newspaper will almost certainly try to tell you that going big is definitely the best option (it's certainly the best option for the paper's sales and revenue figures).

Before making a decision, sit down with the calculator and work out exactly what you'll be up for. Remember, your actual results may vary greatly from the ratios above, but they're a good start.

The only way to really judge which size works for you is to test and measure. That is, run different sizes in the same paper (keeping as many factors the same as you can—same day, same position, same offer, headline, photo, text, etc.) and then precisely measure how many customers respond.

You might also like to test things like how many customers actually buy and how much profit you make from the ad. Work out how many sales resulted directly from the ad, work out how much of that revenue is profit, and then subtract the ad costs.

You'll be surprised how much this reveals. An ad that you thought was working well may turn out to be a dud, and an ad that you thought had flopped may actually be making you a healthy income.

You'll never know until you start testing and measuring and working out precisely how much money each is making (or costing) you.

121. Show the Product in Use

I said before that people don't buy a drill because they want to drill something. They buy a drill because they want a hole.

People buy things because they want a solution to a problem. People buy the services of a chiropractor because they have headaches or back pain. Other people buy a new car because their old one keeps breaking down or is costing them money. No matter what it is you're selling, people want to know that it will fix their problem.

It stands to reason that if you can show the product being used to fix a particular problem that they may have, they'll be more inclined to buy it.

I saw a series of ads on television some time ago that used this technique very well. The product being sold was a car-washing brush that connected to a normal household garden hose. It used detergent that mixed with the water, creating a cleansing foam. Now, there was nothing sensational about that; many products on the market would do the same thing. But the ad went on to show people attaching a brush to clean their boats, house ceilings, etc. There were so many uses for this product that it was sure to solve a number of problems for a number of people.

If your product or service is misunderstood by prospects, or does more than the average person would realize, you need to show the product being used in other ways.

Another frustration for many business owners, particularly those selling tools for home handymen, is that the public will often think you need to have a particular skill or ability to use the product. Often this is not the case and people can use the product to solve their problems.

One client I had sold chain saws. Now when you ask most people about chain saws, they immediately picture a lumberjack or farmer. They wouldn't imagine that the average person could use one. So to overcome this misconception, we had a photograph of an old lady using a small chain saw to prune a branch in her backyard. Immediately people began calling, saying they hadn't realized the average person could be trained in how to use a chain saw.

While it works very well on television, it can also be effective in print ads. Often a series of photographs will convey to readers that this is the answer to their problems. Show your product being used by a number of different people to solve a number of different problems and you're sure to increase the response to your advertising.

122. Put the Photo at the Top—Top 1/3

If you're going to include a photo (from everything we've discussed, you generally should—it increases readership by up to 75 percent), there's no point in sticking it down at the bottom of your ad.

Your photo should be up at the top and it really should take up the top third of your ad.

Of course, there are different ways to approach the layout but this isn't a bad one. Some people consider this the classic ad layout for a larger style ad (when we say larger, we're talking about a third of a page and up. This doesn't really apply to little 10 × 2's—they have a completely different set of rules).

The format is simple. You put your photo at the top, taking up around 30 percent of the space, the headline underneath, then two or three columns of text underneath that. It's been proven that this format (assuming that the picture is truly interesting and the headline grabs) will work well.

This is based on the notion that people are generally more visual than anything else. They'd prefer to see a picture than read a thousand words. This would ring true for 99 percent of people.

Think about it—we live our whole life in pictures, not words. You're reading right now, but in life we see things and make our own interpretations. There are no captions or words to explain what's going on. It's a lot more natural for us to gather information in this way.

The thing is, your picture will be still, not moving. That means that it must be extraimpressive and lifelike. It's worth spending time with a good photographer to get a good shot. It will make your ad come alive.

123. Use a Photo Instead of a Line Drawing

If you've ever looked through a real estate guide you'll understand the importance of this tip. The ads with a photograph of a house always look more appealing than line drawings—those that have been drawn by an artist.

Why? Well, people are used to seeing things a certain way. We don't *see* a house as a cartoon drawing. We see it as it appears in a photograph. Now, this is important because to convince people to buy your product, they need to *picture* themselves owning it, or using it. Most people can't see themselves owning a cartoon.

Your image also plays a large part in the way your business or product is perceived by the public. If you're advertising a Porsche, you won't use a line drawing. It just doesn't project a quality image. A photograph, however, does.

Is there ever an exception to this rule? Well, yes, there are a few. One instance that I can think of would be to show cross sections of technical equipment. For example, if you were trying to show the working components of an engine or gearbox, you may use line drawings, as it might not be practical to try to cut up an engine to show what's inside.

Another example would be a property developer who was preselling apartments in an apartment block that was under construction. Pretty hard to take a photograph of something that hasn't been built yet. Better to show an artist's impression than to have no photographs at all.

These are obvious exceptions. As a general rule, you should never, ever use line drawings in preference to photographs.

Interestingly, while a line drawing looks cheap and shoddy, it often costs more to have the drawing done than it would to have the photograph professionally taken. But people seem to still go with line drawings even though they look like garbage.

The major challenge with a line drawing is not that it looks cheap; it doesn't stand out as a photograph does. Line drawings don't attract the reader's attention. Isn't that the goal of the picture in the first place? To get people interested in reading your ad and finding out more? By always using photographs, you're always giving your ad the greatest chance to succeed.

124. Make Sure the Ad Looks Like Your Business

Have you ever read an ad for a classy restaurant and thought, "Hmmm, that looks nice." You believe the restaurant is classy because in its ad it used lots of white space, the photo is clear and professional, and the typefaces give the impression of some sort of elegance.

Then when you actually visit the restaurant, you find it's just another greasy spoon with teenagers for chefs.

That happened to me a couple of weeks ago. I saw an ad and thought, "Yes, I'll take my significant other out for a nice dinner." You can imagine my surprise when I discovered that the restaurant was nothing more than a fast-food place in a supermarket—that's right—it was in the supermarket.

I was actually quite embarrassed. I'd promised my partner a night of fine food and elegance, only to show up outside a supermarket! Even though it may have been a good restaurant, we definitely didn't eat there and we definitely won't be going back.

It's important to make sure you're giving a fair representation of your business when you write your ad. If your showroom is old and crusty, don't try to pretend that you're ultramodern and new—people will only feel let down and disappointed when they get there.

As you can imagine, this is not the ideal way to start working towards a sale. If people are feeling cheated or unhappy from the start, it makes your job only harder.

Of course, this doesn't mean that you should advertise yourself as "old and crusty"—that'd be stupid. It does mean that you should emphasise your good points without pretending to be something that you're not.

If your business is friendly and fun, get this across in the ad. Even if you're not a graphic designer, you'll be able to tell the newspaper's designer what to do, then judge whether he has achieved the desired effect.

The same goes if your business is serious and professional—make it look that way. You want people to get the right idea from the start, so spend a little time getting the right look.

Once you've got the right look, you should stick to it in all future ads. Don't go changing your logo every week, or the fonts you use. Stay with the same basic graphic design and you'll start to develop a distinctive image. If this also matches the personality of your business, you've got it made.

125. Make Sure Your Picture Tells a Story

Including a photograph in your ad just for the sake of having one is a huge waste of time. You may as well put more text in to help sell, or simply run a smaller ad. But a photo that tells a story is worth its weight in gold.

Providing the story is worthwhile.

Photographs are used for a number of reasons. One may be to show how the product can solve a problem, or you might use one to create interest and arouse curiosity. No matter what the reason, it must convey a message, or in other words, tell a story.

I often laugh when I see people who have a photo of the front of their shops in their ads. It takes up far less valuable space to simply write your address at the bottom of your ad. These people have decided that a photograph would make a big difference to their ad, but the picture they've chosen does not paint a picture in the mind of the reader.

To let you see more clearly what I mean, imagine you needed to put together an advertisement for a women's support group. If you ran an ad with a photograph of a badly beaten woman sitting in a corner sobbing, and a man sitting on a couch with his head in his hands—beside him is an empty whiskey bottle—would you need to say much more? I doubt it. The picture tells you 80 percent of what you need to know.

So, how does this apply to your business or product? If your product makes people feel good about themselves, why not have a photograph of a person's face with a huge smile beaming off the page? Or maybe your service relieves a frustration. You could have two photographs, one of someone experiencing that frustration, another beside it of someone who is relaxed and contented.

There are a million different ways that a photograph can convey a powerful story to the reader. The trick is to be clear on what you want to say. Work out the number-one key benefit of what it is you're selling, and then take a moment to think about what image would get that message across. If you get stuck for ideas, ask other people. Get their input. Then if you still can't think of a worthwhile image, don't bother using one at all. Save your money, run more copy, but never waste money on a picture that doesn't tell a story.

126. Make Sure Your Picture Generates Interest

Telling a story is only half the battle. Your picture must get the reader interested in the first place.

A picture is capable of telling a story, but if that story is dull and boring, you may as well not bother. It has to be something that draws readers in and gets them excited.

Now, there are many different forms of excitement. You can have an agitated excitement with a photograph that you might find offensive, such as a teenage drug addict vomiting in the gutter. Or you might have a happy kind of excitement with a photograph of people having a party at the house they recently purchased. The type of excitement you choose is not important; it's having excitement in the first place that's the key.

So what is it that your prospect is looking for? If you're advertising prestige cars, it could be the look of envy on the faces of the people in your photo who are admiring the car. A gymnasium might show someone looking tanned and toned on a beach, the center of attention among their peers. The point is, the owner of the gym is appealing to something that the prospect is looking for.

It's all about image. It's about having readers see you as the answer to their problems, a professional company that can service their needs. A photograph that causes a little bit of controversy is better than no photograph at all. I'm not suggesting for a moment that you use something that's offensive, just something that will grab the attention of the individual who is scanning the paper.

If you don't have a suitable photograph to use, pay a professional photographer to take one. It costs more but when you consider how much it will cost you to run an ineffective ad, it will probably stack up quite well. More importantly, how much more will you make in extra sales if the photograph really draws people in?

127. Show What Happens When the Product Is Used

There are many industries in the marketplace that do this very well. But there are many more who could, with just a little thought and effort.

In the last few sections we've spoken about solving problems. This technique is about showing the results of the solutions.

As I mentioned, there are a number of industries that do this well. One such business that immediately springs to mind is a weight loss center. Diet companies have been using before-and-after shots for years with great effect. Why does it work? Well, it shows a person before she goes on the program—this person hopefully reminds the readers of themselves, then it shows the same person looking slim and healthy afterwards, the way the readers wish they could look.

Another good example is a company that specializes in skin treatments, particularly acute skin conditions. By showing a close-up of a person's face before he used a particular product, then showing an after-treatment photo, the company owners can convey to the reader the true benefit of the product they're selling.

There are many companies that don't use this type of advertising, but should. A hardware store could show before-and-after photos of people's backyards or the interiors of their homes. Car detailing companies and furniture restoration companies could all do the same.

But let's think outside the box. An accounting firm could have two photographs in its ads. The first could show a business owner looking exhausted, sitting at a desk covered with piles of paperwork. The other could show the same person out on the golf course.

You don't even need before-and-after pictures. You may wish to show how simple a product is to use by illustrating clearly in a photograph the amazing results achieved by ordinary people using your product. Better still if it's a picture of a real customer, someone the reader can relate to.

Think about why people would buy your product or service. Then show them the results achieved by others who had the same problem but who used your product to solve it. This strategy should be explored by anyone who has something to advertise.

Don't be frightened to use this technique, even if you've never seen anyone in your industry use it before. I know some people are put off because they feel that this sort of advertisement comes across as blatant selling. What they don't realize is that people read ads because they're interested in buying something. Don't be bashful, show everyone why they should buy your product, and people will start to do just that.

128. Use Photos of Real Customers

If I tell you that a particular product would solve your problems, you might be inclined to believe me, but chances are you'd like to talk to somebody who had already tried it. That's why testimonials work well in advertising material. Someone who has already experienced a product or service is telling you that it works well.

Hey, presto! Instant credibility.

But the same effect can be gained by using photographs. By putting pictures of *real people* using your product or service, the reader gets the idea that it works.

The majority of people tend to be cautious of trying new things. Even though your product may have been around for some time, if people haven't heard of it previously, they may have reservations about trying it. Average people would rather have someone else try it first then, if it works, they'll give it a go themselves.

So, by showing pictures of real customers using your product, the readers get a sense of, "Hey, this product must be good; other people are using it." The effect is even stronger if they relate to the person in the picture. If they feel that the person in the picture reminds them of themselves, then they'll feel that the product would obviously suit them.

This is why it's important that you use photographs of real people rather than models. People don't relate to models; they relate to real-life people like you and me. You'll notice that diet companies use this technique with great effect. It would be pointless for weight loss companies to have models in their ads, as people expect these people to be thin. If they use a plain-looking everyday human being instead, they're sure to get a better response.

This technique is particularly successful when used in regional centers where there is a good chance that the people reading the ad might know the person pictured in the ad. The same goes for industry journals and magazines. If the person is reasonably well known, it will add credibility to your product or service. This will, therefore, result in more sales.

129. Keep Pictures Simple

You'll remember we spoke at the start of this book about not being too clever. The same goes for the photos you use in your ads. Your picture needs to be simple and easy to interpret.

Just as people won't take time to decipher a clever message, they won't sit there looking at photographs trying to figure out what they're all about.

Your photographs need to have a purpose, a reason for being placed in the ad in the first place. You then need to make sure that the message you're trying to get across is clear in the photo you select.

To work out if the photo you've chosen gives the correct message to the reader, show it to a number of people and ask them what the picture *says* to them. If the answer they give is not the answer you're looking for, you need to choose a new picture.

Another reason for choosing a simple photograph is that the print quality of the publication you're running your advertisement in may not be very good. So a photograph that might look clear when you submit it may look completely different when printed in the final ad. This is particularly true when it comes to a color photo being printed in black and white.

Often the different colors in a photograph help to make it easy to understand. Take away that color and produce it in black and white, and the same photo might now be very confusing.

A simple way to test your photo to see if it becomes less clear in black and white is to photocopy it on a black and white photocopier. As many newspapers tend to make photographs look darker than they should, it's also a good idea to photocopy them darker than normal.

Technical photographs, or those with a lot of background confusion such as factories, often become difficult to decipher when printed in a newspaper. You're best to use a photograph that has limited or large objects in the background. This way it won't confuse the reader who will understand more clearly the message you're trying to get across.

130. Use a Baby, an Animal, Something Sexy, or a Head-and-Shoulders Shot

Not all photographs need to relate specifically to the product or service you're advertising. Sometimes it's worthwhile using a photograph simply to catch the readers' attention to draw them into your ad. When they're into the ad, you can then *sell* them on what it is you're offering.

So let's look at some of the different types of photos you can use.

Now, I don't know anyone who can go past a picture of a really cute baby. While a lot of people would expect women to be attracted to these pictures, I know a lot of men who would find it hard not to stop as well.

A photograph of a happy, smiling baby will normally hold people up long enough to get them reading the first few lines of your ad. It then depends on how well written your ad is as to how far people will continue to read. You might also like to try a photograph of a baby doing something unusual or amusing. This technique works well if you place your headline under a very large photograph, and tie the headline in.

Animals will also attract attention. Unlike the broad appeal of babies, you'll find different types of animals will attract different types of people. This is fine if you're targeting a particular type of prospect.

Cute animal photos like those of puppies or kittens can draw people in, but you don't need to limit yourself to something nice. A photo of a savage dog snarling out of the page with teeth bared will make people look twice. But if you're using this technique, your picture needs to be large and imposing. If you want to save money and still attract attention, the cute animal photos are often a more cost-effective option. But it all depends on who you're trying to reach and what image you're trying to project.

Now for the one you've all been waiting for—something sexy.

There use to be a saying in advertising circles that sex sells. Now while this may have been a popular catch phrase a few years ago, people shy away from using it in today's politically correct society. But just because people don't talk about it doesn't mean that it no longer works.

A recent campaign by a shoe manufacturer featured billboards with scantily clad women in erotic poses with male models who were apparently wearing these shoes. I say "apparently" because the shoes that the ads were meant to be selling were so small you couldn't see them.

The message was meant to be, "If you wear these shoes, beautiful women will fall at your feet." Now, the campaign itself had limited success, but the public outcry against this form of "exploitation" gave the company wide exposure. In fact, despite having seen the billboards a few times, I had no idea what the company was selling until I read the articles about the complaints.

I don't suggest that you go to the extremes that this particular company went to. I don't think that negative publicity is necessarily the way to go. But I do know that subtle images and innuendo can bring great results. Even though people might not admit it in today's society, sex still sells. People are still interested in looking at an attractive male or female and, the more sensual the models look, the more people are drawn to the advertisement.

But you need to be careful that you don't leave people feeling ripped off. If you're trying to say, "Beautiful people use this product or service," then your ad will probably gain high readership. If you try to give the impression that the reader will get some saucy information or gossip from reading your ad, and you don't deliver, your ad will fail badly.

I would only use a picture like this to get people in under the impression that if they use my particular product or service, they'll become more attractive. They will find themselves in some way in the same league as those people that the public admires for their appearance.

If you're going to use a photograph of yourself or your team members, then I would recommend a head-and-shoulders shot. Why? Well, people's eyes are naturally drawn to another person's eyes. So if you run a photograph of a person's face, with her eyes looking out of the page, people will find their eyes drawn to the eyes in the photograph. To achieve this effect, you need to have the eyes big enough to attract attention. This is why I recommend head and shoulders only for this type of photo.

But a word of warning if you're going to use this type: The eyes in the photograph must either look straight out of the page or back into the advertisement. By back into the advertisement I mean if the photo is on the right-hand side of the ad, with the text on the left, then when printed, the eyes in the picture must be facing left, back towards your text.

There's an interesting exercise you can do that will help you understand why this is important. Next time you're in a shopping center, stand still and look up at the ceiling. Stand there for some moments and then look out of the corner of your eye at the number of other shoppers who are also looking up. They do this because they're curious about what it is you're looking at.

The same goes for eyes in an advertisement. If the eyes in your photo look away from your ad, then people looking at the photo will find their eyes being drawn away as well. Bad for you, but great for the ad next to yours.

131. Use Color

Color can be an interesting thing when it comes to advertising. Used well, it will increase the response to your ad dramatically. Used poorly, it will simply cost you money.

So before we look at what works and what doesn't, let's look at the different ways it can be used.

The most obvious relates to flyers or direct mail letters that are printed on colored stock (paper). You can either print black text on the colored page, or print colored text onto colored paper.

"Spot" color is where you use one color, not counting black, in your advertisement. This is common in newspapers that may be printing a certain color on certain pages. They will, however, let you use only that particular color they happen to be using on that page. It's not like you have a choice. You do have the choice, though, of how much of your ad uses this color. You can have your entire ad in this one color (reverse block), or you might have just your headline, logos, or certain words in color and the rest in black and white.

Full color or process color is where you use many colors. For example, you might run a full color photograph, or you might use six or seven different colors in the ad.

So, now that we know what the options are, what works and what doesn't?

Well, studies have shown that print advertisements in full color get a much, much higher readership than other forms of ads. They also cost a lot more. It would seem from most of the studies I've come across that the extra readership gained from using full color far outweighs the higher cost.

But you can't just go throwing color in here, there, and everywhere. You should never use color for your body copy. Readability and comprehension definitely drop off if you do, so always stick to black text, preferably on a white background.

Even when it comes to headlines, it pays to stick to black. The only exception I would make to this rule is if the headline is only two or three words long. Even then I would never use red. Red seems to get lost or overlooked very easily.

Photographs and logos, however, are definitely better in color, if your budget allows.

They certainly stand out and have a higher readership.

Spot color can also bring a higher response to your ads when used sparingly. You'll find that trying to read a block of text when there is a color catching the corner of your eye is quite challenging. I personally don't use spot color. Unlike full process color, which I see as being a good investment, spot color to me is simply a way for newspapers to generate more revenue.

So the hard-and-fast rule around color is this: If you can afford full color then use it, but never use anything for your text other than black. If you choose to use spot color, use it sparingly. Oh, and one final thing about printing flyers or direct mail letters on colored stock: Use only very subtle colors that don't compete with the text.

Anything too bright will be hard on the eyes, causing people to stop reading. And we don't want that to happen, do we?

132. SELL—Don't Just Make It Look Pretty

One of the traps that people fall into when they start designing ads is trying to make everything look good. They try to use clever photographs, print in strange fonts, overdo color, and basically put too many different elements into their layouts.

The only thing your ad should do is sell.

So, let's look at exactly what you're trying to achieve with your ads. First, you want your ad to stand out and be noticed. Once it's noticed you want to draw your readers in. You then want to convince your readers that it would be a really good idea for them to call you or come into your store. You're trying to *sell* them on the idea of doing business with you.

Now that you've learned a bit about using colors and photographs, which fonts to use, and basic layout skills, it's time to look at whether or not the whole thing has a good chance of working.

Sit down and look at your ad objectively. It might even pay to run off a copy and glue it into the publication you're thinking about running it in, just to get an idea of how it will look. Now you need to go through your ad and decide which parts of it sell and which parts don't.

Let's start with your headline. Will it draw people in? Is it easy to read so far as size, color, and typeface are concerned? Then move onto your layout. You need to ask yourself if it's easy to follow. Do any of the elements you've used, such as photographs, logos, and other images, actually distract you from the sales message?"

Is the ad colorful enough to stand out, or is it too colorful and therefore difficult to read? Go through every element like this. Are your photographs interesting? Are your typefaces easy to read? Is there any wasted space? These are all questions you need to ask yourself.

At the end of the day the simpler your layout, the greater the response you'll get. It's not about winning competitions or being creative—leave that to the advertising agencies who aren't spending their own money. No, it's about making sales; it's about calls coming in and putting dollars in the bank. Sure, it looks good to have a classy ad. Why shouldn't you have something that looks classy? But not at the expense of making sales.

If there are any parts of your ad that are not helping you communicate your sales message, get rid of them because they'll just waste your money. Don't dress it up; just make it sell.

133. Don't Print on Dark Colors

It should be very obvious that printing on dark color detracts from the readability of your ad. Apparently it's not that obvious, based on the fact that many people foolishly use this undesirable technique.

Some of the advertisements I've seen involve people printing white writing on a dark background. Now a reverse block headline may work well in certain ads but what I'm talking about is people printing their entire ads in reverse block—body copy and all.

This is sometimes due to the fact that they're printing over a dark photograph. Now, it can be difficult enough to read a headline with large type when it's printed on black, but it's almost impossible when you print small fonts on dark colors. Instead of the crisp, white letters you see on your computer screen, you end up with black blobs.

I read somewhere about a study that was done quite a few years ago where as many as half of the participants in the study refused to attempt to read paragraphs of text printed on a dark background. They complained of poor concentration, headaches, and generally not being able to follow what the ad was trying to say.

So what about black print on more lightly colored backgrounds? Well, some people actually claim that reading black text on a faintly shaded background is preferable to black on white. The slight coloring of the paper, they claim, is easier on the eye than bright white. But studies I have read have shown this not to be the case.

While initially it may appear to be easier to read, over any length of copy people's eyes tend to become tired. So rather than taking the risk that your ad will be hard to read, simply print your copy on white paper. Black on white might not look exciting, but it's effective and easy to read. In advertising, all we want to do is make life easy for the consumer.

Part 5

∎ Final Points to Remember

134. Negotiation

Many people don't realize this, but they are paying too much for their advertising with newspapers and magazines. You see, most people just pay the price that's charged by those publications. What they don't realize is that quite often these prices are open to negotiation.

To understand how to negotiate a better rate, you need to understand the rates in the first place.

Newspapers normally charge what's known as a column centimeter rate. They calculate this by the number of columns wide your advertisement is, multiplied by the height of the advertisement. They then multiply the result by a set dollar amount.

To give you an example, if you are running a two columns wide by five centimeters high—the size of an average business card—advertisement in a metropolitan newspaper at a rate of $35.17, this is how to work out what it would cost you. Multiply the two column widths by the five centimeter height. This would then give you ten column centimeters. You then multiply this by the paper's column centimeter rate, which is $35.17. Your advertisement would therefore cost you $351.70.

But normally the charges don't stop there. Quite often publications will charge you for the artwork. On top of this there can be loading for various pages.

Now, normally the loading is for prime positions: those being pages 2, 3, 5, 7, 11, and so forth. The loading usually applies only to the odd numbers, with the exception of page 2, and will normally apply only to the first few pages, but it can sometimes apply up to page 17, depending on the size of the publication.

In addition, if you want color in your advertisement, you'll pay extra for that. So as you can see, advertising can be quite expensive. The loading for some positions on certain pages can sometimes be up to 50 percent the cost of the advertisement.

If the standard ad costs you $300 and you want to place it on a right-hand page, let's say on page three, then you could actually end up paying $450. This is where many business people fall down—they don't realize that these prices are quite often open to negotiation.

Sometimes you won't get the publication to budge on its prices, but it's always worthwhile getting in there and having a go. First thing you need to do is to arrange a meeting with your advertising rep. Get him to come in and explain exactly what it is that you are paying for, because unless you know the details, it is difficult to negotiate effectively.

With daily newspapers their rates are often higher on weekends, so you could expect to pay on weekends. This is because their circulation is higher. At the end of the day, if your advertisement is going to be seen by a lot more people, it's worthwhile paying a little extra for it.

Now, a lot of newspapers won't budge on their column centimeter rate. That's a price that's set by the newspaper itself, and normally your rep won't be able to help you with this—the newspaper simply won't have the room to negotiate. But as with most businesses, newspapers reward those who spend a lot of money with them over a period of time. You can quite often get a better rate, providing you're doing a lot of advertising with them.

For newspapers to give you a better rate, they require you to sign a contract. For some businesses it's worthwhile signing a contract if they know they're going to spend $70,000 with the paper over the next twelve months. Unless you intend to spend tens of thousands of dollars, you won't find it an advantage being on a contracted rate.

You can also try to negotiate your loading cost. To make sure of a certain position in a publication, you need to pay this, however, it's often open to negotiation. It can sometimes even be a sweetener the rep throws in for free—but only if you ask.

Now let's look at standby rates. As most newspapers don't have a standby rate, it's something that you will need to negotiate with your rep.

The way it works is simply this.

You place an advertisement with them and you run it on a regular basis. The offer that you make to them is that if they have any advertisements being cancelled at the last minute, when they are about to go to print, they can run your advertisement in that position for half the normal rate.

Some newspapers find this very attractive. Someone cancelling at the last minute can be a huge headache for all publications. If they know that they can just slot your advertisement into that position and fill the space, it will make life a lot easier for them.

In that situation they might be happy to give it to you at half price. It's worth your while because your advertisement is still running in the paper, and best of all, you're not paying the full price for it. So in that situation everybody wins. That's one of the first things you should negotiate with the newspapers or magazines that you are advertising in.

Often you will also be able to get your rep to throw in free spot color for your advertisement, providing they are already going to be running color on that page.

The final thing that you need to consider when negotiating with your advertising rep is to get some editorial. What I mean by this is if you are advertising regularly with that newspaper, you should be requesting some free editorial about your business, product, or service.

Keep this in mind, although advertising usually has nothing to do with the editorial department. Your advertising rep can go out of his way talking to the editor and trying to get you a free editorial, but often this just won't be possible. But it is still worthwhile approaching him with the idea, particularly if you have something that is newsworthy.

It's important to remember that everything in advertising is open to negotiation. If you're not getting the best rate for your advertising dollar, you have only yourself to blame.

135. Follow Up

Have you ever run an ad inviting people to phone for a brochure, or for more information? If you're in a business where the buying decision is a longer and more complex one, chances are you have.

The problem is, most business owners simply send out or provide the information, then leave it up to the customer to get back in contact. This is a major mistake and generally leads to failure.

Customers always need a little prodding. Just because they haven't called you back doesn't mean they're a lost cause. It just means that they haven't heard enough reasons to do anything about dealing with you today.

You have to follow them up and give them more reasons to do something then and there. Regardless of how comprehensive your brochure or information is, there are always specific things that will be important to your customers that it doesn't cover.

You need to call them and find out why they are hesitating. More often than not, it's something simple that you can overcome in 30 seconds or less. With a gentle push, the customer comes across the line and buys.

The fact is, the sale often goes to the most persistent salesperson. People are always naturally hesitant to part with their money and will often put off buying until they really have to. If you give them some strong encouragement, they're likely to say, "Oh well, I have to buy some time, I may as well buy from this guy—he seems to know what he's talking about."

If you have a list of unconverted prospects sitting there, the first thing you should do is put this book down and call them. You don't need to do the hard sell. Just call them up and say, "Hi, Mrs. Jones. It's Tim here from Georgie Home Improvements. I'm just calling to check on the progress of the patio we talked about a few weeks ago."

Rarely will the people be rude. They'll probably be quite surprised that you bothered to call and that you actually care. No doubt they'll say something like, "Oh Tim, yeah, we're still thinking about it."

That makes it easy for you to say, "Right. Did you have a look through that information I sent you? Great. What did you think? Is that the kind of price range and patio style you like? I see—well, we do have another patio that looks the same, but it's around $600 cheaper. I could come over tomorrow afternoon and show you the designs in person, if you like."

You'll be surprised how many sales you can reel in this way. There are probably tons of sales waiting to be had right now. These people called you and asked for information for a good reason—they'd like to buy. You just have to call and ask them to do it now!

136. Reach

Reach is a term commonly used in TV and radio. It relates to how many people within the listening or viewing audience your commercial will actually get to, how many people view or listen to your commercial at any given time.

Reach data should always be viewed with frequency data when you are making a purchasing decision from a media supplier. The sales rep you're talking to should have these figures.

So, how do you assess this data when presented with it?

Well, let's say that the schedule being presented to you has a reach of 100,000 people. What this means is that at any given time 100,000 people may be exposed to your message.

What does all this actually tell us?

Well, reach, when viewed by itself, may look impressive. You may feel that it offers excellent value for the money due to the number of people who will potentially be exposed to your ads. But viewed by itself it fails to give you the complete picture. You need more information before you can make an educated decision. You need to understand frequency.

137. Frequency

Frequency data should be viewed in conjunction with reach data. Again, as with reach, frequency is a term used commonly in TV and radio. Let's look at our previous example once again. If our ad has a reach of 100,000 people and a frequency of 1, it means that 100,000 people will be exposed to the message once during the campaign. This schedule is far less likely to get a response than one that has a reach of 50,000 people and a frequency of 4.3.

So frequency means the number of times your commercial message will be viewed or heard by a prospect in the marketplace. The quoted industry figure for ideal frequency is a minimum of 4.3. Now attaining 4.3 can be done in a number of ways through the scheduling of your commercial message.

Media like television and radio have access to research data relevant to your market that enables them to put filters onto a schedule to specifically target the audience you are aiming for.

So let's say that you are a car stereo supplier. Your target audience may be 25–35-year-old males with an income of $35,000 who own, or are in the process of paying off, their own car, and have a mobile phone.

After applying these filters to the research information, your media representative will be able to tell you how many of them are in your market and make recommendations on the best schedule to obtain the optimum frequency for your commercial message.

So in summary, consider how many people are going to be reached by your commercial and how often they are going to be exposed to it. You then have a basis for working out which medium is likely to bring the best results, compare one station to another, and also the likelihood of success for your campaign.

138. Repetition

Repetition relates directly to reach and frequency. It is based on the theory that the more people hear or view your commercial, the more likely they are to make a purchase from you.

This is true of "call-to-action" commercials, commercials that make an offer and then ask the prospect to take action on that offer.

Now, some media people will try to convince you that the more you repeat your branding message (that is your business name, address, and phone number type of commercial) the more likely they are to buy from you! Well, this is a common tactic used to sell you more airtime or advertising space, something aimed at increasing their revenue.

Branding commercials are great if you have a million dollar advertising budget but serve very little purpose for the average business owner. If a commercial does not bring you a response that gives you a great return on investment, stop running it.

Remember, marketing and advertising are an investment, not an expense, and the results from each campaign should be tested, measured, and recorded as carefully as if you had invested in shares on the stock market.

But back to repetition.

People will normally buy from a company they have dealt with previously, or one that's been recommended by a friend. Failing this, they will buy from a company they perceive as being a leader in the field, or one with a long trading history, indicating it's stable.

Considering this, obviously the more often people hear or see your company's ad, the greater the confidence they will have in it. So by saying this, am I condoning, or even encouraging, "image" advertising?

Not at all. You should always use a "call-to-action" type of ad. What I am saying is that the more often people hear or see your offer, the greater the chance of their acting on it.

Think back to a time when you heard or saw an advertisement and thought to yourself, "That sounds good. I should give them a call." Now if you're like most people, you'll still be saying the same thing when you're exposed to the ad for the third time. It's probably going to be after the fourth or fifth time you hear it before you actually act. Therefore, if you want a response to your commercials, repetition is critical.

But how much? Well, this can really be answered only by testing and measuring. The station you're talking to will give you an idea, but you'll only really find out through trial and error.

139. Reply Paid Address

It's been proven that a reply paid address can boost responses enormously, especially if the focus of your ad is on sending in a coupon, or writing in for more information.

These days people tend to use the phone as a tool for seeking information, but, in some cases, the mail is still a valid method.

Simply go to your post office and ask to set one up—it takes about three minutes. They'll give you a number you can advertise in your ads. Your number will be something like Reply Paid 4567.

When people send things to your reply paid address, you pay for the postage. Obviously, you have to work out whether this is going to eat into your profit margin too much and whether you'll attract unqualified prospects who'll never buy.

It does do something important, though: It makes it easier for people to deal with you, which is always a positive thing.

If people can just grab an envelope, stick your coupon in it, and drop it in the mailbox, then they are more likely to do so. It will pull in all those people who think, "Hmmm, maybe."

140. 1 800/0 800 Numbers

1 800 and 0 800 are examples of toll-free numbers. That means if people want to call you, you pay for the cost of the call and they don't have to pay a cent, unless they're calling from mobile phones.

This makes it easier and more likely that people will call you. It's easy to set one up. Just call your phone company, who will be more than happy to get the ball rolling. Of course, you need to take care. One company I worked with had an 1 800 number and it was almost exclusively used by long distance customers who loved to call up and whine.

It was costing the company a fortune to talk to these crackpots who just wanted to whine and complain.

Feature your number at the bottom of your ad. It gives the impression that you are a large company. However, if all of your customers are local, it's probably a waste of time.

141. Print Schedules

If your product is perennial (that is, not seasonal), you don't have to be too concerned about when you run your ad. It's more a question of which day, rather than which time of year.

You'll probably pay different rates for different days. You need to take into consideration the circulation of the different papers and how many more readers you're getting for your money.

Also, major newspapers usually have different lift-out sections each day of the week. You may want to place your ad in one of these special sections. They can yield good results, although many of your competitors might be right next to you.

If your business is seasonal, you need to approach advertising differently. For example, a swimming pool builder would find it fruitless running a "summer ad" in winter. The business owner would need to adapt the appeal to suit the time of year.

The other consideration is major events—for instance, advertising sports merchandise the day before the championship game would work well.

142. Radio Schedules

Radio is a powerful medium if used correctly. The scheduling of your commercial plays a very large part in determining its success. There are some key points to consider when putting a radio schedule together:

1. Consider who you are trying to reach: your target market. It's pointless advertising to people who have no interest in your product or service.

2. Can you reach a large number of these people using the station you've chosen?

3. How frequently does your commercial need to go on the air to get your prospects to act?

4. What times do these people most frequently listen to the station you're advertising on?

Before we go any further, let's look at what a radio schedule is. There are two basic types of schedules that you can choose from.

The first is "run of station." This simply means that the station will decide when your commercials go to air. In other words, the specific time of the day that each commercial will be played. While this is the cheapest option, it's certainly not the best. If your commercials are placed "run of station" they will basically be used as fillers for unsold airtime—that is, the time slots nobody else wants.

Under this system, your commercials could be played early in the morning when nobody is listening, or at other quiet times such as midafternoon. You can occasionally get lucky using this system, but you'll waste a lot of money if you don't.

The second type is "target placed." Using target-placed commercials gives you the opportunity to decide when each commercial is played. This method is more expensive but you also get to decide when your commercials will be played. This greatly improves the chances of your commercials being heard by the right people.

Your local station will have survey figures that indicate the most popular listening times for your potential customers. You need to find out which times your target market is most likely to be listening, then pay for your commercials to be played during those times. As I've already mentioned, this can be more expensive, but there's no point having your ads played at a time when your target market is not listening. Your station's sales representative can tell you which times will suit you best.

As we have discussed elsewhere in this book, the key to having success with any schedule is reach, frequency, and repetition, and a strong *call to action*. So if you are being offered a package by a station that consists of, say, 10 thirty-second commercials over a one-week period, or worse still, over a one-month period, you can be assured it won't work for you and you may as well stand on the sidewalk and burn the money.

A good, solid schedule would be 20 thirty-second commercials placed over five consecutive days, with more commercials in "Breakfast" and "Drive" (I'll explain these terms in a moment). Having said that, if you ran a restaurant and were open for lunch, around lunchtime would be great placement for your commercials.

The station's day traditionally is broken into breakfast (6–9 a.m.), morning (9–midday), afternoon (12–4 p.m.), drive (4–7 p.m.), evenings (7–12 p.m.), and middawn (12–6 a.m.). The times that your audience is listening will dictate at what times your ads go on the air.

The radio stations will be able to give you these figures with the research data they'll have available. Breakfast, morning, afternoon, and drive will usually appear on a schedule as B.M.A.D., and radio reps will often use this jargon. Breakfast usually has the highest listening audience, followed by drive. If your target audience is parents who are at home, with two children going to school, then the morning session traditionally has a high concentration of these listeners.

Be aware that if a package comes out towards the end of the month with a reduced commercial rate, then you can be assured that the station is down on its sales budget for that month and is trying to raise revenue as fast as possible.

If you truly have a product that you want to promote at this time, then great. You can buy airtime at a reduced cost. But if you purchase one of these packages just because it is cheap, it will end up costing you in the long run. You will waste your money on a campaign that hasn't been planned and gets no results.

Above all, remember that the best commercial in the world won't bring results unless it has a solid schedule behind it. Consider your target, the reach, and frequency you'll achieve, the amount of repetition required, and you can't go wrong.

143. Radio Scripting

It's a common misconception that you have to be a great writer, or a wizard with words, to write a commercial that works.

That's rubbish. People who simply knew who they were targeting and how to come up with a good offer wrote many of the most successful commercials. Their writing skills were irrelevant.

Simply running a commercial aimed at new homeowners saying, "Here's how you can cut eight years off your mortgage—guaranteed. We're currently offering a *free* introductory session to the first 14 callers. This session is normally valued at $145" is enough. It doesn't matter what language you use, or even if your commercial is poorly produced.

It's the message that's important.

At the end of the day, people won't buy from you just because you can write witty commercials that a stand-up comic would be proud of. By the same token, people probably won't avoid buying from you just because your commercial sounds as if it was produced on Aunt Laura's $25 gas-driven tape recorder.

As long as your message is clear, quick, and well targeted, your commercial will work. It's really like serving food—if you are serving a delicious meal, it'll taste just as good delivered on paper plates as on your best china. People may prefer it on the china, but if you're serving people hungry for what you've cooked, they'll eat anyway.

There is only one sin you don't want to commit: getting off the point, or rambling on too long. If every word and every sentence says something important for the sale, then fine. If your commercial is full of guff, people will lose interest very quickly.

The same applies if you stray from your initial intention.

Here are some guidelines for creating a commercial that works:

Number of words per commercial: As a rule 65–85 words is the limit for a 30-second commercial. This can vary, however, depending on the style of commercial and how many sound effects you use. One of the most common mistakes that people make when writing their own commercials is using too many words, and then trying to make them fit.

To check that you haven't used too many in your ad, read it out aloud and time it as you read. When reading a commercial, you need to speak only marginally faster than normal speed. While it's possible to read 100 words in 30 seconds by talking very fast, you're better off cutting down on the words and making it easier to understand.

It's important that you realize that radio is a background medium. Most people will listen to the radio while doing something else, such as driving or working in the garden. Understanding this, it's important not to put too much information into your ads.

You should focus only on one theme: the one "big idea" that you want to get across. Trying to explain something that's complex or detailed is a recipe for disaster when advertising on radio. While listing benefits is important in any form of advertising, it's best to focus on the one that consumers will find most appealing.

Opening lines: As mentioned, radio is a background medium. Because of this, you need to get your prospects' attention immediately. A simple way of doing this is by telling them who it is you're talking to. For example, if your commercial is aimed at businesspeople, you could do worse than having an opening line that said, "Attention, businesspeople."

Using the key benefit of your product or service is another great way of getting your target's attention. When looking for the benefit you quite often need to identify a problem that people would like a solution to. Once you've discovered what it is your consumers are dissatisfied with, your opening lines virtually write themselves.

To demonstrate this, let's look at an example. Imagine a commercial which said, "Here's how you can put more fun into ironing." Imagine the same commercial with an opening line that said, "Here's how you can cut your ironing time in half." Do you think this would generate more interest?

The other way to approach your opening line is to invoke curiosity. This is harder to do effectively but better if your product doesn't contain a striking benefit. Here's a good example. "Here's why three out of four Auckland children will lose their hair before they reach 17," or, "Four reasons to call George's Gym before July 15 and say 'I'm a willee-wrinkle-wowee.'" Most importantly, your opening line needs to stop your listeners dead in their tracks.

Another trick is to start your commercial off as if it were an important announcement. For example, "We interrupt our regular program for this important news flash." This is a great way to attract your prospect's attention. It can be even more powerful if the start of your commercial is the opening few bars of a popular song, then you interrupt it.

Finding the right voice for your commercial: This can be more important than you realize. The wrong voice can severely hamper the results your commercial achieves. By taking some time to make this decision, your commercial will have a much greater chance of success.

You may be tempted to voice the commercial yourself. However, unless you have a good voice for radio, you're better off getting someone else to do this for you. This can cause problems for some people, especially those who chose only this form of advertising so they could hear their own voices.

Understand that the reason you're using radio is to get results, not to massage your own ego. There is, however, an exception to this rule. By using the "we're-local" appeal in your commercial, you may be able to get the edge over your "new-to-town" opposition. Yes, I know that I said the quality of production isn't as important as what you say, but why not have the best of both worlds?

You need to keep in mind who you're trying to reach and the type of person they'll find believable. You'll benefit greatly by finding a voice that your target market can relate to. To demonstrate how important this is, imagine using a male voice to talk about period pain. Or having a woman voicing a commercial for impotence. Using the wrong voice can detract from the credibility of your commercial.

You can always request that a local announcer voice your commercial. This will normally be done free of charge if you're running the commercials on that station. This can be beneficial if the announcer has a strong following and good credibility among your target market.

If you decide to use a local announcer, keep in mind that he probably won't be able to use terms such as "us" and "we." If you want the reader to sound like a representative of your company, you may need to source outside talent.

Using music: Should you choose to have music in your commercial, there are a number of things to consider. First, what type of music do your potential clients enjoy? If you're aiming at an older age group, you'll need to use the type of music that they grew up with. It would be detrimental to the effectiveness of a campaign aimed at 50-year-olds to have rap music in your ad. Of course, this would be ideal if you're targeting people aged 20 or under.

You also need to consider the type of music that is played by the station you're using. Of course, the type of music that station plays will generally be the type of music members of your target market prefer to listen to. If they didn't like the music the station played, they'd probably change stations.

Because the majority of people who listen to radio do so for the music, it's a good idea to include it in your commercials. If you're aiming at a younger age group, the more modern the music, the more effective the ad. By making the start of your commercial sound like a popular song, you increase the chances of people paying attention to it. You need to be careful about which music you use. Some songs and instrumentals, particularly those that haven't been around for long, will be covered by copyright laws. To ensure that you're not in breach of these laws, you should check with your radio station representative. You may still be able to use the music, even if it is protected, providing you pay a royalty fee. These fees can be quite expensive, however, so generally you're better off choosing a different song.

Using sound effects: To get your commercial noticed among the host of other things that your prospect may be doing at the time, you need to use impact. One of the most effective ways to do this is by using sound effects. There are literally thousands of options in this area, but there are a few fundamental points you need to consider in choosing the right ones.

When considering the type of sound effect to use, ask yourself this question: If you had the radio on while driving or doing some other task, what sort of noise or effect would make you stop and take notice? When considering the answer, it's a good idea to get a clear mental image of the types of sounds you would normally hear on that station.

People are attracted to loud or unusual sounds. If the sound effect you choose is the type not normally heard on that station, there's a good chance your commercial will make people sit up and take notice.

The effect you use also needs to suit the mood you're trying to create or the product you're trying to sell. For example, if you're trying to promote a nightclub, you'd probably use, as background sound, the sound of people laughing and having a good time. If, however, you were trying to promote the fact that your retail store was busy, you'd still use the sound of a lot of people in the background, but instead of laughter, they'd sound busy and purposeful. Understand that for the nightclub, you want to promote a fun and relaxed atmosphere. For the retail store, however, you want to create a sense of urgency, a feeling of, "I'd better hurry or the stock will be gone before I get there."

The right effect can also assist you in creating the right "mood" for your commercial. You would probably use loud, exaggerated noises if you wanted to create humor in your ad. On the other hand, if you were doing a commercial for violence against women, you'd use more subtle, disturbing sound effects. Try to identify the mood you want before choosing the effect to go with your commercial.

Where to place the sound effects and how loud to have them are two more things you need to think long and hard about. There is no hard-and-fast rule about placement. It's entirely up to you whether you use them just at the start, in the middle, at the end, or all the way through your commercial. Something to consider when you're looking at where to place them is their ability to add disturbing impact to your ad. For example, imagine a commercial for a brake company that started with a woman screaming and the sound of a car crashing, followed by a moment of silence. Careful placement of your sound effects can create a powerful impression.

As to how loud your sound effects should be, once again it's pretty much up to you. There are some things you need to keep in mind, though. A particularly loud and annoying noise, which goes on for long periods of time, may result in people turning the radio off. While it's a good idea to use a loud noise at the start of a commercial, it shouldn't interfere with the prospect's ability to understand what you're saying. You need to make sure that your selling message is not drowned out by the sound effects. Try making the initial noise loud, then fading it out as the presenter starts to speak.

As I mentioned earlier, there are literally thousands of effects to choose from. Most major radio stations will have a library of effects that should contain the one you're after. If they don't have exactly what you need, they can either source it from another station, or possibly create it for you. Once again, your local radio salesperson can assist you with this.

Include a strong, specific call to action: if you don't tell people what to do, they probably won't do anything.

Give them precise instructions on what to do—who to call, which number to use, when to do it, and what to ask for. Here's a good example: "Call Gordon Harris now at 345-6756 and ask for your 45-page personal astrological analysis chart."

By putting a time limit on your offer or sale, you can create a sense of urgency. If people have to act quickly to take advantage of a particular offer, guess what? They will. Make it very clear what it is you want them to do. You also need to understand that because radio is a background medium, people probably won't have time to remember your phone number.

Try giving them your address or perhaps a nearby landmark that they are familiar with. If you have to use a phone number, repeat it at least three times to give your prospects a chance of remembering it. Mention it early on in your ad, then again in the middle, and at the end. By doing this, you're alerting people to the fact that they need to be ready to either memorize the number, or write it down.

You might like to make your phone number the central theme of your commercial. By using your number as a rhyme, or part of a challenge (for instance, "If you can recite this number you'll get a free XYZ."), you can increase the likelihood of your prospects' remembering it. Another technique you can use if you need people to call rather than come into your store is to tell them to look your number up in the phone book.

Include concise and convincing copy: the copy is the actual words between the intro and the call to action.

You don't need to be a great writer to do this part well. It's more important that you get the point across clearly, in as few words as possible, and in logical order.

After you write your first draft, go through and edit viciously—that is, cut out any sentence or word that doesn't need to be there. Remember, you can use only between 65 and 85 words in total, including your introduction and call to action. Next, read it aloud and make sure it flows. Time it as you read to make sure that it will comfortably fit into 30 seconds.

Fianlly, have a couple of people check through and ask them to tell you what they got out of it. Ask them to explain it to you, to make sure you're getting the point across. Ask which parts were boring and don't be afraid of criticism. You didn't set out to be the world's greatest writer anyway, so any comments should be helpful rather than hurtful.

Avoid anything that's hard to understand: Write your commercial in a way that's easy for the consumer to understand. If your offer is long and complex, people won't be able to understand it, therefore, they won't respond to it.

Remember, people aren't interested in playing games trying to decipher what it is you're trying to say. They just want to know if they should bother listening, if they like what they hear, and what they should do.

Don't make things confusing—it'll only obscure your message. Avoid being an artist—be a businessperson.

So you understand the number of words you can use in a 30-second commercial. You also know how to effectively use music and sound effects to add impact to your ads. Let's now take a look at 11 different types of radio commercials, any one of which may suit your product or service.

1. Picture this.

Using words and sound effects, you create a mental picture for the listener. This type of commercial clearly demonstrates a common problem and the way your product or service can provide a solution to that problem.

For example, a commercial for a car breakdown service.

The commercial starts with the sound of a car that won't start. A man and a woman get into an argument about the fact that they'll be late for a party. A voice then explains that if they were a member of Joe Blogg's breakdown service, they'd still have made the party on time. The commercial then cuts back to the couple still arguing.

2. Build a character.

This type of commercial develops a character that then becomes synonymous with your company. This is particularly effective if you're running an ongoing campaign, highlighting different areas of your business.

For example, a character to promote an air-conditioning company.

With the sounds of cattle and chickens in the background, an old farmer starts talking about problems on the land. He complains about the dry weather, the stock looking thin, and generally being miserable. He then goes on to say that the only good thing to happen around his way is XYZ air-conditioning services. He mentions the price and the fact that now he's cool, and he doesn't care when it rains.

3. Use an exaggeration.

While this type is quite humorous, it can be very effective in communicating the key benefit of your product or service. This has the advantage of having consumers associate your product with that benefit.

For example, promoting a new hairdryer.

A lady explains that she has trouble drying her hair with her old, worn-out hair dryer. It's simply not powerful enough. She then starts talking about the new hair dryer she bought from YYY retail store. The listener hears hurricane sound effects as she switches it on.

You could use this type of exaggeration to emphasize the speed of a new computer that types letters before people think of what to write. Or a mechanic that has your beat-up old Chevy sounding like a Rolls Royce. This type of commercial has unlimited applications.

4. Use a familiar theme or character.

Another way to make your commercial stand out is to use the theme music of popular TV shows or movies. You can also use the characters from these shows.

For example, a new line of homes.

Using music from an old Western movie, a voice that sounds like John Wayne starts lecturing his housemate. He explains that the home they're in at the moment isn't "big enough for the both of 'em." He explains that by building a new home with Joe Blogg's Builders, they can both live comfortably.

You can adapt this style of commercial to most businesses. How about the theme music and characters from *Mission Impossible* or *Star Wars*? With a little thought and effort, you could soon identify a theme for your company's radio campaign.

5. Be a bit suggestive.

This is one of the more interesting ways to get your commercial noticed. Make it sound as if there's something naughty going on, using suggestive words, music, and/or sound effects. Make sure you don't get carried away, though, and miss the point. You still need to get the key benefit across, and it has to relate to the commercial itself.

For example, promoting a new bedding store.

The commercial starts with a man and woman grunting and groaning in the bedroom. The moaning then gets louder and louder until finally she says, "I give up. We're never going to get this sheet to fit." An announcer then comes on and explains that if you need new sheets, you should go and see ZXY Bedding.

6. Use humor.

Fun ads tend to be the most popular type, but care should be taken when using a humorous approach. The idea of running the campaign is to sell goods or services, not to make people laugh. This type of commercial is more suited to inexpensive items, as most expensive purchases are not considered a laughing matter. It can, however, be very effective for tradesmen.

For example, advertising a plumbing service.

As the commercial begins, we can hear a man grunting as he goes to the toilet while at a party. You hear the sound of toilet paper being used, then someone knocks on the door to tell him to hurry up because others are waiting. He tells them he's almost finished and you hear him try to flush the toilet. To his horror he realizes that the toilet won't flush. An announcer then comes on promoting Joe Blogg's Plumbing Services. The end line could be something like, "So call Joe today. He'll make those nasty little problems go away."

7. Make it sound like an emergency phone call.

Most people are familiar with the sound of an emergency phone call. This type can be either serious, or tongue-in-cheek. The key is to have the person who's making the call sound flustered, just as they would in real life.

For example, a commercial promoting a first aid course.

The commercial begins with a frantic voice asking the emergency operator how to resuscitate a friend. The operator then tries to talk her through it calmly. The caller then begins to cry, saying that she can't do it, that she doesn't know what to do. You continue to hear the saga being played out as a voice comes over explaining that if the caller had done the XYZ First Aid Course, she would have been able to save her friend's life. The commercial finishes with the caller sobbing frantically because her friend won't start breathing.

8. Telephone talk show.

Here you make your commercial sound like a radio talk show. The announcer introduces the next caller and asks him to speak about today's topic. The caller then goes off on a tangent explaining the benefits of a particular product or service. This is a very common strategy but one that can work well for the right sort of business.

For example, a new clothing store.

The announcer starts off by saying, "And our next caller is Sally from Mitchem. Sally, do you think that the Prime Minister has an image problem?" A female voice then starts to say that she does think he has an image problem and that he should address it by getting his clothes from XYZ Clothing Boutique. The announcer tries to get her back on track, but she goes on to list the benefits of dealing with this particular store.

9. People being interviewed on the street.

Once again this can be used as a serious or humorous type of commercial. Perhaps the most effective way of using it is by actually interviewing people and getting them to give you testimonials. Coordinate with your local radio station to get somebody to come to your store when it's busy. Then ask her to go around and interview your customers. This works well because most people like the idea of being on the radio and will give your store a huge plug. Then pick the best of these and use them as your commercial.

For example, a new food store.

The announcer explains, "We're here at XYZ Cafe Restaurant to find out what it is that makes people come here." He then goes on to interview people who comment on the great quality and range of food, the atmosphere, and the service. The announcer then explains where the store is and its business hours.

10. Radio serials.

You might like to try making your commercial sound like an old-time radio serial. Using phrases and terms that were common from that era, as well as the types of voices and characters that were around then, can make an outstanding commercial. The production department of the radio station can generally make your commercial sound a bit scratchy as well, just to add authenticity.

For example, a new fast-food, home delivery service.

An old army major starts talking to his friend about what he'd like for dinner. He mentions that he'd like some bacon. His friend replies, "Yes, Sir, I'll just go and get that for you." A door closes in the background and immediately opens again with his friend, who's out of breath, saying that he's got the bacon. The major then says that he'd like some tomato paste. The other gentleman replies, "Yes, Sir, I'll just go and get that for you." So it goes on until the major says, "For goodness sake, man, you could've just called XYZ Pizza Delivery." He explains that they have inexpensive home deliveries with your choice of toppings.

As you can see from this example, having a line that is repeated over and over makes the commercial more effective. This was a common theme with earlier radio serials.

11. People talking on telephones or CB radios.

The reason for the success of this type of commercial is that people are used to hearing others on the phone, without seeing them. This is the same with radio advertising—you can hear people, but you can't see them. Two ladies talking on the phone about a new shop that's opened, or two policemen talking about a new car that just went past, are some of the ways this can be used effectively.

For example, a new gymnasium.

One lady comments to her friend about the amount of weight Michele Smith has lost. The other lady says she must be starving herself. As they make catty remarks about her, an announcer explains that you can now lose all the weight you want, at XYZ Gymnasium.

These are just some examples of the types of radio commercials you can choose from. You may have noticed that up until now I haven't mentioned jingles. That is because unless you have an enormous budget, jingles are a waste of money. Large companies like Coca Cola and McDonald's, who pour millions of dollars each year into their advertising, use jingles to good effect. For the average business your money is better spent on specific promotions.

If you find this too hard, there are people who can write your commercial for you. Radio stations have copywriters who write hundreds of commercials a week, like the following. You might also like to consider having a specialist copywriting company do it for you. Whichever you chose, definitely consider using radio; you'll be pleased with the results if you follow these tips.

*** Radio Copy ***

Title: Frosties Ice

Requested Talent (1): Announcer Mike Smith

Requested Talent (2): (Male) (Age: 30+)

Requested Talent (3): (Male) (Age: 30+)

Length: 00:30

Campaign Start Date: (20/11/06)

Campaign Finish Date: (27/11/06)

Station: 2 YZ

——————————————— Copy Text ———————————————

SFX (teeth chattering)

VOICE (2): Move it. Go on, get out of here...

VOICE (3): You Frosties ice have to stop bossing us around. What makes you better than the rest of us ice cubes?

VOICE (2): A hole right through the middle...

VOICE (3): Oh I see, I'm sorry I didn't mean to offend you...

VOICE (2): Now get out of my way...

VOICE (3): Yes sir, right away sir, anything you say sir.

VOICE (2): That's more like it.

ANNCR (1): Frosties ice—a bag full of ice holes. Available at a service station, convenience store, campground, hotel club, or package store near you...

144. TV Schedules

TV schedules are very similar to radio schedules. When electing to use television as the medium to promote your product or service, there are a number of things to consider.

1. Who are the members of your target audience?

2. When are they watching? The television station will have research data on what sorts of people are watching what sort of programs, at what time, and how many of them are watching.

3. How many commercials do you need to run over what period of time to get the frequency you require in order to get a worthwhile response?

Remember, if the programs you choose are high-rating programs, they will cost more to advertise in. But often it is worth paying the extra to target the right audience.

Don't let the station convince you to run a run of station (ROS) schedule. This gives them the right to place your commercials in any time slot and any program that they have space, instead of where it is going to work best for you. Generally, on weekdays the best time to advertise is evenings between 6:00 p.m. and 10:30 p.m.

However, if you want to target small business owners, you might choose a time when there is a specific business program on.

Put most thought into who you're trying to reach. The station itself should be able to help you then with scheduling your ads.

145. TV Scripting

Many creative agencies who produce television commercials are interested in one thing only: winning awards with their ads.

Now this might sound exciting, but the truth is that these awards are based on creative features and technical prowess, not on how many sales resulted from the commercials. Remember, just because commercials win awards doesn't mean they improve the client's sales in any way, shape, or form.

Most of what we spoke about in radio scripts applies to television scripts. The styles of the two and the number of words that can be used are pretty much identical. The only additional consideration is the visuals.

Your commercial must be visually stimulating with a great offer, a call to action, and your contact details. Getting a good commercial produced may cost a little extra, but it will be worth the money in the long run. You needn't spend a fortune on visuals, however. Sometimes the most simple scenes or graphics work the best.

Television stations usually do not have copywriters or marketing strategists as part of their team. So, you may like to consider getting an outside company to write your commercials for you. Don't try to cram too much information into your commercial—be clear, concise, and to the point. Clever advertisements win awards, not customers. They might make people laugh, but they don't put money in your till.

146. TV Storyboarding

OK, so you've worked out the schedule and you've done your script. You now need to develop a storyboard to complete this part of the project.

A storyboard consists of three parts. Let's look at each individually.

The first part is the description of the visuals that will feature in the commercial. By that I mean for each frame of your commercial, you'll have a brief description of what is to happen. For example, you might describe a shot where a young lady enters a bar and orders a drink. You'd list, down the left hand side of the storyboard, "Close-up of woman's face, seductive expression, slight smile."

You would also mention here any cuts to different scenes or any music cuts. For example, "Cut to scene of men sitting at bar. Cut to music."

The second part of the storyboard is the audio description. Here you place your script next to the relevant scene. You need to indicate where the music goes in relation to each scene, and what music goes where. Of course, you'll also indicate who says which lines.

Finally, in between these two columns you place your actual diagrams of what the scenes roughly look like. Now the quality of these can vary quite dramatically, depending on how much work you want to put in, but more importantly, how complex the scenes are.

Obviously, if the scenes are very complex, basic stick figure sketches probably won't get the message across. If people don't understand exactly what you're after, they either won't buy the idea, or the people producing the finished commercial won't deliver exactly what you have envisaged.

Advertising agencies often go to extremes when producing these diagrams. They create elaborate full-color pictures with incredible detail, resulting in huge storyboards. But they fail to realize that people aren't stupid. Their storyboards need to give people only the basic gist of what the commercial will look like; they can then verbally paint the rest of the picture for the client.

Things like who should do the voice-over for the ad and who should appear in the advertisement can be covered closer to the time of filming. This should ideally be done in the preproduction meeting that you have with the director and other technical people. From the client's point of view, they only need to understand the basic concept.

Which brings us to another point: being creative. Now, we've already mentioned a number of times that being too creative with print advertising can be detrimental to the success of your campaign. But often TV advertising is more at fault than print ads. This is because of the creative scope that TV offers the advertiser. You need to create your storyboard and then let it sit for a day or so. Then come back to it and ask yourself, "Do all of these elements help in the sale of the product?" You need to consider if there is a cheaper way to get your message across. As with all forms of advertising, the simpler it is, the more effective it will be.

So when you're putting your storyboard together, the one thing you really need to decide on is whether you are going to do the rough sketches yourself, or are you going to pay an artist to do them for you?

Consider finding a university student to do it for you. Often she will want the experience and would love to add it to her portfolio. She will normally do it for a fraction of the price a full-time artist would charge.

One final word on creating storyboards: Remember that the people who are seeing your ad will probably be sitting at home relaxing. They won't normally have a pen and paper in hand. If you need them to call you or remember your address, it's a good idea to ensure that the details are on screen long enough for the prospect to get them written down.

Alternatively, you can get them to look you up in the White Pages. Always send them to the White Pages and not the Yellow Pages. Why? Well, your opposition's ads are right next to yours in the Yellow Pages, which is most likely not the case in the White Pages.

147. A Guaranteed Way to Get Your Direct Mail Letters to Stand Out

One of the challenges you'll confront when embarking on a direct mail campaign is getting your letters read.

There are many people using direct mail each day, which means your prospects are most likely getting advertising letters on a regular basis. So, unless your direct mail stands out from the crowd, it will end up where most marketing pieces do—in the trash can.

So let's look at ways to make you stand out:

Envelope: There's mixed opinion on whether you should write anything on the envelope.

People will open anything in a plain white envelope with their names on it—it could be a bill, a notice from the government, or a check. Who knows?

If you put a headline or message on the outside of the envelope, you run the risk of people's dismissing the letter before ever opening it. For example, if you received a letter that said, "Inside—your chance to buy a new Falcon," you'd be able to instantly decide whether you needed to read the letter or not. That's before you've seen the pictures or great deals.

Of course, this may produce the desired results. If the person is not in the market for a new car, then what is the point of their reading on?

But sometimes the right headline printed on the envelope will generate a very high response. What about a letter to business owners that says, "Here's how to get better accountancy advice and pay *no* accountant fees," on the outside? If you were a business owner with accounting problems, you'd probably have a look.

Talking about envelopes, there is something else you might like to test and measure. That is, printed envelopes versus handwritten. Handwritten, I've found, often brings a better response because people assume it may be from a friend. This can also backfire if your handwriting is messy, or if you're trying to project a professional image.

Another technique you might like to try is a romantic, scented envelope, or maybe an invitation type of envelope—anything to get people curious enough to open it.

Any of these ideas should make a difference in the number of calls you receive, but there is something else you can do to increase the readership of your letters.

If you place an object inside the envelope, you'll definitely increase its chances of being opened. Often this will mean a higher postage cost, but the results it brings should make it well worthwhile. Things like Minties or large rubber bands create a bulge in the envelope. This has big advantages. First, people will be curious to see what's making the envelope bulge. Second, it will sit at the top of the pile of mail on someone's desk. The reason it will be on top of the pile is because the lump in the envelope will make it difficult to stack other letters on top of it.

Now the idea of putting something in the envelope can be a winner in itself. I remember working with a client whom I instructed to place a small toy dinosaur in each envelope. He complained about how difficult it was to find the dinosaurs, then how much extra the postage cost. But he didn't complain about the results. His response went from 3 percent to 40 percent, due almost entirely to those toy dinosaurs.

The trick is to tie the object into the letter as the next example shows:

Here's how you can pick up 40–50 new customers a week—without lifting a finger

Dear (name),

I've included a toy dinosaur with this letter to stress a point. If you're not using the Internet to promote your business, you'll soon be extinct.

You've probably considered using the Internet before now, or maybe you've got a Web site that's not getting you results. But there is a way to generate business using the Internet.

The Mitchell Financial Directory is one of the leading directories of its kind in Australia. With quality, up-to-date information and resources such as banner advertisements and financial calculators, it's no wonder we get more than 400,000 "hits" each month!

By using powerful layouts and well-written copy, we can create Web sites far more effective than you'd ever imagined possible. You'll be amazed by the results. Like the Brisbane firm who picked up more than 50 new clients as a result of their Mitchell Financial Directory listing.

I've seen companies just like yours achieve these kinds of results, time and time again.

Don't make your decision now. I'll call you in a couple of days to arrange a suitable time when we can meet, so I can explain our services in more depth.

Barry Mitchell

National Marketing Manager

Mitchell Financial Directory

P.S. We're also offering free Internet training for anyone who books an appointment in the next 17 days. Here we will teach you how to "surf the net," send and receive e-mails, and find sites of interest. This training, normally valued at $80, will have you up-to-date with the Internet in no time.

P.P.S. As a special introductory offer we are giving away a free modem to any client who joins our directory during the month of February. This modem would normally cost you $209 but will be yours free if you decided to sign up.

148. It Might Be Corny, but It Works

I always laugh when I hear people complaining about those ads on late night television.

They complain about the "corny" phrases the voice-over person uses, and the funny little "sayings," but while they're complaining, they can still tell you exactly what was being advertised and what great offer was being made. I've even had people complain to me about the ads, then admit that they bought the product that was being offered!

So why do they buy? Simply because the corny sales lines work.

Lines like, "Buy one and get one free" or "Order now and you'll also receive…" actually work! Using lines like this will get people to buy. They might think it's corny or lame, but they'll still buy from you. Isn't that the only thing that really matters? It's not about people liking your ads or thinking you're clever. It's about making sales.

I mentioned at the end of the last section the advantage of putting an object into your envelope. You'll also recall that I spoke about tying the object into the start of your letter so it makes sense. The way to do this might sound corny, but believe me it works.

Let me give you an example:

Harking back to my client who used the toy dinosaur, well, to tie the dinosaur in with their letter we used an opening line that said, "I've included this dinosaur to emphasize a point. If you're not doing business on the Internet, you'll soon be extinct." This might sound a bit lame, but it worked gangbusters for him.

How can you use this in your business? Let's have a look at a few more examples of objects and opening lines that tie them in.

Lollipop—"Life will be sweeter."

Rubber Band—"S-t-r-e-t-c-h your budget."

Bark—"If you're not dealing with us, you're barking up the wrong tree."

Soap—"I've decided to come clean."

Toy dinosaurs—"Don't put up with that prehistoric..."

Wrapping paper—"I'd like to wrap up this deal."

Thermometer—"These deals are sure to get your temperature rising."

Comb—"I've been combing the countryside looking for people like you."

Yo-yo—"Stop your profits going up and down like a yo-yo."

All of these sound a little silly, but they work better than you could possibly imagine. I've seen many times where people are hesitant to use them because they are worried about what others might say. They feel it's too "gimmicky." What they fail to realize is that these silly little techniques really do work.

The same goes for corny old sayings like, "Every dog has its day" and "Slower than a wet week." I know people sometimes view this as being unprofessional, but it doesn't matter if it results in sales. People use these sayings in everyday language, so why not use them in your direct mail letters?

So, how can you use these ideas for your next direct mail campaign? What objects can you include? How can you tie them in at the start of your letter? Answer these questions and you'll be well on the way to amazing direct mail success!

Part 6

■ Just DID It ...

149. Just DID It

I once arrived at a good friend's house to be greeted by an amazing revelation.

He wasn't wearing the traditional Nike, "Just Do It" logo, but instead something that really told me more about him than you'd care to believe. His T-shirt read,

"Just DID it."

And to me it described his attitude toward life and business perfectly. Never did he come to a party telling us of what he was about to do. Never did he show you his plans. All you ever heard or saw were reminders of what he'd done, what he'd achieved, and what he'd changed about himself and the world around him.

So, maybe in business and in life this can become your mantra as well.

To do so you've got to remember this:

You learned to walk by first of all crawling, and you probably took a while to get good at it as well. Then you took that first big step by getting up and falling down. It took much encouragement on your parent's behalf for you to finally learn how to walk, but walk you did.

Advertising is exactly the same. You will first of all crawl, you'll write ads that sort of resemble successful ads, you'll write sales letters that will get a few responses, but you'll have achieved one thing that most will never be able to claim:

You started.

A gift:

By the way, as a gift for having completely read this entire book, and please keep this a secret, as we'll only give it to those who've read the entire book (and to those of you who read from the back to the front, stop cheating and go to the front) my team will be happy to take a look over your first piece to make sure you are on track.

Please check in the back of the book for details of my office nearest to you.

Getting started is at least half the battle.

Getting results is the next half.

Testing and measuring:

Remember back to some of the first things you read in this book; we talked about the value of testing several different smaller ads and measuring the response.

I really want to stress the importance of this to you now, just before you leave me. This, above all else, has catapulted me, and my ads, well above average. Above all else the power of knowing the numbers has helped me show better profits than almost any other ad writer I know.

If you take away only one lesson from this book, it should be to test different strategies and measure the responses.

You have to do this, and here's why:

Still, with all I've taught you, all I've learned about advertising over the years, still a full 80 percent of the ads you write, in fact, 80 percent of the ads I write, are either really bad or just break even.

Only 20 percent of your ads will be *winners*.

But when they do win, boy oh boy will you be excited. Remember this: After testing many different campaigns you'll have a library of winning ads and marketing campaigns that at any point in time you can run to create both sales and profit.

In fact, you'll most probably keep them all running at the same time and grow your business incredibly.

Does marketing become a full-time job, I hear you asking? Take my word that it does, and it's got to be the most profitable job you could ever be involved in.

Just think about it: No more doing a job in your business to save a wage, or save two wages if you're like most business owners who do the work of two people. But focus on bringing money in through leveraged means through advertising.

You write the ads once, and after they're tested and measured, you can run them forever. In other words, do the work once and see the profits come in again and again and again.

That, my friends, is the secret to great results and long-term success in business.

So, without any more words from me...

Go to it. Create your first ads, or revamp the ones you're running now.

Let us know your results, and remember, my team is always available to help you out should you ever get stuck.

Remember, the greatest ad writers of all time weren't the most creative; they weren't the smartest, they weren't the best typists or graphic designers.

The greatest ad writers of all time are the salespeople.

Remember the 1920s definition of advertising is:

Salesmanship in print.

Keep selling.

Getting into *Action*

So, when is the best time to start?

Now—right now—so let me give you a step-by-step method to get yourself onto the same success path of many of my clients and the clients of my team at *Action International.*

Start testing and measuring now.

You'll want to ask your customers and prospects how they found out about you and your business. This will give you an idea of what's been working and what hasn't. You also want to concentrate on the five areas of the business chassis. Remember:

1. Number of Leads from each campaign.
2. Conversion Rate from each and every campaign.
3. Number of Transactions on average per year per customer.
4. Average Dollar Sale from each campaign.
5. Your Margins on each product or service.

The Number of Leads is easy; just take a measure for four weeks, average it out, and multiply by 50 working weeks of the year. Of course you'd ask each lead where they came from so you've got enough information to make advertising decisions.

The Conversion Rate is a little trickier, not because it's hard to measure, but because we want to know a few more details. You want to know what level of conversion you have from each and every type of marketing strategy you use. Remember that some customers won't buy right away, so keep accurate records on each and every lead.

To find the Number of Transactions you'll need to go through your records. Hopefully you can find the transaction history of at least 50 of your past customers and then average out their yearly purchases.

The Average Dollar Sale is as simple as it sounds. The total dollars sold divided by the number of sales. The best information you can collect is the average from each marketing campaign you run, so that you know where the real profit is coming from.

And, of course, your margins. An Average Margin is good to know and measure, but to know the margins on everything you sell is the most powerful knowledge you can collect.

If you're having any challenges with your testing and measuring, be sure to contact your nearest *Action International* Business Coach. She'll be able to help you through and show you the specialized documents to use.

If, by chance, you're thinking of racing ahead before you test and measure, remember this. It's impossible to improve a score when you don't know what the score is.

So you've got your starting point. You know exactly what's going on in your business right now. In fact, you know more about not only what's happening right now, but also the factors that are going to create what will happen tomorrow.

The next step in your business growth is simple.

Let's decide what you want out of the business—in other words, your goals. Here are the main points I want you to plan for.

How many hours do you want to work each week? How much money do you want to take out of the business each month? And, most importantly, when do you want to finish the business?

By "finish" the business, I mean when it will be systematized enough so it can run without your having to be there. Remember this about business; a little bit of planning goes a long way, but to make a plan you have to have a destination.

Once again, if you're having difficulty, talk to an *Action International* Business Coach. He'll know exactly how to help you find what it is you really want out of both your business and your life.

Now the real work begins.

Remember, our goal is to get a 10 percent increase in each area over the next 12 months. Choose well, but I want to warn you of one thing, one thing I can literally guarantee.

Eight out of 10 marketing campaigns you run *will not work.*

That's why when you choose to run, say, an advertising campaign in your local newspaper, you've got to run at least 10 different ads. When you select a direct mail campaign, you should send out at least 10 different letters to test, and so on.

Make sure you get at least five strategies under each heading and plan to run at least one, preferably two, at least each month for the next 12 months.

Don't work on just one of the five areas at a time; mix it up a little so you get the synergy of all five areas working together.

Now, this is the most important advice I can give you:

Learn how to make each and every strategy work. Don't just think you know what to do; go through my hints and tips, read more books, listen to as many tapes as you can, watch all the videos you can find, talk to the experts, and make sure you get the most advantage you can before you invest a whole lot of money.

The next 12 months are going to be a matter of doing the numbers, running the campaigns, testing headlines, testing offers, testing prices, and, of course, measuring the results.

By the end of it you should have at least five new strategies in each of the five areas working together to produce a great result.

Once again I want to stress that this will work and this will make your business grow as long as *you* work it.

Is it simple? *Yes.*

Is it easy? *No.*

You'll have to work hard. If you can get the guidance of someone who's been there before you, then get it.

Whatever you do, start it now, start it today, and most importantly, make the most of every day. Your past does not equal your future; you decide your future right here and right now.

Be who you want to be, *do* what you need to do, in order to *have* what you want to have.

Positive *thought* without positive *Action* leaves you with positively *nothing*. I called my company *Action International*, not Theory International, or Yeah, I read that book International, but *Action International*.

So take the first step—and get into *Action*.

■ ABOUT THE AUTHOR

Bradley J. Sugars

Brad Sugars is a world-renowned Australian entrepreneur, author, and business coach who has helped more than a million clients around the world find business and personal success.

He's a trained accountant, but as he puts it, most of his experience comes from owning his own companies. Brad's been in business for himself since age 15 in some way or another, although his father would argue he started at 7 when he was caught selling his Christmas presents to his brothers. He's owned and operated more than two dozen companies, from pizza to ladies fashion, from real estate to insurance and many more.

His main company, *Action International*, started from humble beginnings in the back bedroom of a suburban home in 1993 when Brad started teaching business owners how to grow their sales and marketing results. Now *Action* has nearly 1000 franchises in 19 countries and is ranked in the top 100 franchises in the world.

Brad Sugars has spoken on stage with the likes of Tom Hopkins, Brian Tracy, John Maxwell, Robert Kiyosaki, and Allen Pease, written books with people like Anthony Robbins, Jim Rohn, and Mark Victor Hansen, appeared on countless TV and radio programs and in literally hundreds of print articles around the globe. He's been voted as one of the Most Admired Entrepreneurs by the readers of *E-Spy* magazine—next to the likes of Rupert Murdoch, Henry Ford, Richard Branson, and Anita Roddick.

Today, *Action International* has coaches across the globe and is ranked as one of the Top 25 Fastest Growing Franchises on the planet as well as the #1 Business Consulting Franchise. The success of *Action International* is simply attributed to the fact that they apply the strategies their coaches use with business owners.

Brad is a proud father and husband, the chairman of a major children's charity and in his own words, "a very average golfer."

Check out Brad's Web site www.bradsugars.com and read the literally hundreds of testimonials from those who've gone before you.

◼ RECOMMENDED READING LIST

ACTION INTERNATIONAL BOOK LIST

"The only difference between *you* now and *you* in 5 years' time will be the people you meet and the books you read." Charlie Tremendous Jones

"And, the only difference between *your* income now and *your* income in 5 years' time will be the people you meet, the books you read, the tapes you listen to, and then how *you* apply it all." Brad Sugars

- *The E-Myth Revisited* by Michael E. Gerber
- *My Life in Advertising & Scientific Advertising* by Claude Hopkins
- *Tested Advertising Methods* by John Caples
- *Building the Happiness Centered Business* by Dr. Paddi Lund
- *Write Language* by Paul Dunn & Alan Pease
- *7 Habits of Highly Effective People* by Steven Covey
- *First Things First* by Steven Covey
- *Awaken the Giant Within* by Anthony Robbins
- *Unlimited Power* by Anthony Robbins
- *22 Immutable Laws of Marketing* by Al Ries & Jack Trout
- *21 Ways to Build a Referral Based Business* by Brad Sugars
- *21 Ways to Increase Your Advertising Response* by Mark Tier
- *The One Minute Salesperson* by Spencer Johnson & Larry Wilson
- *The One Minute Manager* by Spencer Johnson & Kenneth Blanchard
- *The Great Sales Book* by Jack Collis
- *Way of the Peaceful Warrior* by Dan Millman
- *How to Build a Championship Team*—Six Audio tapes by Blair Singer
- Brad Sugars "Introduction to Sales & Marketing" 3-hour Video
- Leverage—Board Game by Brad Sugars
- *17 Ways to Increase Your Business Profits* booklet & tape by Brad Sugars. FREE OF CHARGE to Business Owners

*To order Brad Sugars' products from the recommended reading list, call your nearest *Action International* office today.

The 18 Most Asked Questions about Working with an *Action International* Business Coach

And 18 great reasons why you'll jump at the chance to get your business flying and make your dreams come true

1. So who is *Action International?*

Action International is a business Coaching and Consulting company started in 1993 by entrepreneur and author Brad Sugars. With offices around the globe and business coaches from Singapore to Sydney to San Francisco, *Action International* has been set up with you, the business owner, in mind.

Unlike traditional consulting firms, *Action* is designed to give you both short-term assistance and long-term training through its affordable Mentoring approach. After 12 years teaching business owners how to succeed, *Action's* more than 10,000 clients and 1,000,000 seminar attendees will attest to the power of the programs.

Based on the sales, marketing, and business management systems created by Brad Sugars, your *Action* Coach is trained to not only show you how to increase your business revenues and profits, but also how to develop the business so that you as the owner work less and relax more.

Action International is a franchised company, so your local *Action* Coach is a fellow business owner who's invested her own time, money, and energy to make her business succeed. At *Action*, your success truly does determine our success.

2. And, why do I need a Business Coach?

Every great sports star, business person, and superstar is surrounded by coaches and advisors.

And, as the world of business moves faster and gets more competitive, it's difficult to keep up with both the changes in your industry and the innovations in sales, marketing, and management strategies. Having a business coach is no longer a luxury; it's become a necessity.

On top of all that, it's impossible to get an objective answer from yourself. Don't get me wrong. You can survive in business without the help of a Coach, but it's almost impossible to thrive.

A Coach *can* see the forest for the trees. A Coach will make you focus on the game. A Coach will make you run more laps than you feel like. A Coach will tell it like it is. A Coach will give you small pointers. A Coach will listen. A Coach will be your marketing manager, your sales director, your training coordinator, your partner, your confidant, your mentor, your best friend, and an *Action* Business Coach will help you make your dreams come true.

3. Then, what's an Alignment Consultation?

Great question. It's where an *Action* Coach starts with every business owner. You'll invest a minimum of $1295, and during the initial 2 to 3 hours your Coach invests with you, he'll learn as much as he can about your business, your goals, your challenges, your sales, your marketing, your finances, and so much more.

All with three goals in mind: To know exactly where your business is now. To clarify your goals both in the business and personally. And thirdly, to get the crucial pieces of information he needs to create your businesses *Action* Plan for the next 12 months.

Not a traditional business or marketing plan mind you, but a step-by-step plan of *Action* that you'll work through as you continue with the Mentor Program.

4. So, what, then, is the Mentor Program?

Simply put, it's where your *Action* Coach will work with you for a full 12 months to make your goals a reality. From weekly coaching calls and goal-setting sessions, to creating marketing pieces together, you will develop new sales strategies and business systems so you can work less and learn all that you need to know about how to make your dreams come true.

You'll invest between $995 and $10,000 a month and your Coach will dedicate a minimum of 5 hours a month to working with you on your sales, marketing, team building, business development, and every step of the *Action* Plan you created from your Alignment Consultation.

Unlike most consultants, your *Action* Coach will do more than just show you what to do. She'll be with you when you need her most, as each idea takes shape, as each campaign is put into place, as you need the little pointers on making it happen, when you need someone to talk to, when you're faced with challenges and, most importantly, when you're just not sure what to do next. Your Coach will be there every step of the way.

5. Why at least 12 months?

If you've been in business for more than a few weeks, you've seen at least one or two so called "quick fixes."

Most Consultants seem to think they can solve all your problems in a few hours or a few days. At *Action* we believe that long-term success means not just scraping the surface and doing it for you. It means doing it with you, showing you how to do it, working alongside you, and creating the success together.

Over the 12 months, you'll work on different areas of your business, and month by month you'll not only see your goals become a reality, you'll gain both the confidence and the knowledge to make it happen again and again, even when your first 12 months of Coaching is over.

6. How can you be sure this will work in my industry and in my business?

Very simple. You see at *Action*, we're experts in the areas of sales, marketing, business development, business management, and team building just to name a few. With 328 different profit-building strategies, you'll soon see just how powerful these systems are.

You, on the other hand, are the expert in your business and together we can apply the *Action* systems to make your business fly.

Add to this the fact that within the *Action* Team at least one of our Coaches has either worked with, managed, worked in, or even owned a business that's the same or very similar to yours. Your *Action* Coach has the full resources of the entire *Action* team to call upon for every challenge you have. Imagine hundreds of experts ready to help you.

7. Won't this just mean more work?

Of course when you set the plan with your *Action* Coach, it'll all seem like a massive amount of work, but no one ever said attaining your goals would be easy.

In the first few months, it'll take some work to adjust, some work to get over the hump so to speak. The further you are into the program, the less and less work you'll have to do.

You will, however, be literally amazed at how focused you'll be and how much you'll get done. With focus, an *Action* Coach, and most importantly the *Action* Systems, you'll be achieving a whole lot more with the same or even less work.

8. How will I find the time?

Once again the first few months will be the toughest, not because of an extra amount of work, but because of the different work. In fact, your *Action* Coach will show you how to, on a day-to-day basis, get more work done with less effort.

In other words, after the first few months you'll find that you're not working more, just working differently. Then, depending on your goals from about month six onwards, you'll start to see the results of all your work, and if you choose to, you can start working less than ever before. Just remember, it's about changing what you do with your time, *not* putting in more time.

9. How much will I need to invest?

Nothing, if you look at it from the same perspective as we do. That's the difference between a cost and an investment. Everything you do with your *Action* Coach is a true investment in your future.

Not only will you create great results in your business, but you'll end up with both an entrepreneurial education second to none, and the knowledge that you can repeat your successes over and over again.

As mentioned, you'll need to invest at least $1295 up to $5000 for the Alignment Consultation and Training Day, and then between $995 and $10,000 a month for the next 12 months of coaching.

Your Coach may also suggest several books, tapes, and videos to assist in your training, and yes, they'll add to your investment as you go. Why? Because having an *Action* Coach is just like having a marketing manager, a sales team leader, a trainer, a recruitment specialist, and corporate consultant all for half the price of a secretary.

10. Will it cost me extra to implement the strategies?

Once again, give your *Action* Coach just half an hour and he'll show you how to turn your marketing into an investment that yields sales and profits rather than just running up your expenses.

In most cases we'll actually save you money when we find the areas that aren't working for you. But yes, I'm sure you'll need to spend some money to make some money.

Yet, when you follow our simple testing and measuring systems, you'll never risk more than a few dollars on each campaign, and when we find the ones that work, we make sure you keep profiting from them time and again.

Remember, when you go the accounting way of saving costs, you can only ever add a few percent to the bottom line.

Following Brad Sugars' formula, your *Action* Coach will show you that through sales, marketing, and income growth, your possible returns are exponential.

The sky's the limit, as they say.

11. Are there any guarantees?

To put it bluntly, no. Your *Action* Coach will never promise any specific results, nor will she guarantee that any of your goals will become a reality.

You see, we're your coach. You're still the player, and it's up to you to take the field. Your Coach will push you, cajole you, help you, be there for you, and even do some things with you, but you've still got to do the work.

Only *you* can ever be truly accountable for your own success and at *Action* we know this to be a fact. We guarantee to give you the best service we can, to answer your questions promptly, and with the best available information. And, last but not least your *Action* Coach is committed to making you successful whether you like it or not.

That's right, once we've set the goals and made the plan, we'll do whatever it takes to make sure you reach for that goal and strive with all your might to achieve all that you desire.

Of course we'll be sure to keep you as balanced in your life as we can. We'll make sure you never compromise either the long-term health and success of your company or yourself, and more importantly your personal set of values and what's important to you.

12. What results have other business owners seen?

Anything from previously working 60 hours a week down to working just 10—right through to increases in revenues of 100s and even 1000s of percent. Results speak for themselves. Be sure to keep reading for specific examples of real people, with real businesses, getting real results.

There are three reasons why this will work for you in your business. Firstly, your *Action* Coach will help you get 100 percent focused on your goals and the step-by-step processes to get you there. This focus alone is amazing in its effect on you and your business results.

Secondly, your coach will hold you accountable to get things done, not just for the day-to-day running of the business, but for the dynamic growth of the business. You're investing in your success and we're going to get you there.

Thirdly, your Coach is going to teach you one-on-one as many of *Action's* 328 profit-building strategies as you need. So whether your goal is to be making more money, or working fewer hours or both inside the next 12 months your goals can become a reality. Just ask any of the thousands of existing *Action* clients, or more specifically, check out the results of 19 of our most recent clients shown later in this section.

13. What areas will you coach me in?

There are five main areas your *Action* Coach will work on with you. Of course, how much of each depends on you, your business, and your goals.

Sales. The backbone of creating a superprofitable business, and one area we'll help you get spectacular results in.

Marketing and Advertising. If you want to get a sale, you've got to get a prospect. Over the next 12 months your *Action* Coach will teach you Brad Sugars' amazingly simple streetwise marketing—marketing that makes profits.

Team Building and Recruitment. You'll never *wish* for the right people again. You'll have motivated and passionate team members when your Coach shows you how.

Systems and Business Development. Stop the business from running you and start running your business. Your Coach will show you the secrets to having the business work, even when you're not there.

Customer Service. How to deliver consistently, make it easy to buy, and leave your customers feeling delighted with your service. Both referrals and repeat business are centered in the strategies your Coach will teach you.

14. Can you also train my people?

Yes. We believe that training your people is almost as important as coaching you.

Your investment starts at $1500 for your entire team, and you can decide between five very powerful in-house training programs. From *"Sales Made Simple"* for your face-to-face sales team to *"Phone Power"* for your entire team's telephone etiquette and sales ability. Then you can run the *"Raving Fans"* customer service training or the *"Total Team"* training. And finally, if you're too busy earning a living to make any real money, then you've just got to attend our *"Business Academy 101."* It will make a huge impact on your finances, business, career, family, and lifestyle. You'll be amazed at how much involvement and excitement comes out of your team with each training program.

15. Can you write ads, letters, and marketing pieces for me?

Yes. Your *Action* Coach can do it for you, he can train you to do it yourself, or we can simply critique the marketing pieces you're using right now.

If you want us to do it for you, our one-time fees start at just $1195. You'll not only get one piece; we'll design several pieces for you to take to the market and see which one performs the best. Then, if it's a critique you're after, just $349 means we'll work through your entire piece and give you feedback on what to change, how to change it, and what else you should do. Last but not least, for between $15 and $795 we can recommend a variety of books, tapes, and most importantly, Brad Sugars' Instant Success series books that'll take you step-by-step through the how-tos of creating your marketing pieces.

16. Why do you also recommend books, tapes, and videos?

Basically, to save you time and money. Take Brad Sugars' *Sales Rich* DVD or Video Series, for instance. In about 16 hours you'll learn more about business than you have in the last 12 years. It'll also mean your *Action* Coach works with you on the high-level implementation rather than the very basic teaching.

It's a very powerful way for you to speed up the coaching process and get phenomenal rather than just great results.

17. When is the best time to get started?

Yesterday. OK, seriously, right now, today, this minute, before you take another step, waste another dollar, lose another sale, work too many more hours, miss another family event, forget another special occasion.

Far too many business people wait and see. They think working harder will make it all better. Remember, what you know got you to where you are. To get to where you want to go, you've got to make some changes and most probably learn something new.

There's no time like the present to get started on your dreams and goals.

18. So how do we get started?

Well, you'd better get back in touch with your *Action* Coach. There's some very simple paperwork to sign, and then you're on your way.

You'll have to invest a few hours showing them everything about your business. Together you'll get a plan created and then the work starts. Remember, it may seem like a big job at the start, but with a Coach, you're sharing the load and together you'll achieve great things.

Here's what others say about what happened after working with an *Action* business coach

Paul and Rosemary Rose—Icontact Multimedia

"Our *Action* coach showed us several ways to help market our product. We went on to triple our client base and simultaneously tripled our profits in just seven months. It was unbelievable! Last year was our best Christmas ever. We were really able to spoil ourselves!"

S. Ford—Pride Kitchens

"In 6 months, I've gone from working more than 60 hours per week in my business to less than 20, and my conversion rate's up from 19 percent to 62 percent. I've now got some life back!"

Gary and Leanne Paper—Galea Timber Products

"We achieved our goal for the 12 months within a 6-month period with a 100 percent increase in turnover and a good increase in margins. We have already recommended and will continue to recommend this program to others."

Russell, Kevin, John, and Karen—Northern Lights Power and Distribution

"Our profit margin has increased from 8 percent to 21 percent in the last 8 months. *Action* coaching focussed us on what are our most profitable markets."

Ty Pedersen—De Vries Marketing Sydney

"After just three months of coaching, my sales team's conversion rate has grown from an average of less than 12 percent to more than 23 percent and our profits have climbed by more than 30 percent."

Hank Meerkerk and Hemi McGarvey—B.O.P. School of Welding

"Last year we started off with a profit forecast, but as soon as we got *Action* involved we decided to double our forecast. We're already well over that forecast again by two-and-a-half times on turnover, and profits are even higher. Now we run a really profitable business."

Stuart Birch—Education Personnel Limited

"One direct mail letter added $40,000 to my bottom line, and working with *Action* has given me quality time to work on my business and spend time with my family."

Mark West—Wests Pumping and Irrigation

"In four months two simple strategies have increased our business more than 20 percent. We're so busy, we've had to delay expanding the business while we catch up!"

Michael Griffiths—Gym Owner

"I went from working 70 hours per week *in* the business to just 25 hours, with the rest of the time spent working *on* the business."

Cheryl Standring—In Harmony Landscapes

"We tried our own direct mail and only got a 1 percent response. With *Action* our response rate increased to 20 percent. It's definitely worth every dollar we've invested."

Jason and Chris Houston—Empradoor Finishing

"After 11 months of working with *Action*, we have increased our sales by 497 percent, and the team is working without our having to be there."

Michael Avery—Coomera Pet Motels

"I was skeptical at first, but I knew we needed major changes in our business. In 2 months, our extra profits were easily covering our investment and our predictions for the next 10 months are amazing."

Garry Norris—North Tax & Accounting

"As an accountant, my training enables me to help other business people make more money. It is therefore refreshing when someone else can help me do the same. I have a policy of only referring my clients to people who are professional, good at what they do, and who have personally given me great service. *Action* fits all three of these criteria, and I recommend *Action* to my business clients who want to grow and develop their businesses further."

Lisa Davis and Steve Groves—Mt. Eden Motorcycles

"With *Action* we increased our database from 800 to 1200 in 3 months. We consistently get about 20 new qualified people on our database each week for less than $10 per week."

Christine Pryor—U-Name-It Embroidery

"Sales for August this year have increased 352 percent. We're now targeting a different market and we're a lot more confident about what we're doing."

Joseph Saitta and Michelle Fisher—Banyule Electrics

"Working with *Action*, our inquiry rate has doubled. In four months our business has changed so much our customers love us. It's a better place for people to work and our margins are widening."

Kevin and Alison Snook—Property Sales

"In the 12 months previous to working with *Action*, we had sold one home in our subdivision. In the first eight months of working with *Action*, we sold six homes. The results speak for themselves."

Wayne Manson—Hospital Supplies

"When I first looked at the Mentoring Program it looked expensive, but from the inside looking out, its been the best money I have ever spent. Sales are up more than $3000 per month since I started, and the things I have learned and expect to learn will ensure that I will enjoy strong sustainable growth in the future."

▌*Action* Contact Details

Action International Asia Pacific

Ground Floor, *Action* House, 2 Mayneview Street, Milton QLD 4064

Ph: +61 (0) 7 3368 2525

Fax: +61 (0) 7 3368 2535

Free Call: 1800 670 335

Action International Europe

Olympic House, Harbor Road, Howth, Co. Dublin, Ireland

Ph: +353 (0) 1-832 0213

Fax: +353 (0) 1-839 4934

Action International North America

5670 Wynn Road Suite A & C, Las Vegas, Nevada 89118

Ph: +1 (702) 795 3188

Fax: +1 (702) 795 3183

Free Call: (888) 483 2828

Action International UK

3–5 Richmond Hill, Richmond, Surrey, TW 106RE

Ph: +44 020 8948 5151

Fax: +44 020 8948 4111

Action Offices around the globe:

Australia | Canada | China | England | France | Germany | Hong Kong

India | Indonesia | Ireland | Malaysia | Mexico | New Zealand

Phillippines | Scotland | Spain | Singapore | USA | Wales

Here's how you can profit from all of Brad's ideas with your local *Action* International **Business Coach**

Just like a sporting coach pushes an athlete to achieve optimum performance, provides them with support when they are exhausted, and teaches the athlete to execute plays that the competition does not anticipate.

A business coach will make you run more laps than you feel like. A business coach will show it like it is. And a business coach will listen.

The role of an *Action* Business Coach is to show you how to improve your business through guidance, support, and encouragement. Your coach will help you with your sales, marketing, management, team building, and so much more. Just like a sporting coach, your *Action* Business Coach will help you and your business perform at levels you never thought possible.

Whether you've been in business for a week or 20 years, it's the right time to meet with and see how you'll profit from an *Action* Coach.

As the owner of a business it's hard enough to keep pace with all the changes and innovations going on in your industry, let alone to find the time to devote to sales, marketing, systems, planning and team management, and then to run your business as well.

As the world of business moves faster and becomes more competitive, having a Business Coach is no longer a luxury; it has become a necessity. Based on the sales, marketing, and business management systems created by Brad Sugars, your *Action* Coach is trained to not only show you how to increase your business revenues and profits but also how to develop your business so that you, as the owner, can take back control. All with the aim of your working less and relaxing more. Making money is one thing; having the time to enjoy it is another.

Your *Action* Business Coach will become your marketing manager, your sales director, your training coordinator, your confidant, your mentor. In short, your *Action* Coach will help you make your business dreams come true.

ATTENTION BUSINESS OWNERS
You can increase your profits now

Here's how you can have one of Brad's *Action* International Business Coaches guide you to success.

Like every successful sporting icon or team, a business needs a coach to help it achieve its full potential. In order to guarantee your business success, you can have one of Brad's team as your business coach. You will learn about how you can get amazing results with the help of the team at *Action* International.

The business coaches are ready to take you and your business on a journey that will reward you for the rest of your life. You see, we believe *Action* speaks louder than words.

Complete and post this card to your local *Action* office to discover how our team can help you increase your income today!

Action International

The World's Number-1 Business Coaching Team

Name ....

Position ....

Company ....

Address ....

....

Country ....

Phone ....

Fax ....

Email ....

Referred by ....

How do I become an *Action International* Business Coach?

If you choose to invest your time and money in a great business and you're looking for a white-collar franchise opportunity to build yourself a lifestyle, an income, a way to take control of your life and, a way to get great personal satisfaction ...

Then you've just found the world's best team!

Now, it's about finding out if you've got what it takes to really enjoy and thrive in this amazing business opportunity.

Here are the 4 things we look for in every *Action* Coach:

1. You've got to love succeeding

We're looking for people who love success, who love getting out there and making things happen. People who enjoy mixing with other people, people who thrive on learning and growing, and people who want to charge an hourly rate most professionals only dream of.

2. You've got to love being in charge of your own life

When you're ready to take control, the key is to be in business for yourself, but not by yourself. *Action*'s support, our training, our world leading systems, and the backup of a global team are all waiting to give you the best chance of being an amazing business success.

3. You've got to love helping people

Being a great Coach is all about helping yourself by helping others. The first time clients thank you for showing them step by step how to make more money and work less within their business, will be the day you realize just how great being an *Action* Business Coach really is.

4. You've got to love a great lifestyle

Working from home, setting your own timetable, spending time with family and friends, knowing that the hard work you do is for your own company and, not having to climb a so-called corporate ladder. This is what lifestyle is all about. Remember, business is supposed to give you a life, not take it away.

Our business is booming and we're seriously looking for people ready to find out more about how becoming a member of the *Action International* Business Coaching team is going to be the best decision you've ever made.

Apply online now at www.action-international.com

Here's how you can network, get new leads, build yourself an instant sales team, learn, grow and build a great team of supportive business owners around you by checking into your local *Action* Profit Club

Joining your local *Action* Profit Club is about more than just networking, it's also the learning and exchanging of profitable ideas.

Embark on a journey to a more profitable enterprise by meeting with fellow, like-minded business owners.

An ***Action*** Profit Club is an excellent way to network with business people and business owners. You will meet every two weeks for breakfast to network and learn profitable strategies to grow your business.

Here are three reasons why ***Action*** *International's* Profit Clubs work where other networking groups don't:

1. You know networking is a great idea. The challenge is finding the time and maintaining the motivation to keep it up and make it a part of your business. If you're not really having fun and getting the benefits, you'll find it gets easier to find excuses that stop you going. So, we guarantee you will always have fun and learn a lot from your bi-weekly group meetings.
2. The real problem is that so few people do any work 'on' their business. Instead they generally work "in" it, until it's too late. By being a member of an ***Action*** Profit Club, you get to attend FREE business-building workshops run by Business Coaches that teach you how to work "on" your business and avoid this common pitfall and help you to grow your business.
3. Unlike other groups, we have marketing systems to assist in your groups' growth rather than just relying on you to bring in new members. This way you can concentrate on YOUR business rather than on ours.

Latest statistics show that the average person knows at least 200 other contacts. By being a member of your local ***Action*** Profit Club, you have an instant network of around 3,000 people

Join your local *Action* Profit Club today.

Apply online now at www.actionprofitclub.com

LEVERAGE—The Game of Business
Your Business Success is just a Few Games Away

Leverage—The Game of Business is a fun way to learn how to succeed in business fast.

The rewards start flowing the moment you start playing!

Leverage is three hours of fun, learning, and discovering how you can be an amazingly successful business person.

It's a breakthrough in education that will have you racking up the profits in no time. The principles you take away from playing this game will set you up for a life of business success. It will open your mind to what's truly possible. Apply what you learn and **sit back and watch your profits soar.**

By playing this fun and interactive business game, you will learn:

- How to quickly raise your business income
- How business people can become rich and successful in a short space of time
- How to create a business that works without you

Isn't it time you had the edge over your competition?

Leverage has been played by all age groups from 12-85 and has been a huge learning experience for all. The most common comment we hear is: 'I thought I knew a lot, and just by playing a simple board game I have realized I have a long way to go. The knowledge I've gained from playing Leverage will make me thousands! Thanks for the lesson.'

To order your copy online today, please visit www.bradsugars.com

Also available in the

THE BUSINESS COACH

Learn how to master the six steps on
the ladder of success

(0-07-146672-X)

INSTANT REPEAT BUSINESS

Build a solid and loyal
customer base

(0-07-146666-5)

THE REAL ESTATE COACH

Invest in real estate with
little or no cash

(0-07-146662-2)

INSTANT SALES

Master the crucial first minute of
any sales call

(0-07-146664-9)

INSTANT PROMOTIONS

Create powerful press releases, amazing
ads, and brilliant brochures

(0-07-146665-7)

INSTANT
SUCCESS

Real Results. Right Now.

Instant Success series.

INSTANT CASHFLOW
Turn every lead into a sale
(0-07-146659-2)

INSTANT PROFIT
Boost your bottom line with
a cash-building plan
(0-07-146668-1)

INSTANT ADVERTISING
Create ads that stand out and sell
(0-07-146660-6)

INSTANT LEADS
Generate a steady flow of leads
(0-07-146663-0)

INSTANT TEAM BUILDING
Learn the six keys to a winning team
(0-07-146669-X)

BILLIONAIRE IN TRAINING
Learn the wealth building secrets
of billionaires
(0-07-146661-4)

SUCCESSFUL FRANCHISING
Learn how to buy or sell a franchise
(0-07-146671-1)

INSTANT REFERRALS
Never cold call or chase after
customers again
(0-07-146667-3)

INSTANT SYSTEMS
Stop running your business and start
growing it
(0-07-146670-3)

Your source for the strategies, skills, and confidence every business owner needs to succeed.